Desks, Bookcases & Entertainment Centers

Working Furniture for Your Home

from the editors of *Woodworker's Journal*

1970 Broad Street • East Petersburg, PA 17520
www.FoxChapelPublishing.com

Desks, Bookcases & Entertainment Centers: Working Furniture for Your Home is a compilation first published in 2008 by Fox Chapel Publishing, Inc. The patterns contained herein are copyrighted by *Woodworker's Journal.*

Our friends at Rockler Woodworking and Hardware supplied us with most of the hardware used in this book. Visit rockler.com. For subscription information to *Woodworker's Journal magazine,* call toll-free 800-765-4119.

Woodworker's Journal
Founder & CEO: Ann Rockler Jackson
Publisher: Larry N. Stoiaken
Editor-in-Chief: Rob Johnstone
Art Director: Jeff Jacobson
Senior Editor: Joanna Werch Takes
Field Editor: Chris Marshall
Illustrators: Jeff Jacobson, John Kelliher

ISBN 978-1-56523-363-8

Publisher's Cataloging-in-Publication Data

Desks, bookcases, entertainment centers : working furniture for your home / from the editors of Woodworker's journal. -- 1st ed. -- East Petersburg, PA : Fox Chapel Publishing, c2008.

p. ; cm.
(The best of Woodworker's journal)
ISBN: 978-1-56523-363-8

1. Desks--Patterns. 2. Bookcases--Patterns. 3. Entertainment centers (Cabinetwork)--Patterns. 4. Cabinetwork. 5. Furniture making. 6.Woodwork--Patterns. I. Title. II. Series. III.Woodworker's journal.

TT197 .D47 2008
684.104--dc22 2008

To learn more about the other great books from Fox Chapel Publishing, or to find a retailer near you, call toll-free 800-457-9112 or visit us at www.FoxChapelPublishing.com.

Printed in China
First Printing: July 2008

Note to Authors: We are always looking for talented authors to write new books in our area of woodworking, design, and related crafts. Please send a brief letter describing your idea to Acquisition Editor, Fox Chapel Publishing, 1970 Broad Street, East Petersburg, PA 17520.

Introduction

As we progress into the twenty-first century, I'm sure our lives will continue to become more technologically sophisticated. Right now, we can receive our e-mails from almost anywhere, watch our favorite shows in digital clarity, and drive cars partially on rechargeable power. But, all of that wizardry doesn't change some of our basic tendencies. For one, we probably always will be creatures who accumulate and save. The digital age hasn't replaced our desire to collect printed books and magazines, store photos on shelves, or hang on to treasured collectibles. We also still need a quiet, dedicated place to sit, gather our thoughts, and write out bills. And, new media gadgetry has to be stacked, organized, and stored, just like everything else.

Thank goodness woodworking can help us keep one foot firmly grounded in the past while we march boldly into the future. Some of woodworking's most classic projects—bookcases and desks—are as useful today as they've ever been. Regardless of whether you still pen your letters longhand or use your desk mostly as a computing station, the desk projects in this book have you covered. If you're ready for a good challenge, build one of the high style desks featured here: a Federal Secretary Desk by Dick Coers or Chris Inman's Queen Anne Writing Desk. Rick White's Santa Fe Desk should be a bit more approachable for the novice woodworkers, but it doesn't compromise one bit of eye-catching appeal.

Rick White and Bill Hylton offer two different versions of computer desks, or you can take computer storage in a different direction with Rick's Compact Computer Cabinet. Mike McGlynn, our former master of Arts & Crafts furniture, created a cherry stereo cabinet that's both classically designed and eminently functional. We're also including three different entertainment center projects that have long been reader favorites. One could be perfect for your den or family room.

Woodworker's Journal editor-in-chief Rob Johnstone assures me we could print a bookcase project in every issue, and his rationale is simple: every home needs them, and their shelf space tends to be in short supply! That's why you'll find five uniquely different bookcases featured here. Chris Inman's Knockdown Bookcase is frugally designed, rock-solid and attractive—perfect for dorm life or just life on the "go." Rick White's Modular Barrister's Bookcases will give you the freedom to expand your bookcase collection along with the collections they store. And, for a more rigorous shop workout, build the mahogany veneered, fluted Heirloom Bookcase or Paul Lee's Itasca Bookcase. It's detailed with an array of shop-made moldings inspired by urban architecture. Rick White rounds out the collection with a handsome Walnut Library Bookcase.

The next time a desk, bookcase, or media organizer sifts to the top of your project list, reach for this book first. I'm confident you'll find just the solution you're looking for... and you won't need a Web browser to do it. Enjoy!

Larry N. Stoiaken, Publisher

Acknowledgments

Woodworker's Journal recently celebrated its 30th anniversary—a benchmark few magazines ever reach. I would like to acknowledge both the 300,000 woodworkers who make up our readership and Rockler Woodworking and Hardware (*rockler.com*), which provided most of the hardware, wood, and other products used to build the projects in this book.

Our publishing partner, Fox Chapel, did a terrific job re-presenting our material, and I am especially grateful to Alan Giagnocavo, Paul Hambke, John Kelsey, and Troy Thorne for their commitment to our content.

Larry N. Stoiaken, Publisher

Contents

74

10

52

80

142

Federal Secretary Desk

Federal styling, an American response to various European influences, relies on a combination of simple elements to create an elegant complete design. With that goal in mind, our secretary features oval inlays and book-matched burl veneer, together with tapered legs and slender, light-colored inlay strips.

by Dick Coers

On a project like this, with so many details and complicated steps, you'll need to be organized. Two good pieces of advice before you start: First, work from the floor up. Second, have all your materials, including the burl veneer and specialty hardware, on hand before you make your first cut.

Take your time when choosing stock for the four legs (pieces 1). They'll look best if there are no cathedral spikes in the grain, especially after the inlay is applied. To keep a uniform appearance, use stock with growth rings running at a 45° angle across the bottom face.

After cutting the legs to the dimensions shown in the Material List on page 3, orient them so the best color and figure face forward. Then follow the Technical Drawings on page 8 and the sidebar, at right, to lay out and cut the tapers. Note all eight tapers stop shy of the top of the legs where the desk aprons (pieces 2 and 3) will be attached.

Quick and Easy Leg Tapering

Make a bed from ¾" plywood, 10" longer than your workpiece and wide enough to accommodate a toggle clamp. Rip another 4"-wide piece for the jig's fence and cut two small pieces to make a stop for the jig bed and a mounting block for the toggle clamp. Mark the starting and finishing points for a taper on one leg (see Technical Drawings, page 8), and place it on the bed with the stock you wish to remove hanging over the edge. Mount the fence and stop block against the edge of the leg (the fence will be positioned at an angle, relative to the jig bed). Toggle-clamp the leg in place and raise the blade up high. Set the jig against you saw's rip fence, and align the fence as necessary. Slide the jig along the fence to cut the tapers.

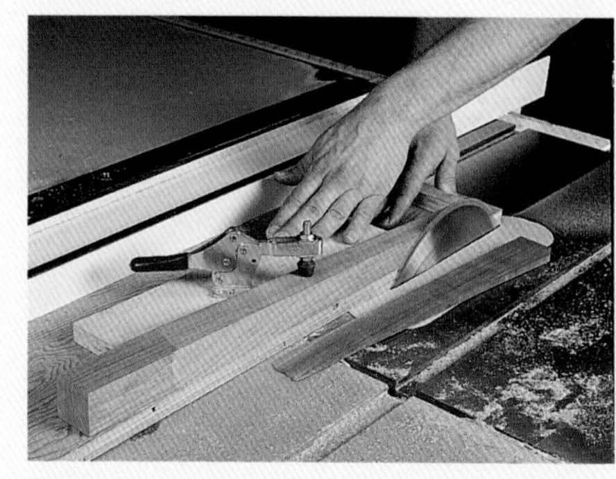

The nicely tapered legs on this classic design were produced using this simple jig.

Rip the aprons to size from walnut veneered plywood. The bottom of the aprons are accented with a solid piece of ⅜" molding (piece 4). Glue it in place and shape the bead profile on your router table, as shown in the Bead Molding Detail on page 3.

Making Floating Tenon Joinery

The aprons are secured to the legs with mortise and tenon joinery, but in this case the tenons (pieces 5) float—that is, they aren't an integral part of either piece. As such, it is necessary

As you open the door on the desk, door supports slide smoothly out into position to support it.

Specialty brass hardware combines with classic inlay and dovetail details on this Federal-style Secretary Desk.

Forming the Oval Accents

To allow for the offset of the router bit and rub collar, use a small machine nut as a guide when tracing around the oval inlay.

Federal styling relies on simple elements combined to create an elegant, complete design. To that end, our secretary uses oval inlays together with tapered legs and slender, light-colored inlay strips. The key to getting the ovals and strips to fit well is to use a template to guide your router. However, the space between the outside edge of the rub collar and the router bit must be accommodated (see inset). One trick is to use a machine nut to offset your pencil as you trace a line around the outside of the oval. Cut the template opening on your scroll saw and rout a few oval shapes with your new template and rub collar to test the fit. Expect to make a few adjustments—and possibly even a few templates—before your oval inlay fits perfectly. It's worth the effort to be precise.

After a few adjustments to the template, the ovals should fit perfectly in the scrap wood test piece. A precise template is imperative here.

to form matching mortises in both the legs and aprons.

Follow the Technical Drawings to lay out the mortises. Now, install a ⅜" straight bit in your router table and set the fence to the dimensions shown on the drawings. Use a stop block and a piece of masking tape to give you the proper size mortise, then test your set-up on some scrap before milling the leg and apron mortises in several passes. Make the floating tenons to snugly fit the mortises. Next, use a pocket hole jig and bit to drill pocket holes in the top edges of the aprons (see Technical Drawings for locations). These holes will eventually hold face frame screws (pieces 6) to attach the legset to the rest of the desk. With this done, complete the inlay and stringing (pieces 7 and 8) in the legs, following the sidebars shown here.

Building the Legset Assembly

With the inlay and decorative stringing completed, sand the aprons and legs, starting with 100-grit and finishing with 220-grit papers. Dry-fit and temporarily clamp the legs and aprons together. With the assembly square and plumb, cut the corner braces (pieces 9) to size and predrill and countersink for their screws (pieces 10). When everything fits, remove the clamps and glue and screw the legset together.

Making the Walnut Frame

A flat frame (pieces 11, 12, and 13) serves as a transition between the base and desktop. The front joints are mitered, while the back ones are simple butts held with screws. The miter joints

Leg, Door, and Drawer Inlays

Use a router bit with a rub collar and a template to form the grooves on the tapered legs, drawer, and door. Make some test cuts on scrapwood first to verify your set-up.

As with the decorative ovals, above, forming the grooves for the slender inlays is easy with a router, rub collar, and a jig. Use the Technical Drawings to make jigs for all of the inlays. To form the long thin inlays, start with a piece of ¾" stock, slicing it on your table saw a hair wider than the groove it will fill. Lower the blade and rip strips to the depth of the groove, test fitting as you go. It is imperative to use a zero-clearance insert in the table saw for this operation. Anytime you fit a strip of inlay into a tiny groove, try slightly tapering the edges of the strips to ensure a better fit. Use a file to remove just a bit of wood.

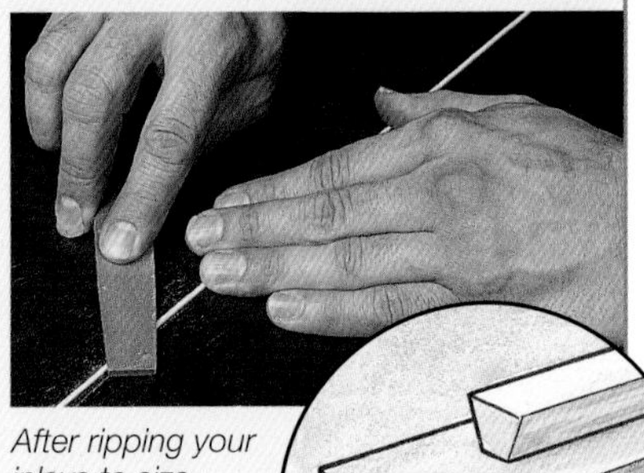

After ripping your inlays to size, taper their edges to ensure a good fit and provide room for glue. Use a file to form the bevels, as shown in the inset.

Legset Exploded View

Material List – Legset

		TxWxL
1	Legs (4)	$1\frac{5}{8}$" x $1\frac{5}{8}$" x $22\frac{7}{8}$"
2	Front & Back Aprons (2)	$\frac{3}{4}$" x $2\frac{5}{8}$" x $35\frac{5}{8}$"
3	Side Aprons (2)	$\frac{3}{4}$" x $2\frac{5}{8}$" x $17\frac{3}{4}$"
4	Bead Molding (1)	$\frac{3}{8}$" x $\frac{3}{4}$" x 110"
5	Floating Tenons (8)	$\frac{3}{8}$" x $\frac{3}{4}$" x 2"
6	Pocket Hole Screws (8)	#8 x 2"
7	Leg Inlays (2)	$\frac{1}{40}$" Oval inlay
8	Stringing (1)	$\frac{1}{8}$" x $\frac{1}{8}$" x 80"
9	Corner Braces (4)	$\frac{3}{4}$" x 3" x 9"
10	Screws (24)	#8 x 2"
11	Legset Frame Front (1)	$\frac{3}{4}$" x 3" x $39\frac{1}{4}$"
12	Legset Frame Sides (2)	$\frac{3}{4}$" x 3" x $21\frac{1}{4}$"
13	Legset Frame Back (1)	$\frac{3}{4}$" x 3" x $33\frac{1}{4}$"
14	Biscuits (100)	#20
15	Drawer Supports (2)	$\frac{3}{4}$" x $\frac{3}{4}$" x $15\frac{1}{4}$"

Bead Molding Detail
(Section View)

Floating tenons are a unique feature in this design. Use a stop block and masking tape to start and stop your mortises.

are reinforced with #20 biscuits (pieces 14). Dry-fit the frame, then glue, and clamp it together. Now add the drawer supports (pieces 15) with glue and clamps (see Exploded View).

With a belt sander, smooth the frame to 220 grit before routing the ogee profile on the front and side edges. Set the frame upside down on the workbench and center the legset (side-to-side) on it. Align the back edges so they're flush with each other, then extend the pocket screw holes into the frame and set this assembly aside.

Building the Carcass Sides

Cut the carcass sides (pieces 16) and top (piece 17) from a single sheet of veneered plywood, to preserve their grain pattern. Use a plywood-cutting

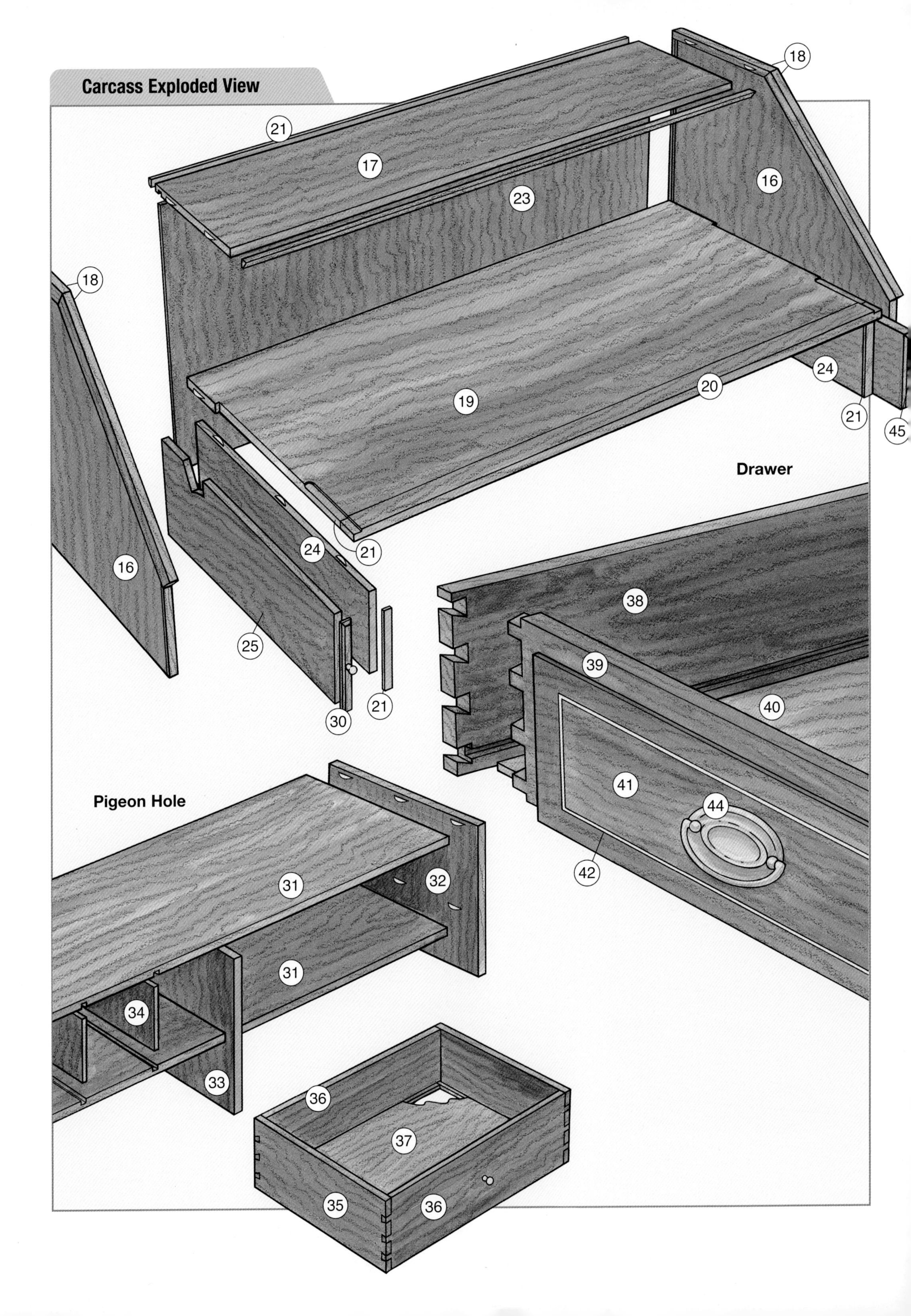

Carcass Exploded View
21
17
23
16
18
18
19
20
24
21
45
21
24
16
25
30
21
Drawer
38
39
40
41
44
42
Pigeon Hole
31
32
31
34
33
36
37
35
36

Material List – Carcass

	TxWxL
16 Carcass Sides (2)	¾" x 20⅜" x 13½"
17 Carcass Top (1)	¾" x 11⅜" x 36¾"
18 Carcass Edge Banding (1)	¾" x ¾" x 96"
19 Carcass Writing Top (1)	¾" x 18" x 36¾"
20 Brace (1)	¾" x 2" x 36¼"
21 Banding (1)	⅛" x ¾" x 60"
22 Specialty Door Hardware (1 Set)	Brass
23 Carcass Back (1)	¼" x 14½" x 37¼"
24 Drawer Cavity Dividers (2)	¾" x 4" x 19⅞"
25 Door Supports (2)	¾" x 31 5/16" x 20"
26 Door Edge (1)	¾" x ¾" x 124"
27 Door (1)	¾" x 11 5/16" x 35 5/16"
28 Burl Door Veneer (2)	1/32" x 13" x 19"
29 Plain Door Veneer (1)	1/32" x 13" x 37"
30 Door Support Endcaps (2)	¼" x ¾" x 31 5/16"

Material List – Pigeon Hole Unit

	TxWxL
31 Pigeon Hole Top & Shelf (2)	½" x 10" x 35⅛"
32 Pigeon Hole Sides (2)	½" x 10" x 8 13/16"
33 Pigeon Hole Large Dividers (2)	½" x 10" x 8 5/16"
34 Pigeon Hole Small Dividers (3)	¼" x 10" x 4⅜"
35 Pigeon Hole Drawer Sides (4)	½" x 3⅞" x 10"
36 Pigeon Hole Drawer Frt & Bk (4)	½" x 3⅞" x 11 5/16"
37 Pigeon Hole Drawer Bottoms (2)	¼" x 9⅝" x 11"
38 Large Drawer Sides (2)	½" x 3⅞" x 19⅞"
39 Large Drawer Front & Back (2)	½" x 3⅞" x 33 11/16"
40 Large Drawer Bottom (1)	¼" x 33 3/16" x 19⅜"
41 Large Drawer Face (1)	3/32" x 4" x 33⅞"
42 Large Stringing (1)	⅛" x ¼" x 168"
43 Key Pull (1)	Brass
44 Drawer Pulls (2)	Brass, ⅝" Dia.
45 Drawer Support Pulls (2)	Brass, ⅜" Dia.

Adding Solid-Hardwood Edges

The exposed edges of the top and angled edges of the sides are covered with hardwood banding (piece 18) that is mitered to length (see Technical Drawings) and applied with glue and clamps. Stretchable plastic packing tape makes a great clamp here. After spreading glue on the parts, wrap one edge of the tape around the opposite edge of each panel. Press the first few inches firmly so it gets a good grip on the plywood. Stretch the tape tightly as you apply it across the face, over the banding, and down the other face of each piece. When the glue dries, trim the banding flush with the plywood. Use a sharp cabinet scraper to shave the banding edges flush. Then, cut the proper angle on the front edge of the top.

Time for Some Minor Milling

The sides are attached to the legset frame with screws. The writing top (piece 19), and the carcass top are joined to the sides with biscuits. Refer to the Technical Drawings before laying out and machining these biscuit slots, then apply a hardwood brace (piece 20) to the front edge of the writing top with glue and biscuits. Then, apply hardwood banding (piece 21) to all the exposed edges of the walnut plywood.

You'll find dimensions on the Technical Drawings for making a notch in each side of the writing top. The notches are for the door hardware (pieces 22), and they can be cut on the band saw. Apply hardwood banding to the sides of these slots too, then machine biscuit slots in the ends of the writing top. The last bit of machining for the writing top is to rout mortises for the door hinges. You will also need to pare a chamfer into the leading edge directly in front of the hinge mortise. Check the Technical Drawings for more details.

We recommend walnut plywood for the carcass back (piece 23). It may be undersize in thickness, so select an undersized straight router bit to match. Refer to the Technical Drawings to find the groove locations and dimensions, then mill them in the carcass sides and top, and also in the frame for the back panel. Make sure to end the stopped grooves at the correct locations.

blade in your table saw to cut these parts to shape (see Technical Drawings), following the dimensions provided in the Material List, above.

Use double-sided tape to temporarily hold the sides together, taping them in the same orientation they will appear on the desk. Now make the angled front edge cuts on the sides (see Technical Drawings).

Carrying Out the Dry Assembly

Cut the drawer cavity dividers (pieces 24) and door supports (pieces 25) to size. In order to mount the door hinge hardware to the door supports, you need to drill a shallow mortise into the sides of the supports with a large Forstner bit (this will create right and left pieces) and finish by cutting the shaped notch onto each support (see the Technical

Drawings). Now you're almost ready to start dry-assembling the carcass.

The drawer cavity dividers are joined to the writing top by biscuits. Use the Technical Drawings to locate and cut the biscuit slots in the drawer cavity dividers, writing top, and the carcass sides and top.

Final-sand all of the inside surfaces, then dry-fit and clamp the carcass together. It's a good idea to apply finish to the inside surfaces before gluing up the carcass. Be sure not to get stain or finish on any area you will need to glue up later. After a dry-fit, glue, and clamp the carcass together, checking for squareness. When the glue cures, secure the carcass to the frame by extending the frame's pilot holes into the sides and drawer cavity dividers.

Making the Door

The door is the most difficult and time-consuming part of the project, especially when you consider the veneer work involved. You don't want any mistakes, so make a 6"-wide template—the same dimension as the door from the writing top to the carcass top. This piece will help you test the fit of the hinge leaf and the lid support linkage before you get started on your burl-veneered masterpiece.

Apply solid-hardwood door edging (piece 26) to the edges of the door blank (piece 27), securing it with glue and clamps. Miter the corners of this banding so no end grain shows. Flush up the banding with the plywood after the glue dries, using scrapers and a sanding block to avoid rounding over the edges. The veneer will telegraph any errors, so take your time. Leave the lid oversized by 1⁄16" all around (that's the way it's listed in the Material List), for final trimming after the veneer work is completed. Your final trim will leave a 1⁄16" gap on each side.

Balance the door construction by gluing veneer (pieces 28 and 29) to both sides of the plywood. It's best to do this clamping with a veneer press (see sidebar page 7), or you can use bricks or sand bags on top of scrap plywood to apply even pressure to the panel and veneer. Cover the door with a sheet of wax paper to keep the veneering glue from sticking to things it shouldn't.

If you use a veneer press for this operation and glue both veneer faces at once, be sure to apply equal pressure to all areas of the panel. As you tighten your clamps, work from the center out to the edges to eliminate any air pockets or pooled glue. Scrap-wood crossbearers with curved bottom edges will help you keep the pressure evenly applied.

Prepping for the Hardware

After the veneering glue is dry, flush-trim the veneer with an ultra sharp knife. Set your table saw to 22½° to trim the top edge and 90° to trim the sides. Then sand the edges smooth with just a hint of a roll back where the veneer meets the edge.

Using the scrap template you made earlier as a guide, trim the sides of the door for the door hinge support hardware (piece 22), as indicated on the Technical Drawings. Cut the rabbets for the support linkages on your router table, using an extra-tall fence for good support. Use a sharp chisel to pare out the recess to 30° from vertical, (providing clearance for the hinge knuckle when the door closes). Connect the hardware to the door support pieces you prepared earlier. There is a bit of hand work involved when final-fitting the hinge support hardware, so dry-fit the hinges as you go.

Cut the door support endcaps (pieces 30) to size and sand them. Use two-sided tape to temporarily attach each endcap to a large piece of scrap while you mill the cove profile on their front faces. Do this on the router table with a bearing-guided bit. When they're completed, epoxy the two endcaps in place.

Making the Pigeon Hole Unit

Most of the pigeon hole assembly elements (pieces 31 through 34) are joined with lap joints in the center and simple butt joints and biscuits at the ends and top. The three small dividers are contained in small dadoes. Use your table saw to nibble out the six dadoes that hold the small dividers in place and your router table to mill the interlocking slots. Before moving on, cut the biscuit slots. All of the dimensions are shown on the Technical Drawings. Again, it is a good idea to pre-finish this unit before you glue it up (mask off the joints). When the finish is dry, glue the assembly together, checking for squareness as you tighten the clamps. Give the outside a final sanding, then apply finish.

Technical Drawings

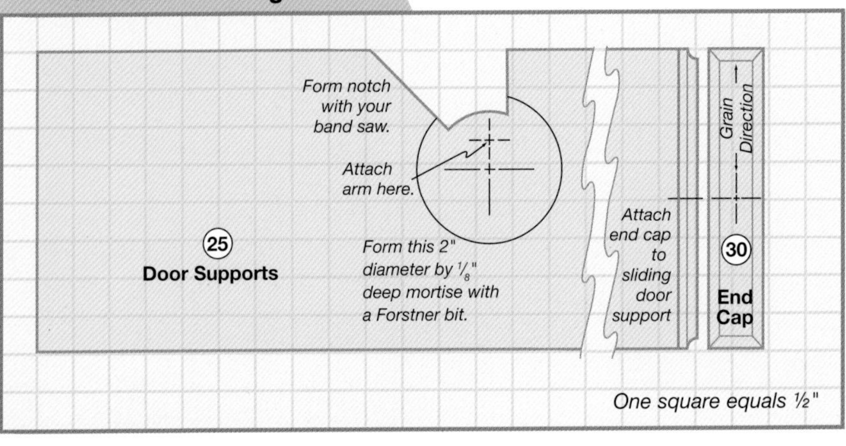

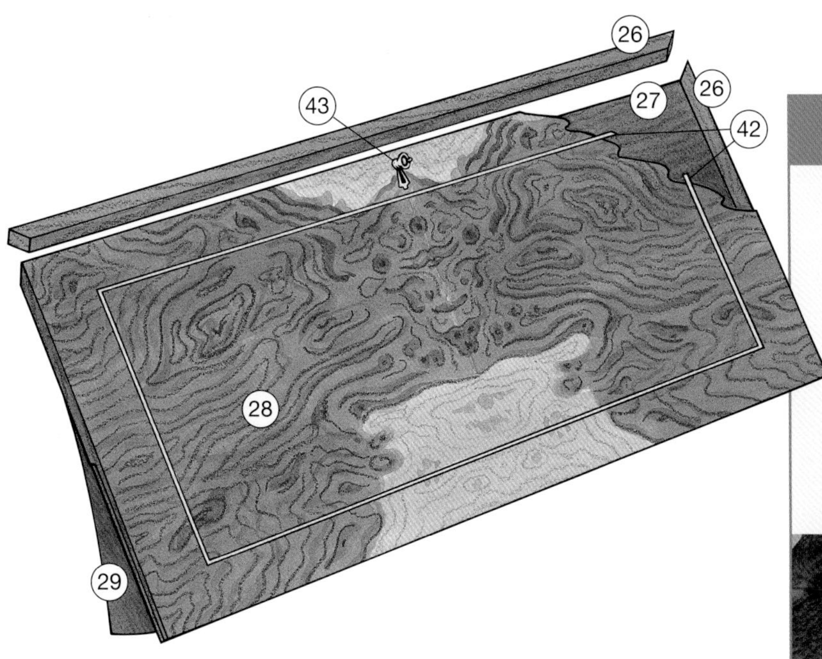

Building the Drawers

Cut stock for the drawers (pieces 35 through 40) and join the sides to the fronts and backs with through dovetails. We used a Keller Dovetail jig with two different sizes of bits (see the Technical Drawings for the dimensions and the photos on the facing page for milling details), but any similar dovetailing jig will work just as well. If you don't own a dovetail jig, you can cut them by hand. Use a ¼" bit in your router table to cut stopped grooves for the bottoms (see the Technical Drawings), then glue up and clamp all three drawers.

For aesthetic reasons, we decided to cover the dovetails on the front face of the large drawer. After planing some walnut (piece 41) to 3⁄32" thickness, center it on the drawer front before gluing and clamping it in place. When the glue dries, use a flush-trim bit to clean the edges.

Adding Final Touches and Finish

To continue the striping theme established on the front faces of the legs, follow the same technique used there to apply stringing (piece 42) to the door face and the face of the large drawer. All of the locations and dimensions are shown on the Technical Drawings.

Now you're ready to finish the rest of the bare surfaces. Remove all the hardware and thoroughly sand the project. Apply three coats of finish, sanding between coats with 400-grit wet/dry paper. Either lacquer or satin varnish would make a durable and attractive topcoat for this desk.

When the finish is dry, locate the key pull according to the Technical Drawings and follow the manufacturer's instructions to install it. Drill pilot holes for the key pull, the drawer support pulls and the drawer pulls (pieces 43, 44, and 45), and screw them in place at the locations shown on the Technical Drawings. Finally, apply a little wax to the door supports so they slide easily. Then breathe a big sigh of relief at completing such an ambitious project! This one is sure to become a family heirloom.

Burl Veneer

If this is the first time you've ever ordered burl veneer, you'll be surprised when you receive it. Burl veneer is definitely not ready to use right out of the box. Because of the many different grain directions, there's a tremendous amount of stress in the veneer. Never fear—waves, and even holes, are quite acceptable. But the first step in readying the veneer for use is to get it flat.

Do this by soaking your wavy panels in glycerine-based veneer treatment. Once it's saturated, start forming a big sandwich. This begins with a piece of flat ¾" melamine-covered MDF, cut at least ⅛" bigger all around than the sheet of veneer. On top of this, place a sheet of fiberglas window screen and six sheets of newspaper to prevent bonding between the paper and burl. Place the wet veneer on the screen, then complete the sandwich with more screen, newspaper and plywood. Clamp everything tight with a set of curved cauls to form a press.

Fill larger holes in the burl veneer with cut-outs of similarly colored veneer. Place a piece of masking tape behind the hole and glue the new piece in place.

Replace the newspaper after four hours and again after another eight. Do this twice a day for about a week. In extreme cases, you may have to go through this entire process twice, but it's well worth the effort as it makes the rest of the veneering work much easier.

A slick way to book-match the veneer with a straight, clean joint is to sandwich the two pieces between MDF panels. Hold them tightly together and slice them off on the table saw.

When the veneer is dry, fill any holes, holding your piece up to the light to spot them. Filling them now prevents them from trapping gobs of glue later. On larger holes, take trimmings from the edge of the sheet where it will be cut off, and place them on your bench. Align the hole over them, match the colors, and trim to fit. Use masking tape on the top side to hold these trimmings in place.

Now clamp the veneer back in its press and keep it there until you're ready to glue the veneer to the plywood panel.

Technical Drawings

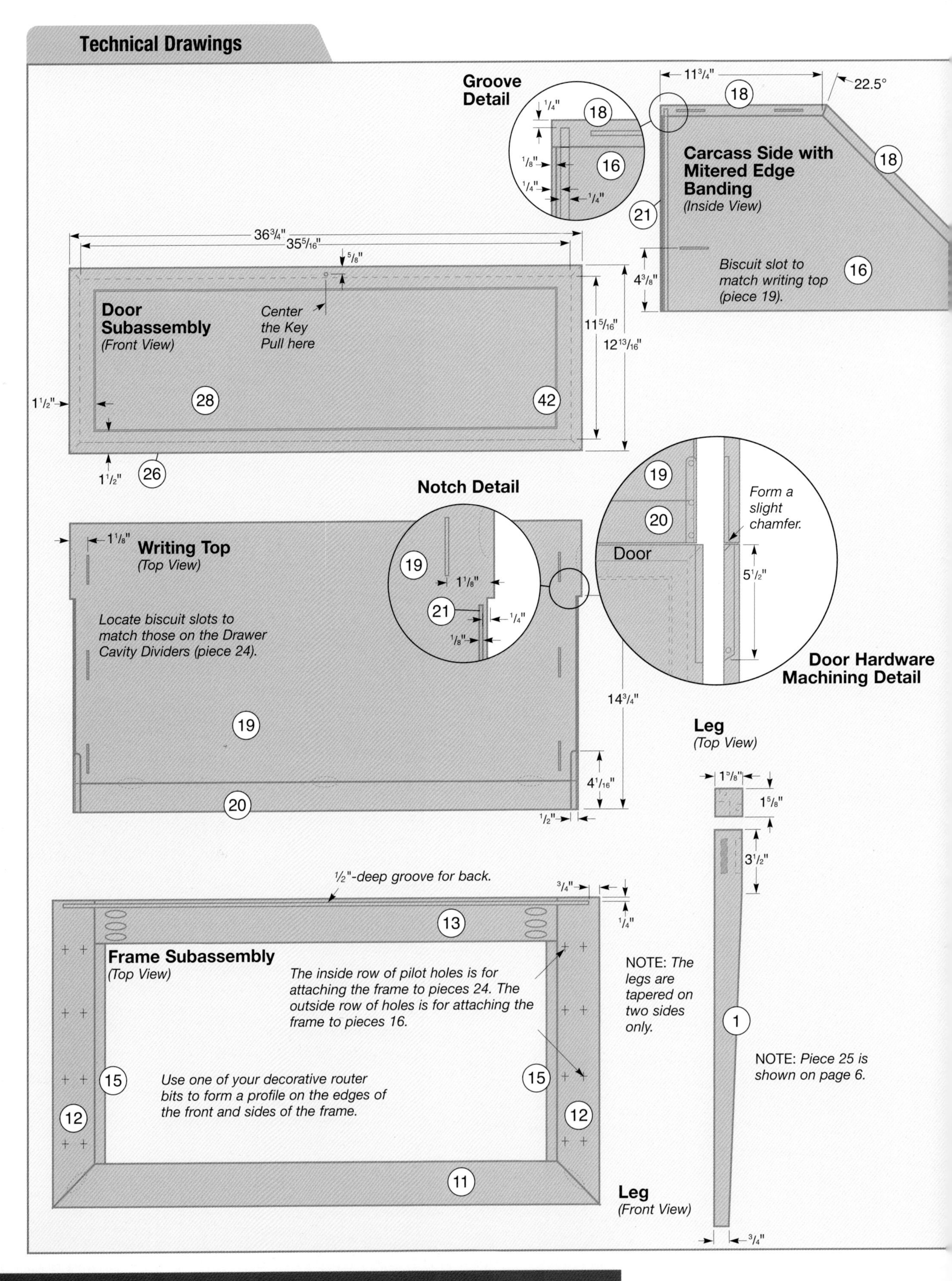

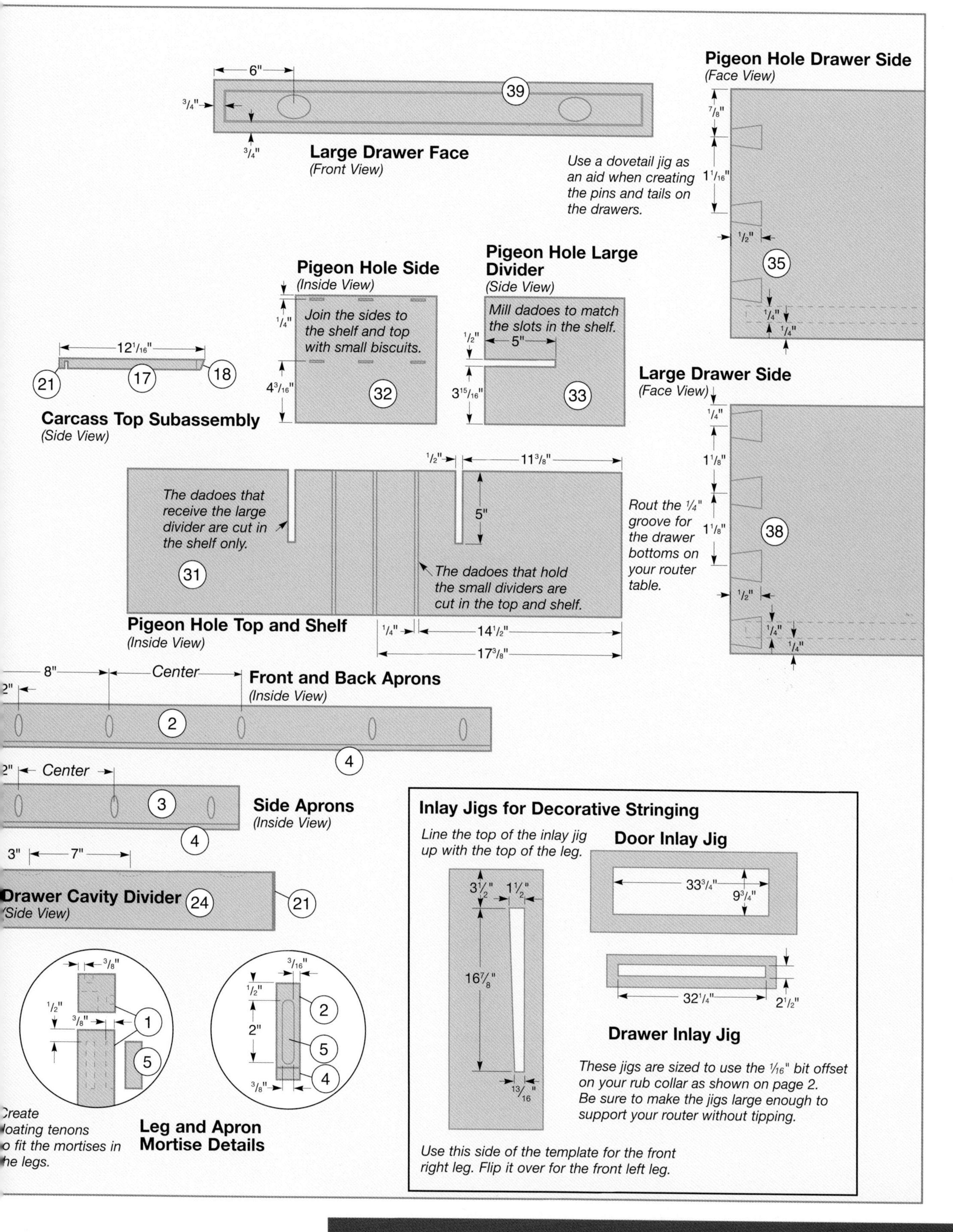
6"
3/4"
39
3/4"
Large Drawer Face
(Front View)
Pigeon Hole Drawer Side
(Face View)
7/8"
Use a dovetail jig as an aid when creating the pins and tails on the drawers.
1 1/16"
1/2"
35
1/4"
1/4"
Pigeon Hole Side
(Inside View)
1/4"
Join the sides to the shelf and top with small biscuits.
4 3/16"
32
Pigeon Hole Large Divider
(Side View)
Mill dadoes to match the slots in the shelf.
1/2"
5"
3 15/16"
33
12 1/16"
21
17
18
Carcass Top Subassembly
(Side View)
Large Drawer Side
(Face View)
1/4"
1 1/8"
1 1/8"
38
Rout the 1/4" groove for the drawer bottoms on your router table.
1/2"
1/4"
1/4"
1/2"
11 3/8"
The dadoes that receive the large divider are cut in the shelf only.
5"
31
The dadoes that hold the small dividers are cut in the top and shelf.
Pigeon Hole Top and Shelf
(Inside View)
1/4"
14 1/2"
17 3/8"
8"
Center
Front and Back Aprons
(Inside View)
2
4
Center
3
Side Aprons
(Inside View)
4
3"
7"
Drawer Cavity Divider
Side View)
24
21
3/8"
1/2"
3/8"
1
5
3/16"
1/2"
2"
2
5
4
3/8"
Create floating tenons to fit the mortises in the legs.
Leg and Apron Mortise Details
Inlay Jigs for Decorative Stringing
Line the top of the inlay jig up with the top of the leg.
Door Inlay Jig
3 1/2"
1 1/2"
16 7/8"
13/16"
33 3/4"
9 3/4"
32 1/4"
2 1/2"
Drawer Inlay Jig
These jigs are sized to use the 1/16" bit offset on your rub collar as shown on page 2. Be sure to make the jigs large enough to support your router without tipping.
Use this side of the template for the front right leg. Flip it over for the front left leg.

Queen Anne's Writing Desk

No furniture is more refined than Queen Anne, and this desk is full of the graceful curves that characterize the style. If you've never taken on the challenge of making cabriole legs, now's the time. Our instructions will walk you through an abbreviated "crash course." It's also a great project to splurge for some premium mahogany.

by Chris Inman

For an English monarch whose reign lasted a scant twelve years, it's remarkable that the legacy of Queen Anne's rule can be found in nearly every furniture store today. The irony is she couldn't have had more than an inkling that a new style was in the offing, since it actually evolved after her death, during the reign of King George I. For some reason, furniture built in this style became known in America as Queen Anne, even though it was labeled Georgian in its native country.

The cornerstone of Queen Anne design is the cyma or S curve, which is most clearly seen in cabriole legs and ogee moulding. Queen Anne furnituremakers also popularized shell carvings and the curved bonnet tops seen on many chests and secretaries.

The desk in this article has many features typical of Queen Anne style. The cabriole legs, which may appear difficult to make, are actually easier than you might think. To help you out, we've laid out a step-by-step approach to cutting and shaping the legs on the Technical Drawing on page 18. If you want even more detailed information on building Queen Anne furniture, take a look at the book "Queen Anne Furniture: History, Design and Construction," by Norm Vandal.

The materials for this desk do add up, but the $400 that you'll spend on the lumber will result in a desk that you'll see priced in a furniture store for more than $2,000. You'll need 8 board feet of 3" x 3" mahogany for the legs, another 16 board feet of 3" x 5" stock for the curved aprons, and 12 board feet of 3/4" material for the desk top. If thick mahogany isn't available in your

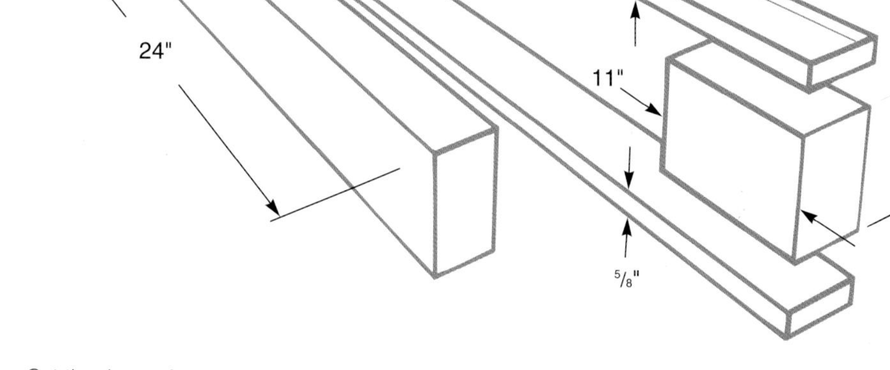

Cut the drawer front directly from the front apron. Rip the top and bottom off the stock, then cut the drawer front from the remaining middle piece. Glue everything but the drawer front back together and you'll have a perfect grain match when the drawer is installed.

After cutting the tenon shoulders, lay out the curved aprons with a template, and band-saw each one to shape.

area, give an Internet lumber source a try. You can use scrap wood for the drawer parts and the support frame. The desk takes approximately 50 hours to build and finish.

Laying the Groundwork

Begin by making a template for the legs (pieces 1). Transfer the leg pattern from the Technical Drawings on page18 onto some thin plywood and cut it out with a band saw. Mill and size your leg stock, then trace the leg shape onto two adjacent sides of each leg blank. Always align the back side of the template with the same edge of the stock for both outlines. Next, layout the mortises for the apron joints as shown in the Elevation Drawing on page 14.

Use a plunge router, a fence and a 3⁄8" straight bit to rout 1"-deep mortises 1 1⁄8" from the back edge of each leg. Make shallow passes to reach full depth, then square the mortise ends with a chisel. Once you've made them the legs, turn your attention to the aprons.

Making the Aprons

Like the legs, the aprons (pieces 2, 3, and 4) are formed from thick stock with a band saw. Cut your 3" x 5" stock long for now and plane it square, but keep it oversized.

Now make the drawer opening, which creates the piece used for the drawer front by cutting the front apron (piece 2) apart. Clamp your table saw fence 3⁄4" from the blade and rip the top and bottom edges off the apron. Keep these pieces labeled so you can rejoin them in the same order later. Plane the outside strips to 5⁄8" in width and plane the inside piece to 3". Cut the 24"-long drawer front from the inside piece (see Elevation, page 11).

Lay out the front apron pieces in order, but rather than gluing them back together just as they were cut, move each inside piece about 1⁄8" closer together to make up for the wood lost in the two crosscuts. Mark this alignment and glue the pieces back together, making sure everything lines up perfectly.

The front apron should end up 4 1⁄4" wide, although if it's off a hair that's not a problem. Take the other three aprons now and rip them 1⁄16" wider than the front apron, then plane them to match. Cut all the aprons to their finished lengths.

The aprons will soon be curved, so it's easier to cut the tenons now while the stock is square. To cut the shoulders, clamp a set up block to your table saw fence and position the fence so the set up block is 7⁄8" from the blade. Raise the blade 2 3⁄8". The front and back aprons are too long and heavy to let hang over the table saw edge during these cuts, so use a roller stand to support the outboard end of the stock. Now cut the front shoulders and, when you've finished, lower the blade to 1⁄4" and cut the back shoulders.

Next, make thin plywood templates for the aprons. Trace the curves onto the top edge of each apron after aligning the templates with the tenons. Be sure to trace the tenon cheeks, too.

Set up your band saw with a 3⁄8" hook-tooth blade for cutting the apron profiles. As you cut, pay close attention to the saw and the wood, slowing down if the blade seems stressed and always brushing the outside edge of the layout lines (see Figure 1). You may want to set up a roller stand to help support the longer aprons as they extend beyond the saw table. When you're done cutting, scrape and sand the apron faces smooth, then pare the tenons to 3⁄8" thick.

Adding the Apron Transition Pieces

In order for the legs and aprons to gracefully blend together, a transition piece (pieces 5) is added to each joint. Make a template for this piece from stiff cardboard or hardboard, then trace this shape eight times onto 1"-thick mahogany resawn from the apron waste. Cut out the transition pieces with a band saw and sand their contoured edges with a drum sander. Next, glue them to the aprons, making sure the end of each piece aligns with the end of the tenons.

Plane and sand the faces of the transition pieces to conform with the aprons, then use a back saw to extend the apron tenon shoulders across the transition pieces. Remove the cheek waste with a chisel. A few passes

*Quick*Tips

"Nearly" Mahogany for Projects on a Modest Budget

If you like the look of Honduras Mahogany but feel the price is too steep, consider substituting clear Spanish cedar. When finished clear, it has similar characteristics to mahogany—just as rich and deep, with a bit of character, too. The cedar is available in fairly wide or thick boards (not as wide as mahogany), and it is a little lighter in weight.

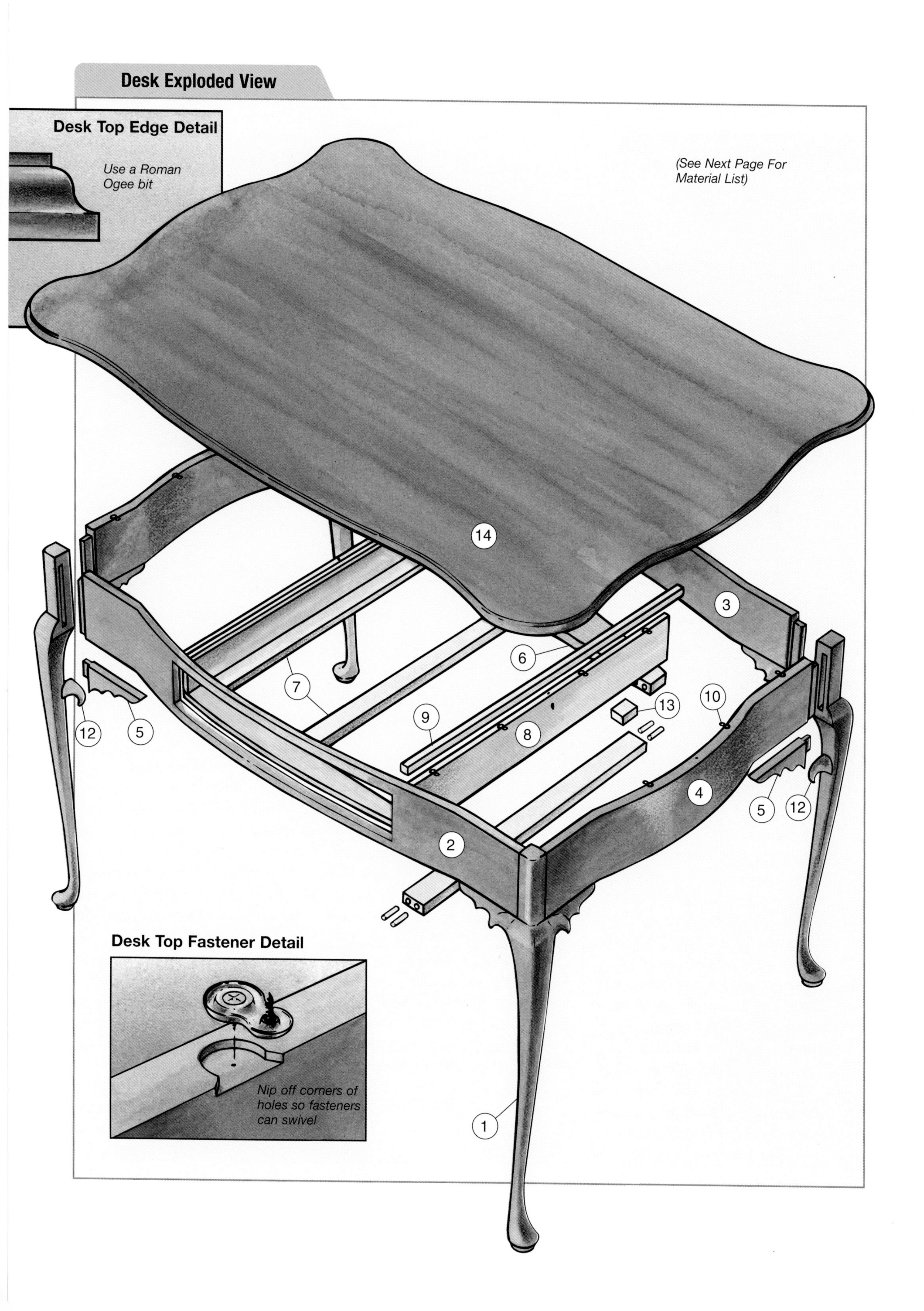
Desk Exploded View
Desk Top Edge Detail
Use a Roman Ogee bit
(See Next Page For Material List)
14
3
6
7
13
10
9
8
12
5
4
5
12
2
1
Desk Top Fastener Detail
Nip off corners of holes so fasteners can swivel

Also, nip off the points on the desk top holes so the fasteners will swivel freely.

Adding the Knee Brackets

Knee brackets (pieces 12) are added to the sides of each leg to blend the legs into the aprons. Make a template for this piece and trace the shape onto some 1⅛"-thick stock. Make sure one side-grain edge of each knee bracket is square so you can get a good joint with the legs. Band saw the knee brackets to shape, then hold each piece in position to trace the curve of the knee onto the knee brackets. Now rough in the curve with a very sharp ¾" chisel—it's helpful to make a carving platform from a piece of scrap and a 1¼"-long drywall screw (see Knee Bracket Details, page 14). Hold the platform in a vise, then drill a pilot hole in the back of each knee bracket. Make sure the pilot holes are positioned in what will be the fat part of the knee brackets. Mount each knee bracket on the platform and carve them to shape.

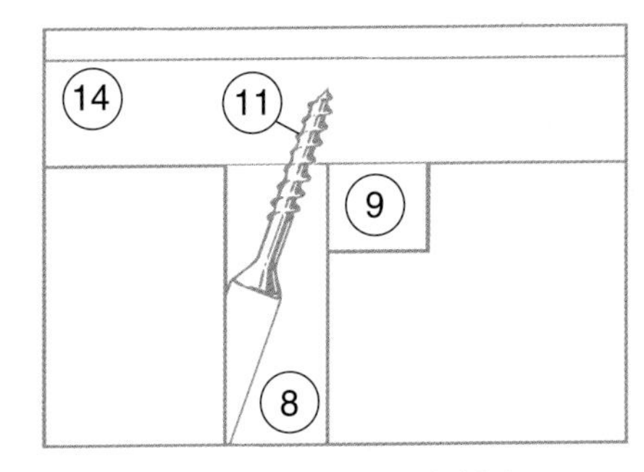

Figure 3: *When installing the hold down screws, first drill angled pilot holes, then counterbore them so the screws will be firmly seated.*

Hold each knee bracket up to a leg and drill a 1⁄16" pilot hole in a concealed place. Now spread glue on the side of the knee brackets, keeping the glue at least ¼" from their back edges, then secure the brackets to the legs with a 1¼" brad. Don't glue the knee brackets to the aprons—if you do, the likelihood of the pieces splitting is very high. Once the glue dries, blend the knee bracket into the legs with chisels and files.

Making the Drawer

Retrieve the drawer front (piece 15) that was cut from the front apron earlier and trim and plane its edges to fit into the drawer opening. Leave a gap of about 1⁄32" on both ends and 1⁄16" on the top. Cut the back (piece 16) and sides (pieces 17) for the drawer from ⅝"-thick secondary wood.

The dovetails for this desk drawer were made with the help of a Leigh jig, however there are plenty of inexpensive jigs on the market that will help you cut similar dovetails. You may need to alter the dimensions of the drawer sides specified in the Material List to comply with your jig's requirements. Rout half-blind dovetails for the front joints and through dovetails for the back. Once the joints are done, insert the drawer front in the drawer opening and trace both the inside and outside curves of the front apron onto its top edge. Be sure to leave the joint area at each end of the drawer front flat or you'll mess up the dovetails.

To hold the bottom (piece 18) in the drawer, rout ¼"-wide grooves in the front, back and sides. Use a ¼" x ½" slot cutter for routing the groove in the drawer front, then rout matching ¼" x ¼" grooves in the other walls with a straight bit and a router fence. Remember to stop the grooves ¼"

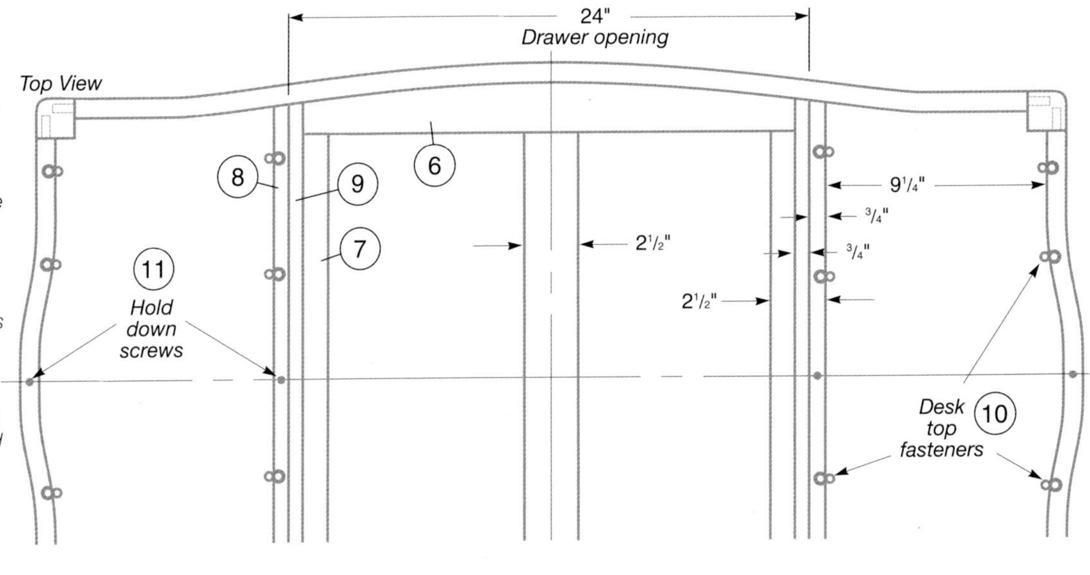

Figure 2: *Center the drawer support frame in the desk and trace the apron curve onto the stiles (pieces 6). After band-sawing the curve on the frame, glue it in position. Add the alignment walls (pieces 8) and retaining strips (pieces 9), then drill the shallow holes for the desk top fasteners and the counterbored pilot holes for the hold down screws.*

One sign of a well-made table is the transition from the apron into the legs, which should be natural and smooth. Another indication is that the builder allowed for wood movement in the top. Several fastener styles are available, so use whatever you have on hand.

short of passing out the ends of the front and back to avoid exposing a hole in the sides of the drawer.

Cut your plywood bottom to size and test the fit of the drawer assembly. Glue the dovetails together when everything fits properly, and check to make sure the drawer is square.

After cleaning up the joints, slip the drawer into the opening and make any adjustments to get it to slide easily. Once the drawer fits, slide it in almost all the way, leaving it protrude about 1⁄32", and glue the drawer stops (pieces 13) to the frame behind the drawer. After the glue dries, belt-sand the drawer front even with the front apron. Now drill holes for the drawer pulls, but don't install them until the finishing is completed.

Building the Writing Surface

Panels the size of this desk top (piece 14) are often prone to warping. Even though mahogany is a very stable wood species, you can guarantee your top remains flat by making it with a number of narrow boards. Pick pieces that are similar in color and grain and, as much as possible, alternate their end grain directions. Joint the edges and glue the boards together, alternating the clamps above and below the panel to prevent any cupping. Wipe off the glue squeeze-out with a damp rag.

Plane the surfaces of the desk top to even the joints, then belt-sand the panel smooth. Use an orbital sander to refine the top surface to 180 grit.

Create a template for tracing the corner detail onto the top's four corners. To accurately position the pattern on the top, draw crossing lines down the middle of the panel, one going with the grain and one across the grain. These lines separate the top into four equal corner sections. Now lay your pattern on the top so its edges align with the layout lines in one corner. Trace around the pattern, then do the other three corners. Cut out the top profile with a jigsaw, and use a palm sander to smooth the edge. Shape the edges with a router and an ogee bit.

Drill 3⁄32" pilot holes in the aprons for the desk top fasteners, then install them with the screws provided. Turn the desk top upside down and flip the base assembly over onto it. Next, center the base on the top and drill pilot holes for the other half of the desk top fasteners—use masking tape on your bit to indicate the proper depth. Your desk construction is now complete.

Finishing Details

Mahogany is a very open-grained wood. If you'd prefer a level, close-pored finish, the pores must be filled. Choose a reddish grain filler, and thin the filler as outlined in the manufacturer's instructions. Work in sections, brushing it on the desk. Wipe up the excess with a dry cloth, then let the filler dry overnight. Wipe off the desk again the next day to remove any residue. The process for filling the grain takes a fair amount of elbow grease.

Sand your desk through 220 grit to get it nice and smooth. Since the mahogany available today isn't very dramatic or colorful, it's nice to stain it a deeper reddish-brown. For natural-looking colors, water based aniline dyes work well, and you can mix the colors to get the exact shade you want. Wear latex gloves while applying the stain, otherwise you'll have colored fingers for the next week. One drawback to using water-based stains is that they raise the grain. To minimize this issue, before staining wipe the bare wood with distilled water, and sand off any grain that raises with 220-grit paper.

Varnish was often used as a finish on original Queen Anne furniture. For a speedy and smooth application, you can spray on varnish with good results. If you're not set up for spray gun finishes, a conventional brushed finish is also fine, or try one of the new gel-style rubbing varnishes. Whichever approach you take, keep an old pro's trick in mind as you work with varnish—let the first coat dry for one day, the second coat two days, the third coat three days, and so on. This will guarantee a hard, completely dry finish. When it's all done, attach the top to the base and mount the drawer pulls.

By now you have an absolutely beautiful masterpiece. If this is your first Queen Anne project, you've covered some exciting new ground. From here you'll be able to undertake many other pieces from this period, and hopefully your legacy will be as long-lived as Queen Anne's.

Technical Drawings

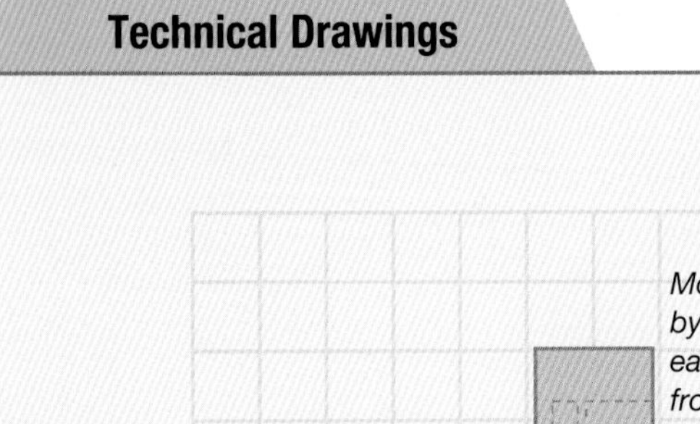

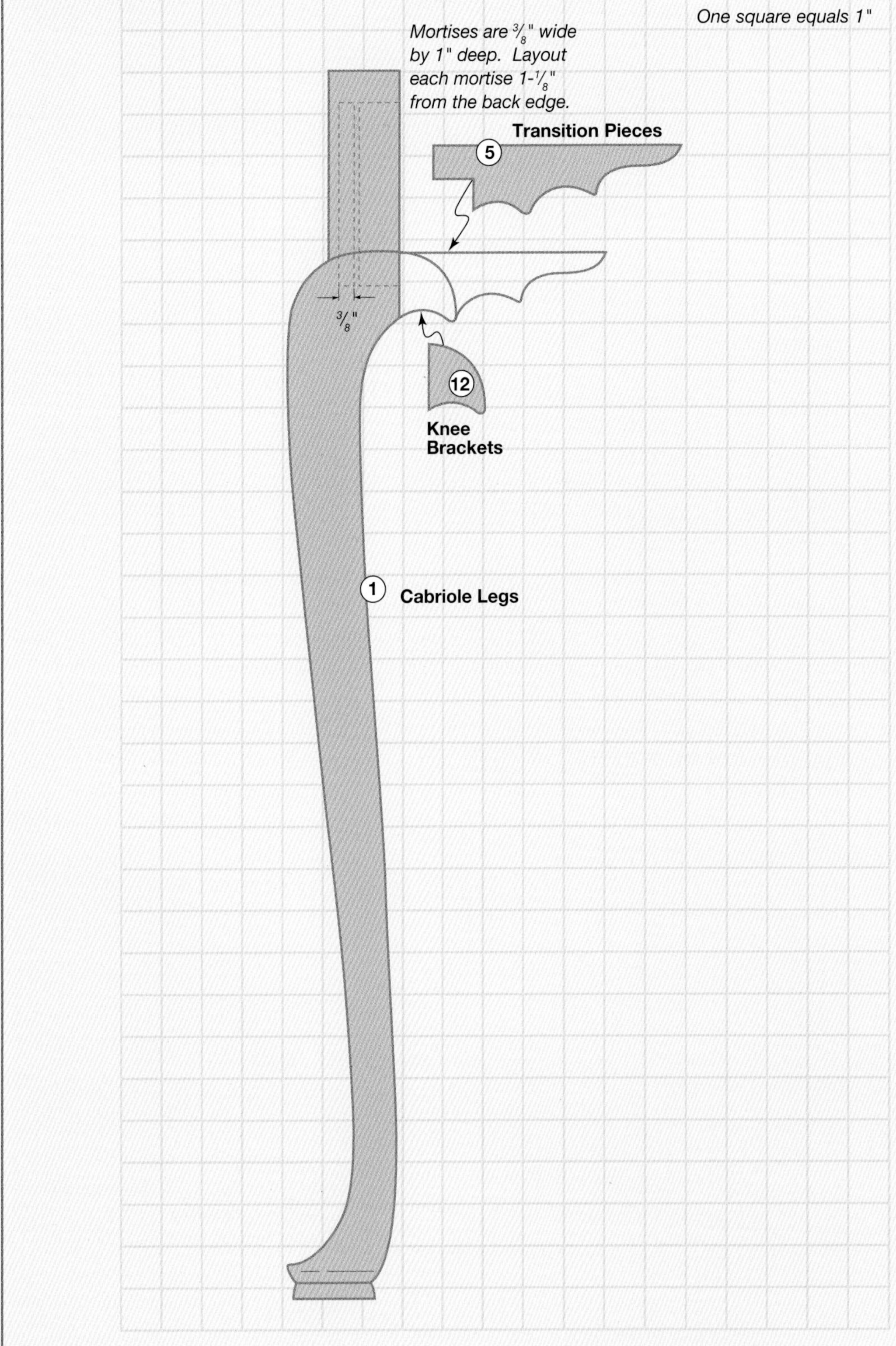

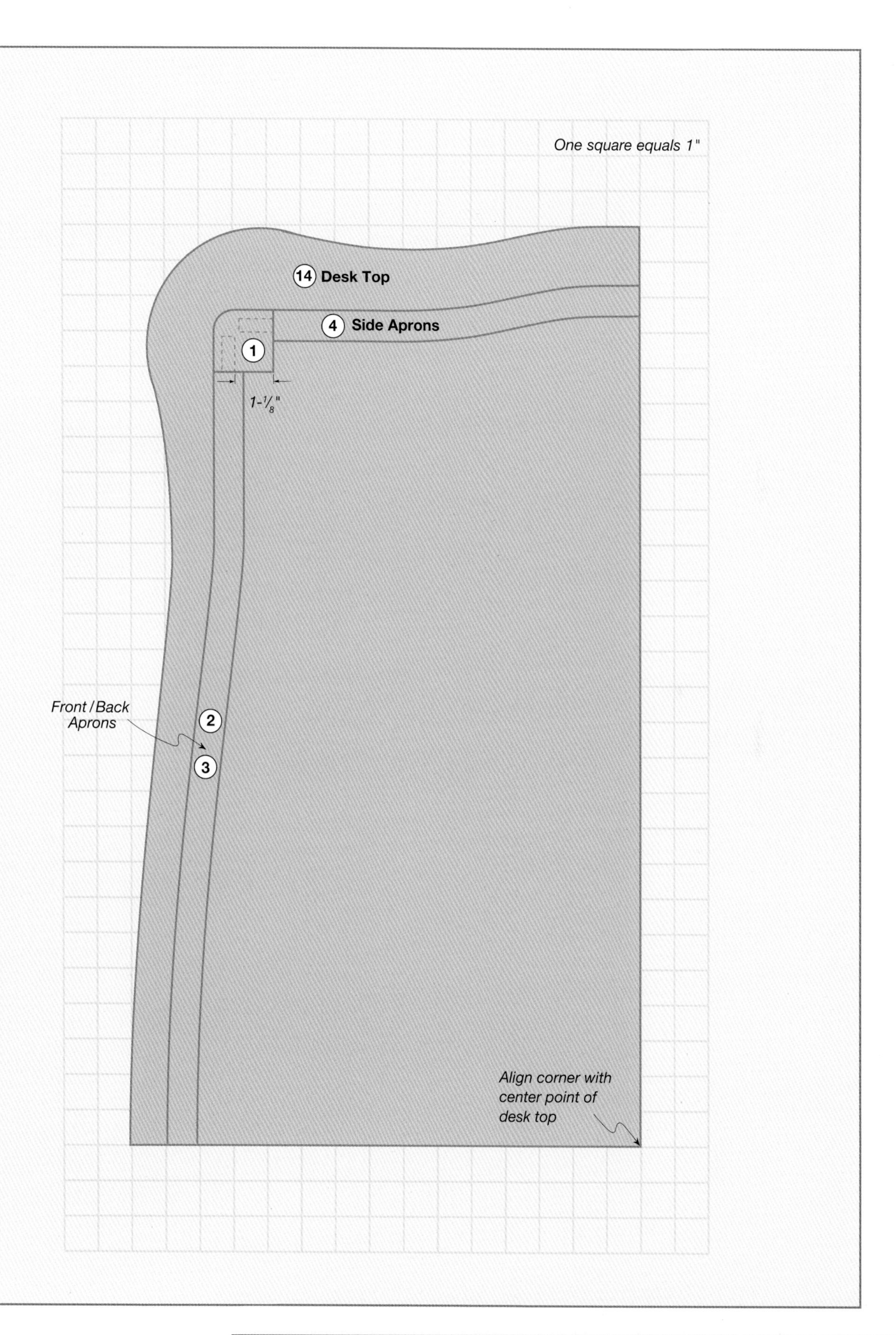
One square equals 1"
14 Desk Top
4 Side Aprons
1
1-1/8"
Front / Back Aprons
2
3
Align corner with center point of desk top

Santa Fe Style Desk

The popularity of southwest style furniture is growing by leaps and bounds, and we've captured its rich, traditional look in this desk design. The front apron, stretchers, and backsplash have an elegant stepped lift, and the overall appearance is understated without being stark. Buy some white ash and give this desk a try.

by Rick White

As it turns out, they do a lot more than punch cattle and drill for oil in the old southwest. Among other things, it's a place where artists and woodworkers have created a rich identity that's completely unique to this part of the country. When I was in Santa Fe a few years ago, I was struck by all of the desert colors, the rough textures of the buildings and the unusual furniture styles. The furniture construction reminded me of the mission pieces that are so popular now, but the distinctive southwestern motif completely separates this more ornate style from its plainer-looking eastern cousins.

This desk is used mostly for writing letters and paying bills, although I built it with enough space to fit a small computer. To keep paperwork and accessories organized I included a few cubbyholes and drawers. In addition, there's a special feature—one you can't see in the photographs. A secret compartment in the desk top will stow important items, like money and keys. If you look at the Exploded View Drawing on page 25, you'll see the compartment clearly.

I chose white ash for the desk because it gets that bone-dry look featured on many of the southwest pieces I saw. The desk requires 7 board feet of 2"-square stock, 18 board feet of ¼"-thick material, 25 board feet of ¾" lumber, and 15 board feet of ½"-thick ash. There's also a small bit of plywood for the hidden parts.

As you can see in the photos, some of the tenons go completely through the legs, which is a trademark of mission furniture pieces as well as those from the southwest. Even though most of this work is done on a table saw and drill press, we recommend sharpening a couple of your favorite chisels for the finer detail work.

Mortising the Legs

To get the best match, always try to cut your desk legs (pieces 1) from the same piece of stock, ripping the edges of the board to get the straightest grain possible. Once the pieces are ripped, joint two adjacent sides on each leg, then plane them to their finished size. Now cut the legs to length and lay out the mortises as shown in the Elevation Drawings on page 23. On the through mortise layouts, be sure to label the shallow haunch areas and draw your lines completely around the legs. The haunched joints may seem like extra work, but they ensure that your aprons and legs will never twist away from each other. To help align the drill bit when boring out the mortise waste, draw a line down the center of the mortise layouts.

Now chuck a ½" bit in your drill press and clamp a fence to its table to align the bit with the center of the mortise layouts. Drill all the mortises 9⁄16" deep first, then re-adjust the drilling depth for the through mortises. When drilling the through holes, bore into the legs from both sides to avoid tearout.

Clean out the mortises with your chisels, again working from both sides of the legs. On the side walls of all the mortises, keep your chisel square to the stock, but undercut the end walls a hair to help fit the tenons.

Cutting the Tenons

Now that the legs are made, cut pieces to size for the aprons (pieces 2, 3, and 4) and stretchers (pieces 5 and 6). The front apron measurement is a little longer than the back apron to allow for cutting away the drawer front later.

To cut the tenons, install a ½" dado blade in your table saw. Raise the blade 1⁄16" and set the fence for cutting cheeks for the through tenons on the side aprons and stretchers (see Figure 1). Next, raise the blade to ¼" and cut edge shoulders on the side apron tenons, then raise the blade to ⅝" and cut edge shoulders on the side stretchers. Now raise the blade to ¾" and reset the fence for cutting haunches on the aprons. Remove the waste between the apron through tenons with a hand saw and chisel.

Figure 1: *Chamfer the ends of the tenons by tilting your blade 45° and clamping a clearance block to the fence to align the workpiece with the blade.*

Lower the dado blade back to 1⁄16" and set the fence for cutting ½"-long tenons on the front apron, back apron and back stretcher. Once the cheeks are cut, raise the blade to ¼" and cut edge shoulders on these pieces.

The ends of the through tenons are chamfered to add a decorative appearance. Tilt a standard table saw blade 45°, then clamp a clearance block to the fence (see Figure 2). Adjust the setup to cut ⅛"-deep chamfers. For the inside edges on the double apron tenons, form the chamfers with a file.

Decorating the Aprons and Stretchers

The patterns for the aprons and stretchers shown on the Technical Drawings on pages 30 to 31. The drawings detail the decorative shapes and V-groove lines on these pieces.

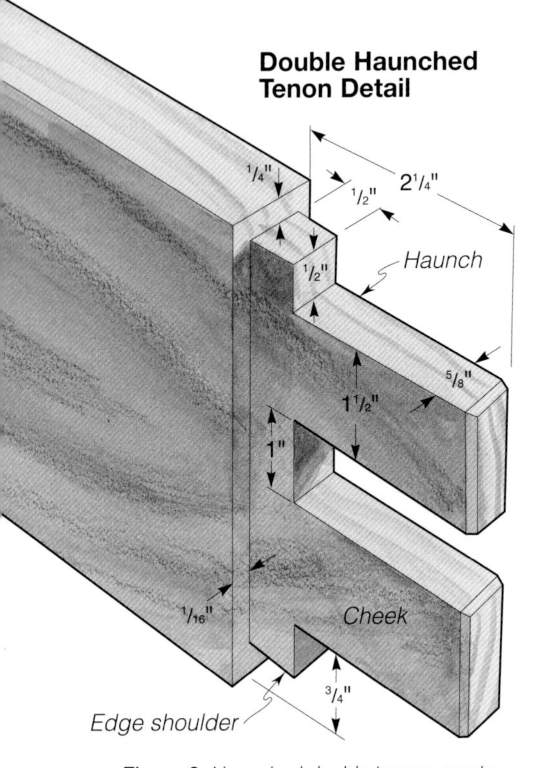

Figure 2: *Haunched double tenons create a strong joint and guarantee that the aprons and legs will never twist out of alignment.*

Cut out the patterns, then trace the outside shapes and the routing lines onto your stock. (Note: the stretchers have decorative lines on both sides, while the aprons feature lines on the outside only.) Lay out the routing lines on the legs as well (see Technical Drawings on page 23).

Now chuck a ½" V-grooving bit in your router and install a straightedge guide. Using the guide to center the bit on each line, rout to a depth of 3⁄16". Once all the V-grooving is done, bandsaw the outside shapes on the aprons and stretchers. Smooth the edges, then rout a ⅛"-deep chamfer on all the stretcher and leg edges, and all but the top inside edge of the aprons.

Notice that the front apron is a little long to accommodate cutting out the drawer front (piece 17). Now is the time to remove that piece. Lay out the drawer on the front apron (see Technical Drawings on page 23) and cut it with your table saw. Set the drawer piece aside and cut the remaining front apron pieces to a length of 12".

The free ends of the front apron are supported in the desk assembly by two apron supports (pieces 7). Cut the supports to size, then set up a ⅜" dado blade in your table saw to form ⅜" x ⅜" tongues on each end of both pieces as shown in the Elevation Drawings on page 24. After cutting the tongues, use the dado blade to cut slots in the front and back aprons to fit the tongues on the apron supports.

To allow the desk top to expand and contract freely, it's held to the base with table top fasteners (pieces 8). You should prepare for this hardware by cutting a ⅜"-deep slot on the inside surface of the aprons and on one face of each apron support. Set the fence ½" from the blade, and be sure to avoid cutting into any of the through tenons.

Assembling the Base

Glue together the sides of the base assembly first and, after they dry, join them with the front and back pieces and the apron supports. It's wise to take a wet rag and clean the glue off the through tenons right away. Later, if you see glue that you missed, use a sharp chisel to slice it off.

A common technique on southwestern furniture is crosspinning the mortise and tenon joints. In earlier times, when glue wasn't as dependable as it is today, these pins provided insurance against loosening joints. Today they aren't needed so much, but we still like the look. However, here's an easier, more modern method.

First drill 7⁄32" pilot holes with ⅜" counterbores in the legs so the holes are centered on the through tenons. Next, lay out a ⅜" square around each hole and use a chisel to square the counterbores. Now drive a #8-1¼" wood screw (pieces 9) into each pilot hole to pin the joints. To cover the screws, rip a ⅜" x ⅜" x 24" strip and cut it into ½"-long plugs (pieces 10). Put a few drops of glue into each square hole and drive in the plugs. After the glue sets, cut off the excess and sand the plugs flush.

There's just one more piece to add to the base assembly to make it structurally sound. Make a spanner (piece 11) to fit between the apron supports in your drawer opening (see Elevation Drawings) and clamp it into place. Now drill two 7⁄32" countersunk pilot holes through the apron supports into each end of the spanner and drive in #8-1¼" screws to secure the parts.

Making the Top and Cubbyholes

The desk top (piece 12) is made up of five boards that are jointed and glued together. Build your panel a little wider and longer than the finished size, then cut it down later. Scrape off the glue when it dries to a rubbery consistency and, after the panel sits overnight, sand its surfaces smooth.

You'll also need to join several boards for the cubbyhole structures (pieces 13, 14, and 15). It's important that the grain in all the cubbyhole pieces run parallel with the grain in the top, otherwise they're likely to split with seasonal movement. RIck made a 60"-long by 12"-wide panel and cut it into the various pieces the following day.

The cubby sides and dividers are secured to the desk top with tongue and dado joints (see Elevation Drawings on page 132). Lay out the dadoes in the top and chuck a ¼" bit in your router, setting it to cut ¼" deep. Now make a T-square jig for routing the dadoes in the top (see Figure 3). Align the bit paths in the jig with the layout lines on the top and rout the dadoes, making sure to start the dadoes ½" from the top's back edge.

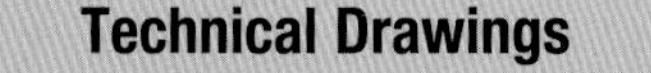

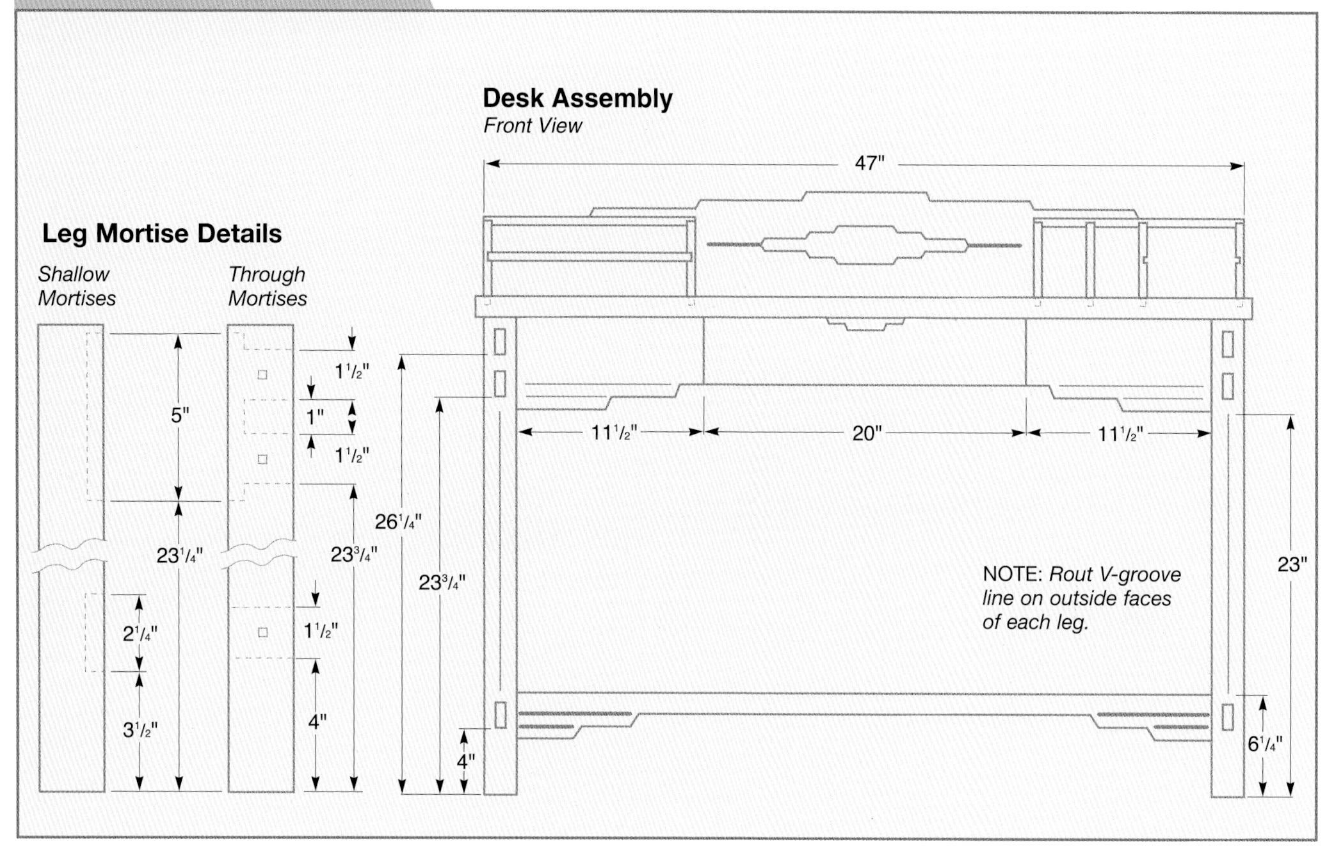

Lay out the access hole for the secret compartment as shown in the Elevation Drawing on page 24, and drill through each corner of the layout with a ½" bit. Now cut the hole with a jigsaw, then smooth the edges with a file and rout around the opening with a ½" roundover bit.

Finish up your work on the top panel by routing its side and front edges with a ¾" roundover bit, but cut with the lower part of the bit only (see Figure 4). Sand the edges thoroughly to remove any saw marks, then sand the whole top to 120 grit.

The panel for the cubbyholes has dried by now, so sand it smooth and cut it into the pieces listed in the Material List on page 24. Use the full-size patterns to lay out the shape on the front edge of the shelf and one of the dividers, and use a jigsaw to make the cuts. Once this is done, install a ½" dado blade in your table saw to cut the ¼"-deep dadoes and rabbets in both top pieces and in some of the sides and dividers (see Elevation Drawings on page 24). As always, be sure to clamp a wood face to your fence to protect it during the rabbet cuts.

Now replace the ½" dado blade with a ¼" blade, and raise it ⅛" to cut the bottom tongues on the cubbyhole sides and dividers. Keep the wood face clamped to the fence and slide the fence right up to the blade. Cut the cheeks first, then flip the pieces up on their front edge to cut a ⅛"-deep shoulder on the front of each tongue.

Sand all the cubbyhole pieces to 120 grit, then assemble them on the desk top. When the glue dries, cut the drawer runners (pieces 25) and glue them into place, then rout the top edges of both cubbyhole structures (except for the back edge) with a chamfering bit.

We've left cutting the backsplash (piece 16) until now because, for the best appearance, it has to fit your desk exactly. Cut the backsplash to fit behind the cubbyholes on your desk top, then cut out the full-size pattern—be sure to cut out the interior opening on the pattern as well. Center the pattern on your backsplash and trace it onto the wood (be sure to trace the interior opening and the V-grooves on both sides of the stock). Now rout the V-grooves with a straightedge guide just as you did earlier on the aprons and stretchers. Next, place a back-up board underneath the backsplash and drill through the board with a ½" bit at each turn of the interior opening (see Figure 5). Use a jigsaw to cut the opening from hole to hole, then cut the decorative top edge. Once the edges are smooth, rout both sides of the opening with a chamfering bit.

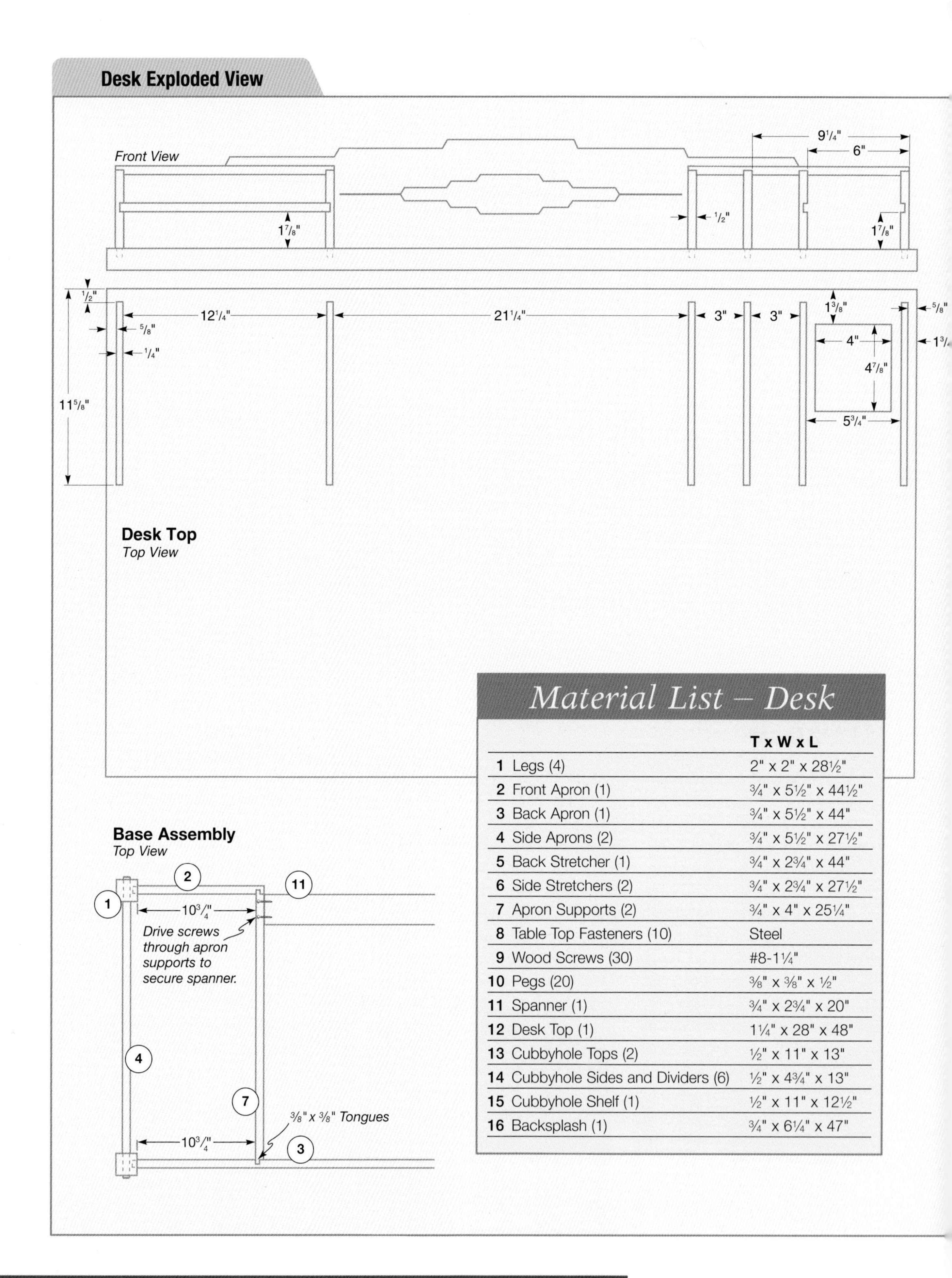

Material List – Desk

		T x W x L
1	Legs (4)	2" x 2" x 28½"
2	Front Apron (1)	¾" x 5½" x 44½"
3	Back Apron (1)	¾" x 5½" x 44"
4	Side Aprons (2)	¾" x 5½" x 27½"
5	Back Stretcher (1)	¾" x 2¾" x 44"
6	Side Stretchers (2)	¾" x 2¾" x 27½"
7	Apron Supports (2)	¾" x 4" x 25¼"
8	Table Top Fasteners (10)	Steel
9	Wood Screws (30)	#8-1¼"
10	Pegs (20)	⅜" x ⅜" x ½"
11	Spanner (1)	¾" x 2¾" x 20"
12	Desk Top (1)	1¼" x 28" x 48"
13	Cubbyhole Tops (2)	½" x 11" x 13"
14	Cubbyhole Sides and Dividers (6)	½" x 4¾" x 13"
15	Cubbyhole Shelf (1)	½" x 11" x 12½"
16	Backsplash (1)	¾" x 6¼" x 47"

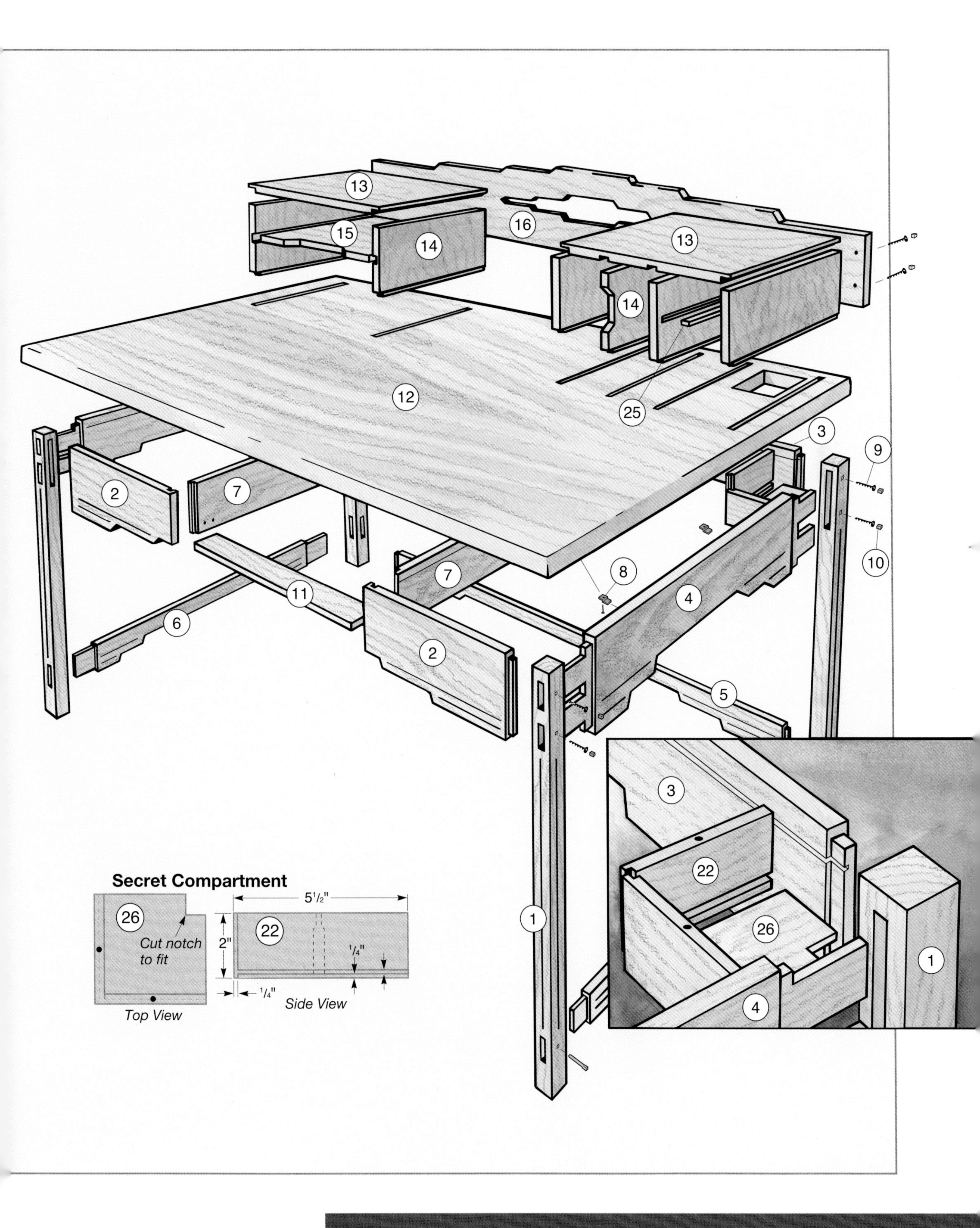
13
15
14
16
13
14
12
25
3
9
2
7
10
8
7
11
4
6
2
5
3
22
26
1
1
4
Secret Compartment
26
Cut notch to fit
Top View
5½"
2"
22
¼"
¼"
Side View

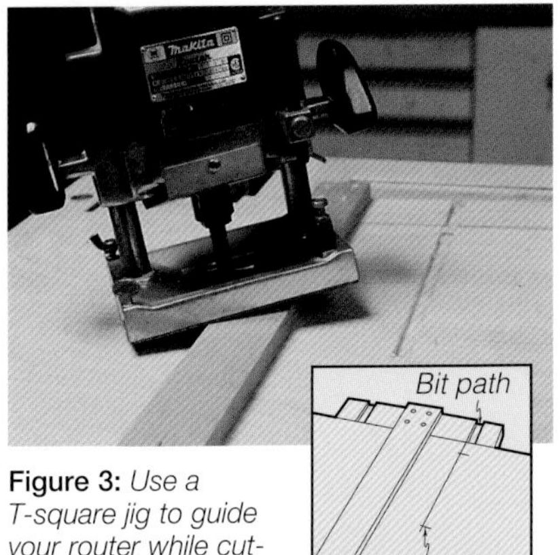

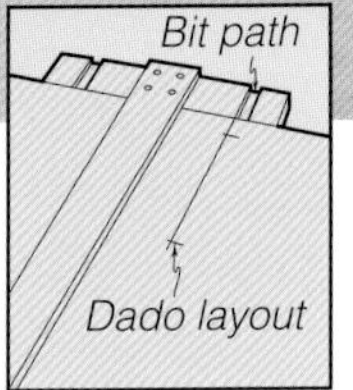

Figure 3: *Use a T-square jig to guide your router while cutting dadoes in the top.*

Clamp the backsplash into position on the desk top and drill four counterbored pilot holes into each cubbyhole structure. In addition, drill four counterbored pilot holes up into the backsplash from underneath the desk top. Square the counterbores in the backsplash and drive a #8-1¼" screw into each hole. Finish up by gluing plugs into the backsplash holes.

Making the Drawers and Secret Compartment

Begin work on this stage by cutting the fronts (pieces 17 and 18), backs (pieces 18 and 19) and sides (pieces 20 and 21) of the drawers, but be sure to measure your drawer openings first to see if these sizes fit well in your desk. Cut the walls (pieces 22) for the secret compartment while you're at it.

There are many different joints you can use for the drawers in this project. Rick decided that sliding dovetails on the large drawer and double rabbets on the small cubbyhole drawer would serve well. For a thorough discussion on drawer joints, turn to page 28.

For routing the dovetail slots in the large drawer, use a ½" dovetail bit raised 5⁄16" (see the Drawer Elevation on the next page for the layout). You may want to hog out some of the initial waste with a straight bit first, then switch to the dovetail bit. When cutting the tails, always test your setup on scrap wood first, with the bit partially buried in the router table fence. After you get a good test fit, cut the tails on the drawer back and sides.

The rabbet joints for the small drawer and secret compartment pieces are cut using a ¼" dado blade in your table saw. As with any cut where the fence is set right next to the blade, clamp on a wood face for protection.

Once the joints are formed, switch to a ½" dado blade and cut the drawer runner grooves in the small drawer sides (see Elevation Drawings on page 27). Now cut out the full-size patterns of both drawer fronts to trace the shapes onto your stock, then cut the shapes with a jigsaw. File and sand the edges smooth.

Cutting grooves for the bottom panels (pieces 23, 24, and 26) can be done with a ¼" straight bit in your router table. During this operation, be sure to avoid routing beyond the dovetail slots in the large drawer front, although you should rout the full length of all the other pieces (except for the large drawer back, which doesn't require a groove).

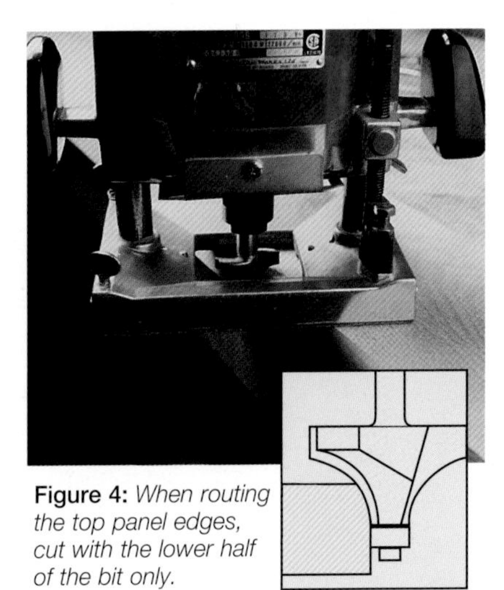

Figure 4: *When routing the top panel edges, cut with the lower half of the bit only.*

Figure 5: *To form the opening on the backsplash, first drill relief holes at every inside corner, then use your jigsaw to cut from hole to hole.*

Cut the bottom panels for the drawers and check the fit of the parts. When everything fits correctly, glue the drawers together. On the large drawer, secure the bottom to the back wall with a screw, and on the small drawer, be sure to extend the drawer runner grooves through the back with a chisel after the glue dries.

The bottom of the secret compartment must fit snugly around the right rear leg of the desk. Cut the piece to size, then remove one corner. Drill counterbored pilot holes in the walls for screwing the compartment to the desk top, then glue the unit together and screw it into place.

Install the drawer slides (pieces 27) in the desk and on the large drawer. Once you have the drawer operating properly, disassemble the hardware to give your desk a final sanding. Apply several coats of brush-on lacquer, sanding lightly between coats to remove any dust nibs. Now put the desk together for the last time and attach the top to the base with tabletop fasteners securing these parts.

If you fall in love with the design of your new desk, maybe its high time to take a trip to Santa Fe and investigate other furniture you could build to go along with this one.

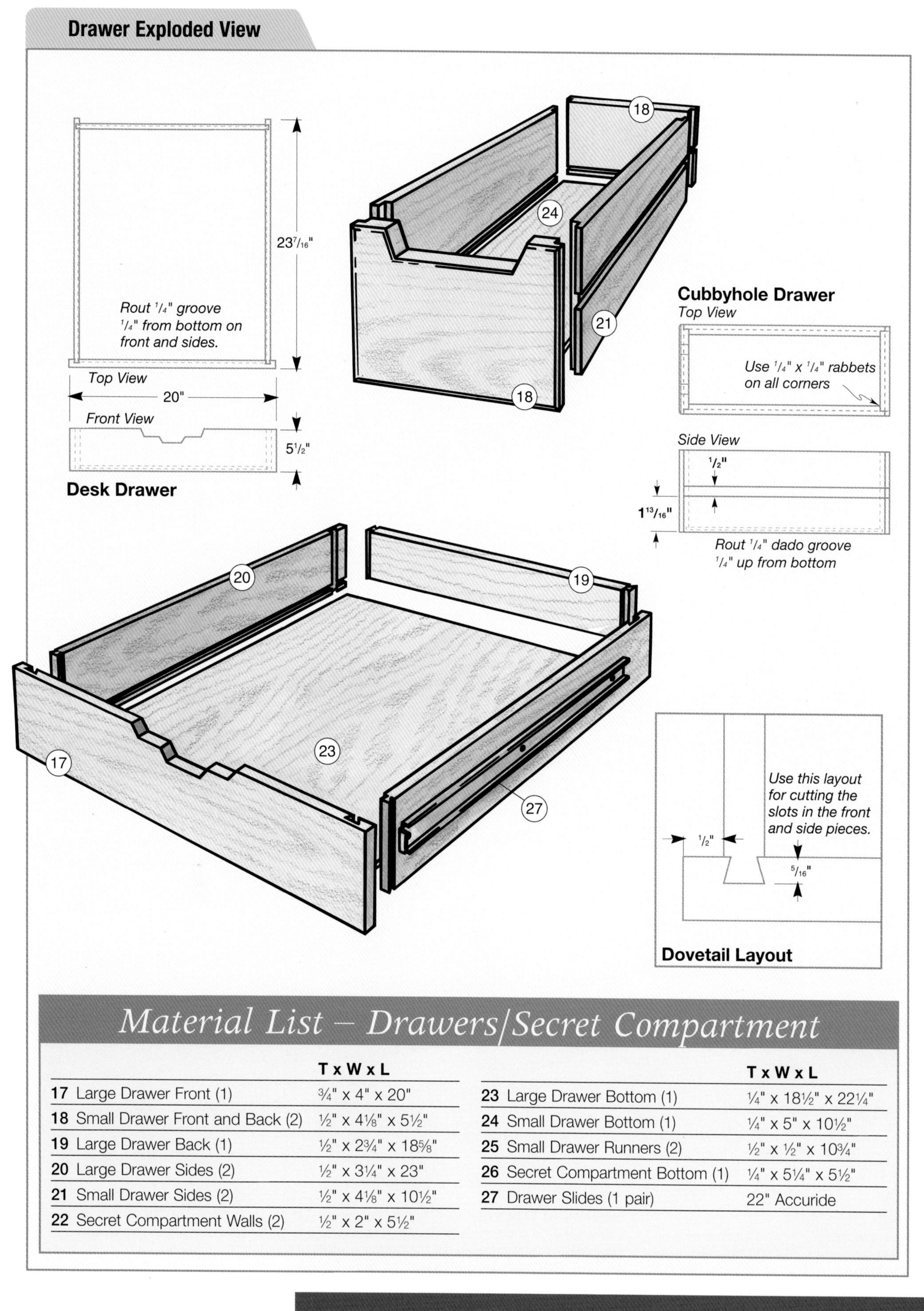

Material List – Drawers/Secret Compartment

	T x W x L
17 Large Drawer Front (1)	¾" x 4" x 20"
18 Small Drawer Front and Back (2)	½" x 4⅛" x 5½"
19 Large Drawer Back (1)	½" x 2¾" x 18⅝"
20 Large Drawer Sides (2)	½" x 3¼" x 23"
21 Small Drawer Sides (2)	½" x 4⅛" x 10½"
22 Secret Compartment Walls (2)	½" x 2" x 5½"
23 Large Drawer Bottom (1)	¼" x 18½" x 22¼"
24 Small Drawer Bottom (1)	¼" x 5" x 10½"
25 Small Drawer Runners (2)	½" x ½" x 10¾"
26 Secret Compartment Bottom (1)	¼" x 5¼" x 5½"
27 Drawer Slides (1 pair)	22" Accuride

Matching Drawer Joints to Projects

Drawers serve many functions, but it's not always necessary to build them to survive a hurricane. In some circumstances, using a lighter duty construction method is more efficient, saving both time and materials. The key is understanding the type of stress the drawer will undergo during its lifetime, and then selecting an appropriate joint for the application. If, on the other hand, you're building a reproduction piece, by all means use dovetail joints. If you're making a basic cupboard drawer, then consider some of the options discussed below.

The first thing to figure out is what type of drawer you plan to build (see drawings below). Each type has requirements that make some joints inappropriate, and the use of drawer slides also affects the joint selection.

Inset
This classic, drawer style requires accurate fitting.

Overlay Drawer
An excellent choice for hiding gaps and slide hardware.

False Front Drawer
For production speed and adjustability, nothing beats this technique.

Strength and Good Looks

Among drawer joints, dovetails are the strongest and most visually appealing. They'll withstand considerable pulling forces on a drawer front, and the large amount of gluing surface between the pins and tails guarantees a durable bond. The classic through dovetail joint is suited to drawers where you want to show the joinery, whereas half-blind dovetails hide the joinery from in front. A typical inset drawer has half-blind dovetails on the front and through dovetails on the back, as is always true of overlay drawers that feature dovetail joints.

Learning to cut dovetail joints takes time and practice, and even after you develop these skills, dovetails require more time to make than most machined joints. Dovetail jigs for use with routers definitely speed production, but they are most efficient to use on larger jobs because of their long set-up procedure.

While dovetails are clearly the elite drawer joint, the more modest box (also called finger) joint provides very much the same capabilities, with the distinct advantage of being easy to cut on a table saw. If you're after production speed, strength and an interesting appearance, the finger joint is an excellent alternative. And if you're using plywood for the hidden drawer sides and back, finger joints are the ideal choice.

Speed and Utility

With drawer slides that float effortlessly on ball bearings or nylon rollers, the necessity for a rock-solid drawer joint is diminished. Since these drawers operate with such a light touch, little stress is put on the joints. Given this drawer slide technology, simpler joints make sense for the production woodworker.

A simple dado joint is always fine for a drawer back since little stress is directed here. When used on the front of a drawer, however, the dado joint must be pinned with a few brads to create a mechanical connection between the two pieces of wood. Pulling on a drawer front that's just dadoed and glued to the sides will eventually break the bond. Gluing a plywood drawer bottom into the sides and front will reinforce this structure immensely. The dado joint is highly suited for plywood construction, where you'll benefit from some side grain to side grain glue bond. In hardwood, the joint is entirely side grain to end grain, so you have to depend on a tight fit and the wonders of modern glue.

A step above the simple dado is a tongue and dado joint. The additional shoulder in this joint strengthens the drawer against racking. Like the dado joint, this one works best for the back of a drawer or for a false front drawer. If you do use the tongue and dado joint for the back of a drawer, you can increase its strength by moving the joint further from the end of the board and

Through Dovetails
Generally considered the strongest and most attractive drawer joint, through dovetails were once the standard even on production projects.

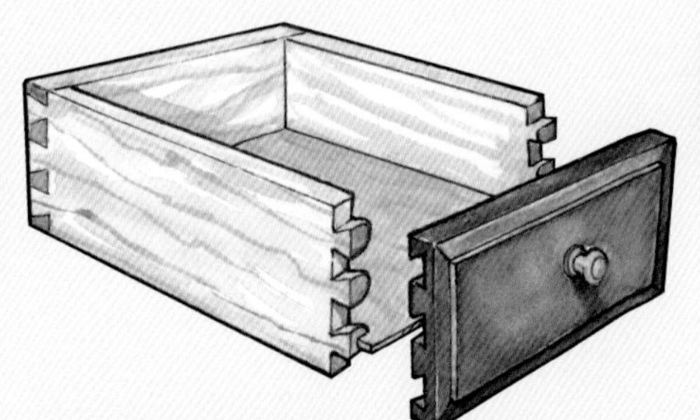

Half-blind Dovetails
Usually half-blind dovetails are cut on the drawer front only, but with modern routing methods many woodworkers use them on the back as well.

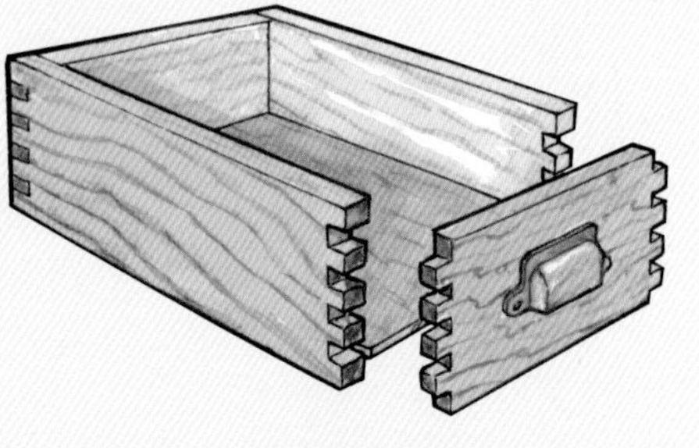

Box (Finger) Joints
Taking a close second place to dovetails for overall strength, box joints are easy to cut on the table saw and are ideal for small production runs.

Dado Joint

Tongue & Dado

Locked Rabbet

gluing in a plywood bottom. Cut both parts with the same dado blade by setting the fence for the dado cut first, then shifting the fence to make the rabbet cut for the tongue.

The locked rabbet joint is commonly used on commercially made drawers. If properly done, it's a strong joint and, even though there isn't good side grain to side grain contact between the pieces, there is so much surface area contact that yellow glue holds the drawer together just fine. The small tongue strengthens the joint mechanically, like the pins in the dado joint, so that the stress of opening and closing the drawer isn't borne entirely by the glue bond. There are lots of shoulders in this joint, so concern about racking is minimized, particularly if a plywood drawer bottom is installed. The locked rabbet is cut in three easy steps with a standard table saw blade or a ¼" dado blade, depending on the thickness of your stock. All you have to do is reset the blade height and fence position for each cut.

Drawer Joints For The Desk

The southwest desk featured previously provides a good example of how to adapt drawer-making techniques to fit a particular need. The large main drawer will get lots of use and requires a durable joint at the front with a strong mechanical connection. The small cubby hole drawer, on the other hand, will probably get very light use and only contain small items, so a simpler joint is adequate.

To make the cubby hole drawer quickly and without fuss, a double rabbet joint is fine (see two photos, below). Gluing a plywood bottom into its grooves will strengthen it further.

Since side-mounted slides are used on the large drawer, the front must extend past the side walls by ½". This configuration lends itself to an excellent but seldom used drawer joint: the sliding dovetail (see three photos, below). This joint is made entirely with a router and dovetail bit, and one router table set up usually works for both front and back joints.

Step 1: *Clamp a clearance block to your router table fence to safely cut the dovetail slots.*

Step 1: *When cutting a rabbet in the drawer front, clamp a protective wood face to your saw fence.*

Step 2: *When routing the tails, use a 5" or taller fence to keep the workpiece stable.*

Step 2: *Secure the joint by spreading glue in the rabbet and then driving brads in at alternating angles.*

Step 3: *A snug, but not tight, joint is best. If the joint is too tight all the glue will be forced out.*

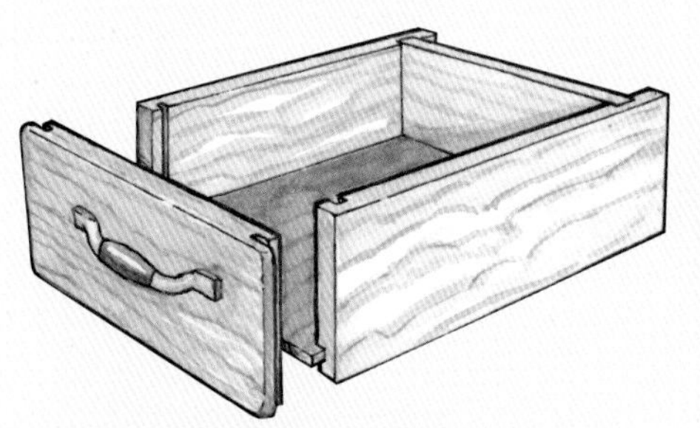

Locked Rabbet Joints
Locked rabbets are well suited to drawers made with plywood. They're easily cut on the table saw and provide lots of gluing area.

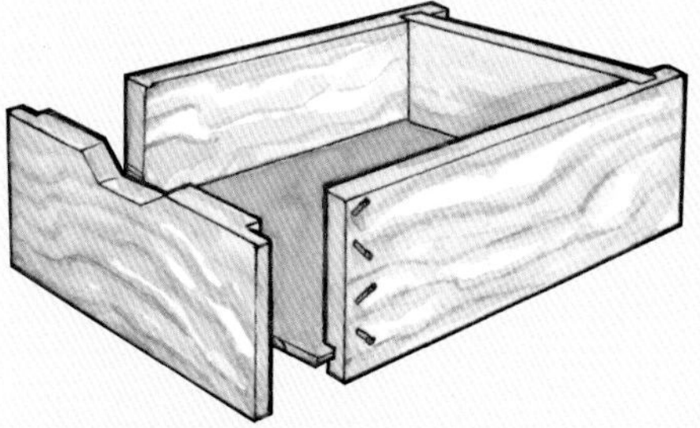

Pinned Rabbet Joints
Pinned rabbet joints are fine for light-duty drawers, and when a drawer bottom is glued in, the structure becomes even stronger.

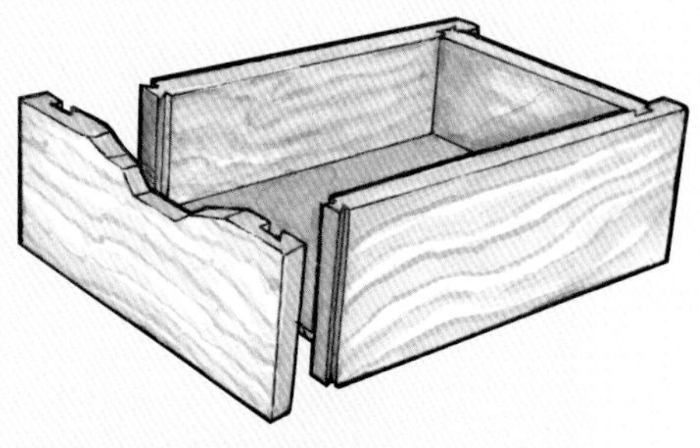

Sliding Dovetail Joints
Sliding dovetails are a perfect compromise. They create more strength than a dado joint but are just as easy to cut on a router table.

A Cherry Arts & Crafts Stereo Cabinet

In the spirit of the Arts & Crafts movement, furniture should be beautiful, well-made and functional. This custom piece captures those tenets while using both traditional and state-of-the-art joinery.

by Mike McGlynn

My old friends Chuck and Linda Lee have a beautiful Craftsman bungalow in LaCrosse, Wisconsin. For a small Midwestern town, LaCrosse has a surprising number of classic Craftsman and Prairie School houses. I've built a few small pieces of furniture for them in the past and was delighted when they asked for a freestanding book and stereo cabinet. The other pieces I've built for them were traditional, wedged tenon, Craftsman style, all constructed of solid cherry with an oil finish. This piece would follow in the same style.

Selecting Solid Hardwood

Unlike a lot of pieces I build, this cabinet was going to be almost entirely solid wood. The shelves and the back were not. Solid wood construction requires careful wood selection. I sorted through at least 2,000 board feet of lumber to come up with the stock to make the six main panels of this cabinet. I selected for color, figure and to avoid sapwood on faces that showed.

Back in the shop, I roughed out the boards to about 1" over width and 3" overlong and let them sit for a week to adjust to the shop's atmosphere.

My first step in milling the wood was to face joint all the boards flat on one face. This is where careful selection of flat boards will pay off. On a board that is over 70" long, it doesn't take much warp before you have a board that ends up too thin at the ends by the time you get one face flat. After flattening, I ran the boards through the planer, but left them 1⁄16" thick. I'd take this off with a wide belt sander after the panels were glued up. If you don't have access to a wide belt sander, take the boards to their final dimension, but your planer needs to be really sharp to avoid chip-out.

I make my panels an inch or two wide and a few inches long so that I can trim them after I'm done sanding them to thickness. This also helps to prevent damaged edges. I jointed, ripped, and jointed all of my boards, then laid them out to biscuit joint. The only caveat here is to make sure the biscuits won't appear when the panels are cut to size. I learned this the hard way when one of the biscuits appeared on the side of one of the through tenons. Luckily, I was able to patch it with a small Dutchman. Gluing up the panels was a matter of biscuits, Titebond® and plenty of bar clamps. An advantage of oversized panels is I don't worry about clamp pads. I always scrape off the squeeze-out before it gets hard. When the panels were dry I took them to a friend's shop to run through a wide belt sander. A word of warning is warranted about using someone else's wide belt sander. Not to look a gift horse in the mouth, but not all wide belt sanders are created equally, and they are certainly not all maintained equally. A good wide belt sander is a great thing, but a bad one can totally ruin your parts. When using an unfamiliar wide belt, start by running a test piece through and make sure it dimensions evenly and doesn't get burned. Never use a grit coarser than 120 for the final pass; 220 is better.

Ultra-accurate Machining

Next, I sanded my panels with a random orbital sander and 220-grit paper, after raising the grain with a damp rag. At this point, I cut the end panels and the top and bottom to size. I didn't cut the two dividers to size yet. I'd do that when I could measure their exact size on the project. Theory is one thing; fact is another.

I always joint one edge of the panel, cut the other edge parallel but oversize, cut off both ends, and then joint off the saw-cut edge to size. Cutting the ends first prevents chips at the corners. It's also important to prevent chip-out on the bottom side of the end panels. I have a table

> **QuickTips**
>
> Solid wood construction requires careful wood selection.
>
> Acclimatize your lumber before and as you machine your parts.
>
> Always glue up your panels oversized in both length and width.
>
> Plan ahead when placing biscuit joints to prevent them from "peeking out."

I used both centuries-old joinery techniques like the wedged mortise and tenon (right) and brand-new joinery such as biscuits and pocket-hole joints (left).

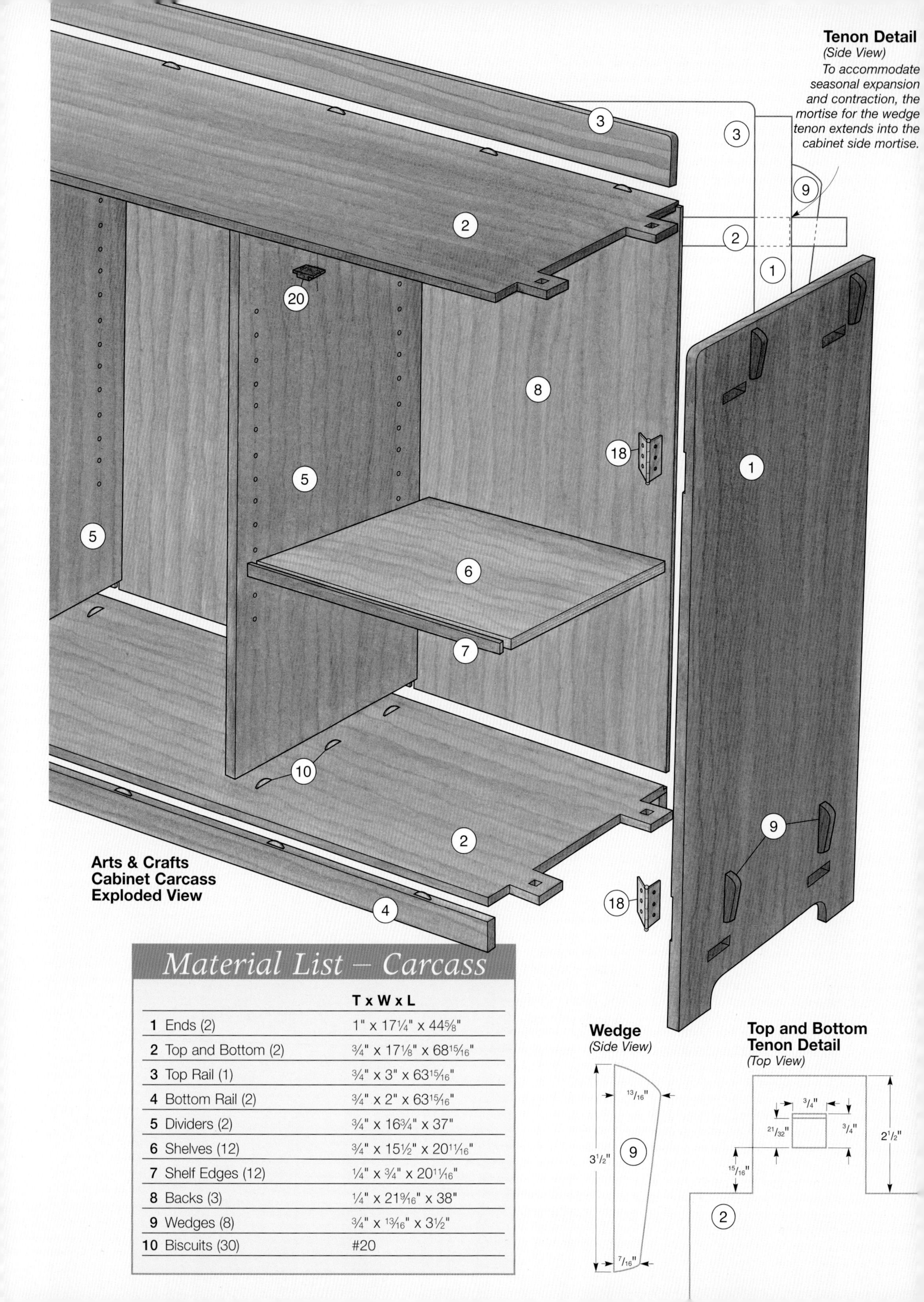

Material List – Carcass

	T x W x L
1 Ends (2)	1" x 17 1/4" x 44 5/8"
2 Top and Bottom (2)	3/4" x 17 1/8" x 68 15/16"
3 Top Rail (1)	3/4" x 3" x 63 15/16"
4 Bottom Rail (2)	3/4" x 2" x 63 15/16"
5 Dividers (2)	3/4" x 16 3/4" x 37"
6 Shelves (12)	3/4" x 15 1/2" x 20 11/16"
7 Shelf Edges (12)	1/4" x 3/4" x 20 11/16"
8 Backs (3)	1/4" x 21 9/16" x 38"
9 Wedges (8)	3/4" x 13/16" x 3 1/2"
10 Biscuits (30)	#20

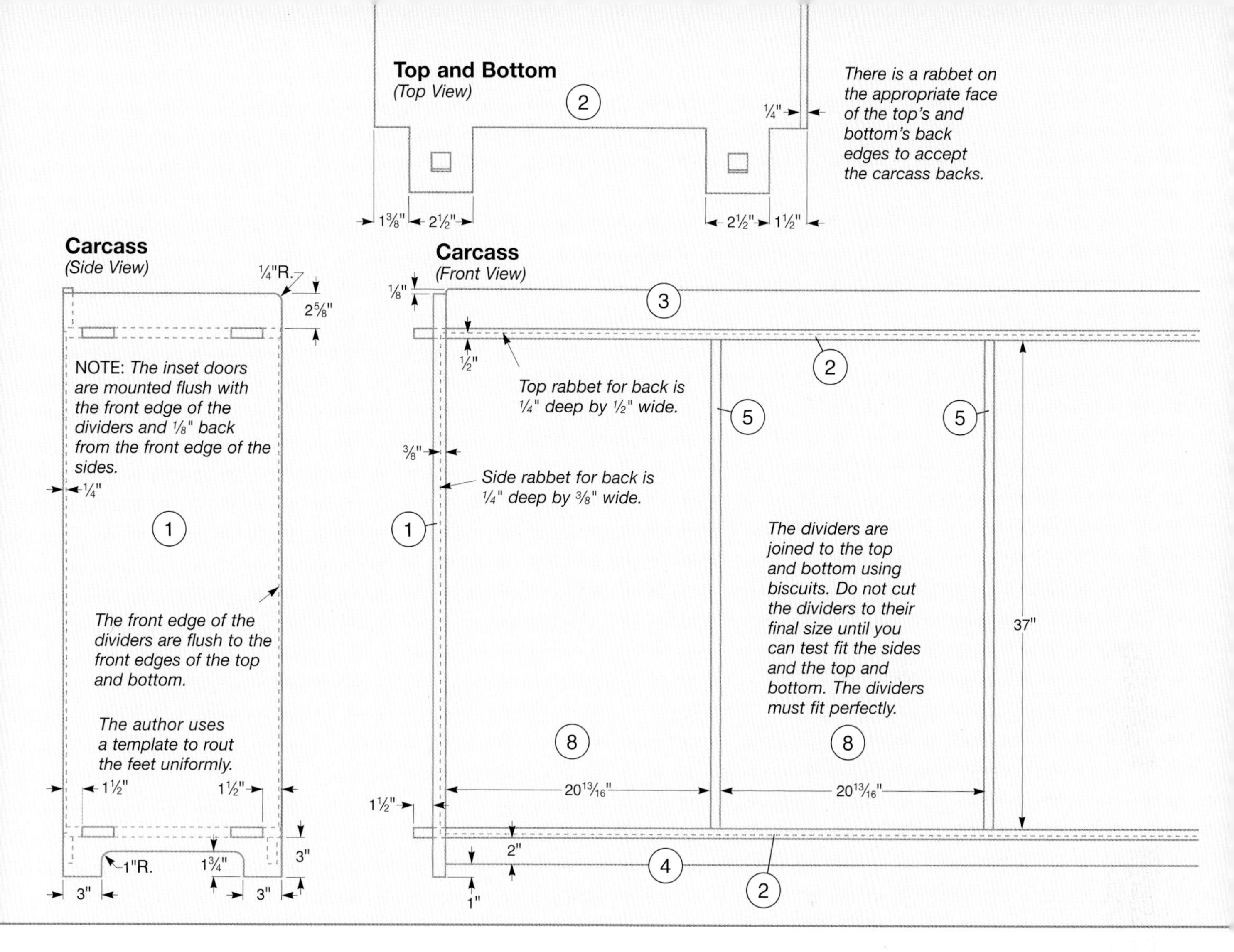

Tight-Fitting Mortises ... There Are No Shortcuts

saw with a scoring blade, but a piece of blue masking tape covering the insert's saw kerf and a sharp blade help as well. The most challenging and time-consuming part of this cabinet is cutting and fitting the through tenons and their matching mortises. I cut the tenons first and then sized the mortises to them.

As can be seen from the photos, I used a router with a pattern bit and a template to make the tenons. I laid out the tenons with my template, band sawed away most of the waste, clamped the template in place, and routed the tenons to size. It is best to saw away most of the wood and use controlled climb cuts to do this shaping. This prevents the possibility of some catastrophic blowout that will ruin the piece. When I was done routing, I used a very sharp chisel and cleaned out the inside corners left by the router.

QuickTips

Whenever possible, don't confuse theory and fact: measure the pieces of wood after you've cut them, too.

Blue masking tape is a cool, quick "zero-clearance insert" trick.

Controlled climb-cuts are a great way to avoid catastrophic blowouts.

Laying out the Mortises

Laying out the mortises is the most precise task on this cabinet. They must be laid out using a very sharp pencil and a good square. As with the dividers, it's important to use the actual dimensions of the tenons, not the theoretical. It's possible the top and bottom may be a slightly different thickness than what is called for in the plans and, depending on the accuracy of the template, there may be a slight difference in width. To get the best look, the gap between the mortise and the tenon can be only a few thousandths of an inch. After carefully measuring the thickness of the top and bottom, I laid out the lines on both sides of the end panels. Of course it should go without saying that these lines need to line up exactly with one another. To lay out the mortise sides I laid the top or bottom on the end panel and marked directly off the tenons. Again, I transferred these lines to the other side of the panels. Now it is time for the fun to begin.

Chiseling the mortises requires three things: sharp chisels, steady hands, and patience. The first step is to cut out the outline of the mortises. I started by chiseling a cut 1⁄32" inside my layout line. I then lifted that chip out, all the way around. Then I made a second, deeper pass and carefully pared straight down exactly on the layout line. With the inside already relieved, this chip popped straight out with no chance of the chisel drifting outward. Once I had done this procedure on both sides of the panel, I used a ½" drill to remove the bulk of the waste. By chiseling out both sides first, I prevented any split-out from the drill. I was then left to carefully chisel out the remaining waste. I did this from both sides of the panel. I slightly undercut the walls so there would be less binding when the cabinet was assembled. The interior and exterior faces are where it needs to fit tight. Without fail, there will be some final fitting to get the tenons to slide home with a nice, tight fit. I accomplished this by using a combination of sanding sticks, files, and chisels.

The last step of the mortise and tenon work was to cut the mortises for the wedges. The key to having wedged tenons work well is to make sure the mortise and wedge have exactly the same slope to them. This required laying out the sloped mortise on both sides of the tenon. To accomplish this, I laid out the mortise opening on the top side of the tenon and then, using a sliding bevel and combination square, transferred the cut lines down the sides of the tenon and around to the bottom. You will notice in the drawing that the inside face of the mortise is 1⁄16" inside the vertical face of the end panel. This is done so that no matter what the humidity is, the wedge will always seat tight. I cut the mortises out using the same technique I used to cut the other mortises. Once again, I slightly undercut the angled face of the mortise for a tight fit.

To ensure the wedges turned out the same,I made a template of ¼" MDF and tested it to fit in the actual assembled mortise. When it fit right, I used the template to lay out my wedges on a strip of wood I milled to the width of the mortise. I found it's easiest to lay out the wedges on one edge of a board that I had jointed square. In this way, my inside face was already done. I rough cut the wedges using a band saw and finished them using a sanding block and a plane.

The top, bottom, and ends of the cabinet have a rabbet to accept the three backs. The rabbet is easy to cut on the

Pattern and template routing are great ways to ensure uniformity of furniture components.

Ian Kirby's Take on Template Routing

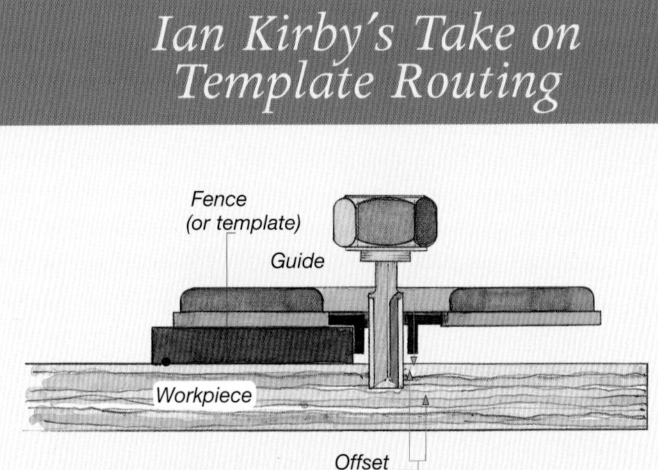

The guide collar is, in effect, a much reduced router base. It runs against a template. The guide is the outer surface of the collar. The fence is the template. The offset is the distance from the outside of the guide collar to the bit's cutting circle. If you use a bearing-guided (top or bottom) router bit, there is no offset to accommodate.

With this guide system you can:

1. Make practically any shape, recess, or hole in or through a board.

top and bottom as it goes all the way through. I cut this rabbet with two careful passes on the table saw. The rabbets in the end panels are stopped at both ends. I cut these rabbets on the router table and finished them off with a sharp chisel.

The last steps for the end panels were to profile the feet and round over the upper corner. The feet were easily profiled using a template and router after cutting away most of the waste with a jigsaw. To round the top corner, I laid out a nice radius and rasped and sanded to the line.

At this point, I carefully dry-assembled the ends to the top and bottom. When I say carefully, I REALLY mean it. The very thing that took so much time and skill on this job ... the through tenons ... can really bite.. you at this point. There is a tendency for the end panel face to chip out when the tenons are pushed through. To prevent this, I put a tiny break, no more than 220 sandpaper, on the outside corners of the mortises, and took my time tapping the ends into place. Then I tapped the wedges in to hold the assembly together.

*Quick*Tips

Chiseling mortises requires three things:

Sharp chisels, steady hands, and patience. The key to wedged tenons working well is to make sure the mortise and wedge have exactly the same slope to them.

Make an MDF template of the wedge and fit it to perfectly match the assembled mortises.

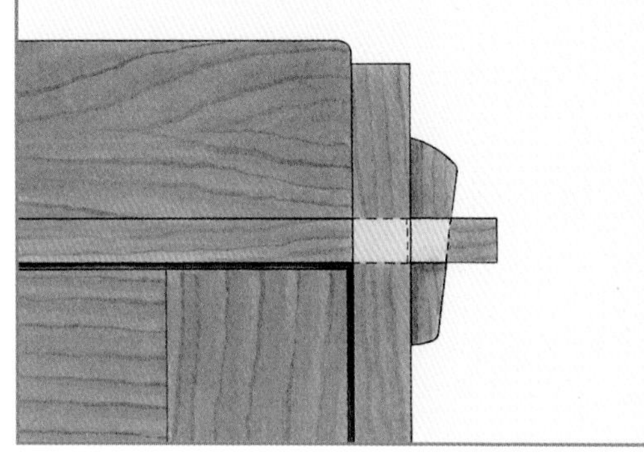

With the carcass together I could measure for the length and width of the dividers. Measure for length at the end panel to prevent errors from subtle warpage of the top and bottom. After measuring, I cut the dividers to length and width.

While the carcass was still dry-assembled, I cut out and fit the top rail and the two bottom rails. In a bow to modern technology, I double pocket-holed the end of all these rails. The top rail got a subtle little roundover on its top corners, as it's ⅜" taller than the sides. Once I had cut and fit my dividers and rails, I disassembled the cabinet.

The dividers are attached to the top and bottom with a combination of biscuit joints and screws. I carefully laid out the biscuit joints on both the dividers and the top and bottom. I've found there is no better place to screw up biscuit joints than when joining one panel to the middle of another. It is easy to align the biscuit joiner with the wrong layout line—so take your time. After biscuiting, I drilled and countersunk the screw holes in the bottom.

When I finished the joint prep, I rubbed my pieces with a damp cloth to raise the grain and sanded and detailed all of the parts with 220 sandpaper. It's important to keep in mind which edges and where they need to be broken.

To put the carcass together, I began by attaching the dividers to the bottom using biscuits, glue, and screws. Attaching the dividers to the top is a little more difficult since there aren't any screws. I used four bar clamps with Mastodon extenders attached to them. Once the glue cured, I glued the two bottom rails and the top rail into place. Before I attached the end panels, I used a sharp utility knife to cut a glue relief groove into the ends of the top and bottom. I found it was best to attach one end at a time. To attach the ends, I carefully put glue on the ends of the top and bottom, tapped the end panel into place, drove in the wedges, and installed the pocket screws. I then repeated this process with the other end. At last the cabinet was starting to look like something other than a pile of parts.

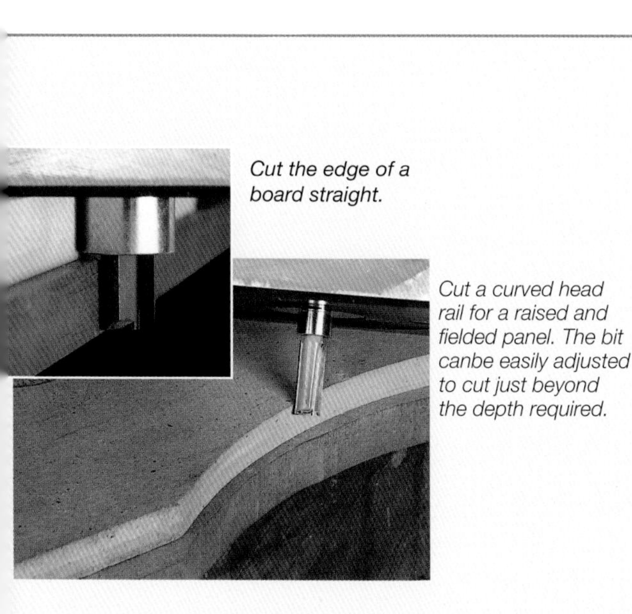

Cut the edge of a board straight.

Cut a curved head rail for a raised and fielded panel. The bit canbe easily adjusted to cut just beyond the depth required.

2. Cut the edge of a board straight.
3. Make a rabbet or a groove parallel to the edge of the template.
4. Make an inlay and a matching recess in the workpiece. This setup works well for straight cuts. When you use guide collars with a shaped template, the template has to be adjusted to compensate for the offset.

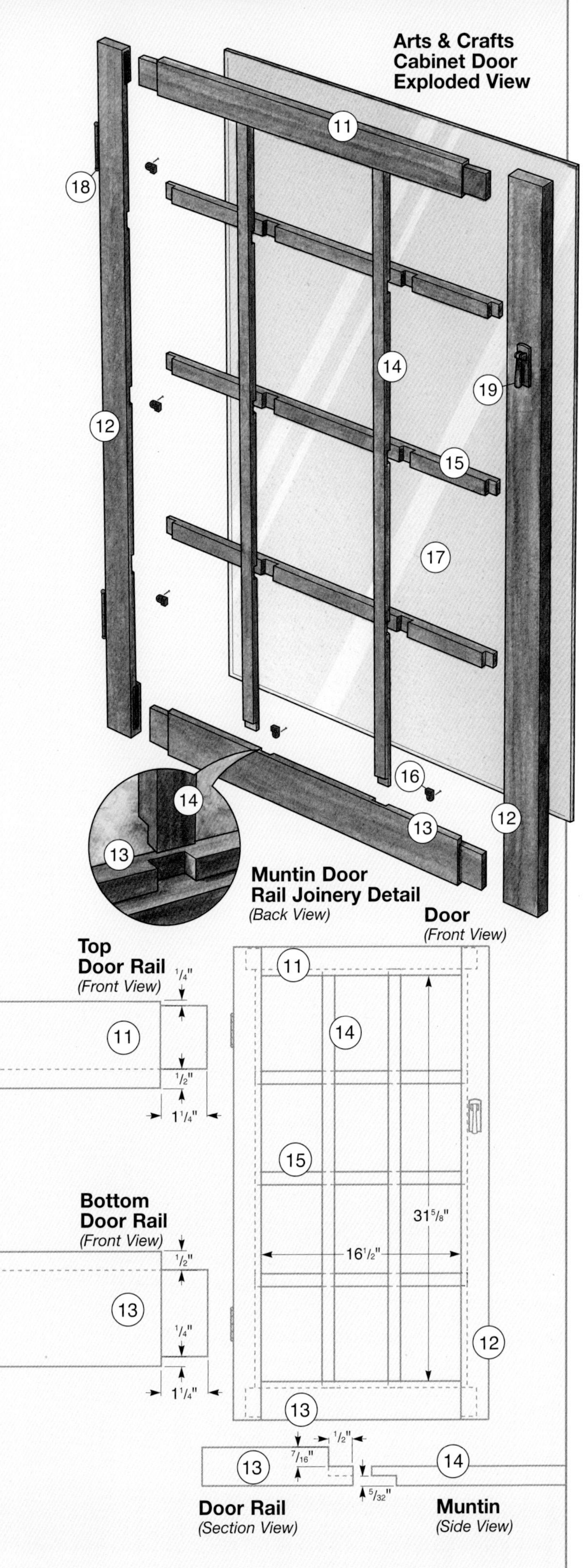

Material List – Door

	T x W x L
11 Top Door Rails (3)	¾" x 2¼" x 18¾"
12 Door Stiles (6)	¾" x 2¼" x 36⅞"
13 Bottom Door Rails (3)	¾" x 3" x 18¾"
14 Long Mullions (6)	5⁄16" x 1" x 32⅝"
15 Short Mullions (9)	5⁄16" x 1" x 17¼"
16 Glass Retainers (30)	Rubber
17 Door Glass (3)	¼" Measure to fit
18 Hinges (6)	Stickley
19 Pulls (3)	Stickley
20 Magnetic Catches (3)	Low profile

Shelf and Door Basics

With the carcass assembled, I drilled the shelf support holes. My usual method is to use a shop-built guide with 1" spacing. It's important to keep in mind that the end panels stick out ⅛" further than the dividers, and that the doors are fully inset. I drilled my front row of holes 1½" behind the front edge of the dividers.

The shelves themselves are made of plain-sliced cherry veneered MDF with a ¼" solid wood front edge band. To me, it's simply not worth it to invest the time and money into making solid wood shelves when all you really ever see is their front edge.

Making the Doors

The doors are the last major part of the cabinet. I started the doors by milling all my wood to dimension and then cutting the pieces to length. I built these doors with mortise and tenon joints, but you could choose to use floating tenons. It's important the joint is quite a bit deeper than the glass rabbet. On these doors, the glass rabbet is ½" deep from the inside edge, so I made the mortises 1¼" deep. As with the back rabbet, it's easier to cut the glass rabbet before the doors are assembled, rather than after. Once the rabbets had been cut I glued up the doors, taking time to make sure they were square and flat.

The grid, I found, is easiest built as a unit, then installed into the doors. One trick with these grids is to make them out of thicker material—7⁄16" thick as opposed to the 5⁄16" finished thickness—and run them through a wide belt sander after they're assembled. This extra thickness allows the depth of the lap joints to be slightly off and not matter. The lap joints are best cut with a very accurate dado setup. I sanded all the edges of my strips before I started the fitting process so that the fit didn't change later. Once I had a tight fit on a piece of scrap, I laid out the

Jigging up to cut the notches on the muntins is one of those repetitive woodworking tasks you want to take your time on. Get it right the first time and the rest of the job will come easily.

laps on one each of the horizontal and vertical pieces. Using a stop block on my miter gauge, I then cut all the laps. It's important to keep in mind that the dado goes on the back of the vertical pieces and on the front of the horizontal pieces.

Once the grids were glued up and sanded to thickness, I laid them in the doors, carefully checked for alignment, and used a sharp layout knife to mark the end laps—both on the door and the grid ends. I cut the laps on the frame with two very careful passes on the table saw. The laps on the frame were cut with a trim router mounted on a shop-made base, and chisels. Because I had done this work very methodically and carefully, a perfect, tight fit was obtained. With glue in the mortises, I mounted the grids in the doors. When the glue had cured, I went over everything to make sure all the joints were perfect and flush.

Fitting and hinging the doors was the last stop before finishing. I placed each door in its opening to make sure it was square and the gap was even. I corrected any problems with a sharp block plane. In keeping with the Craftsman theme, I used Stickley butt hinges. There are two important things to keep in mind when mounting the hinges. The first thing is that the center door is mounted to one of the dividers whose front edge is ⅛" inset from the end panels where the other two doors are mounted. To get the doors to line up, the end panel mortises must be ⅛" deeper, from their front edge, than the mortises in the divider are from their front edge. The second thing to keep in mind, and this is a personal aesthetic opinion, is that for there to be an even gap all the way around, the hinge mortises should be somewhat less than half the depth of the closed hinge. As an example: If the hinge gap is to be 1⁄16", and the thickness of the closed hinge is ⅛", then the mortise should be 1⁄32" deep. I cut the mortises on the doors first with a trim router and chisels. I then shimmed the doors in place and marked the carcass mortises directly off the doors. Again, I used the trim router and chisels to cut the mortises. My figuring and marking seemed to have been correct, and the doors mounted up perfectly. When I was satisfied with the fit, I disassembled everything and got ready for finishing.

The first step to finishing was to go over everything and touch up any areas that needed it with 220 sandpaper. To match the other pieces I had made, this cabinet has an oil finish. The oil finish I have been using lately is the Sam Maloof finish. This finish seems to have all of the positive qualities of other oils, with better build. I applied three coats with a day or so in between, and rubbed out the final two coats with a fine Scotchbrite® pad.

When the finish was dry, I installed the backs (with the grain running vertically, for best visual effect), put the glass in the doors, installed the door catches the doors and attached the door pulls.

To me this cabinet entails all of the things that I love about Craftsman furniture. First, it is a very functional design that serves a purpose without compromise. Second, it has details, such as the wedged tenons, that are purely functional and aesthetically pleasing at the same time. Last, it is a cabinet that is fairly simple in appearance, yet takes a lot of attention to detail to get it to turn out right. The simple thing done right is often the best.

Router Magic
HYLTON
FURNITURE
HYLTON
Classic Joints with Power Tools
WOODWORKING WITH THE ROUTER
HYLTON
ILLUSTRATED CABINETMAKING

Computer Desk

Sooner or later, a busy woodworking writer needs to get his desk organized. But what if the current desk doesn't cut it? If you're due for a new desk too, this project will give your router a good workout—and trust us—the end result will be well worth the effort.

by Bill Hylton

The patented Burgess Edge is created with these two, two-part router bits. Using this system to put hardwood edges onto veneered panels has several advantages.

Until recently, my computer, monitor, keyboard, mousepad and power strip shared a 27" by 48" table-top with pens and pencils, files and papers and an ever-changing assortment of stuff: oversized coffee cup,staplers, staple puller, loupe, tape measure, joint samples, loose paper clips, a Band-Aid® or two, a couple of brass screws...well, you get the picture. (And yeah, it isn't pretty.)

For a long time, I've wanted to expand my computer table to provide more room for papers and reference materials. I also wanted to position things so I'd be more comfortable using the computer for long periods.

Having resolved to make a new desk, I looked on the Web for ergonomic guidelines. As well, I searched for examples of other people's solutions. I considered stand-up desks,worktables, and variations of traditional desks. What I settled on is an eclectic mix of features that suit me. You should easily be able to stretch and/or compress the basic layout to accommodate the computer system you use, your stature,and your work habits.

The basic form is a traditional pedestal desk. It's deep enough to accommodate a typical computer system, placing the monitor directly in front of the keyboard. The desktop is at typical tabletop height (29½"), but the monitor sits on a platform several inches below that level, and it supports the keyboard via a sliding, tilting, pivoting tray. Hiding behind a door in the left pedestal is the CPU, standing on a sliding platform. In the right pedestal there's a file drawer for important papers, a drawer for CDs and such, and a pencil drawer that matches one over the top of the CPU door.

I used soft maple and maple-veneered plywood for all the exposed components, Baltic birch plywood for the drawer boxes and odds and ends of MDF, particleboard, and plywood for shims, templates, and jigs. Necessary hardware includes cross-dowels and connector bolts to join the monitor platform to the pedestals, Accuride® slides for the drawers, a pair of cup hinges for the door and pulls for the door and drawers.

Tooling Notes

I do a lot with routers. On this project, I did everything from some panel-sizing cuts, to mortising, to edge-banding using my routers. Several specialized router bits were particularly useful, and I want to highlight them.

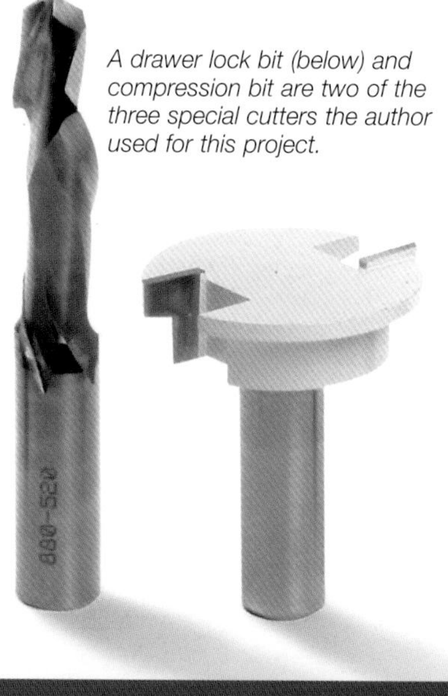
A drawer lock bit (below) and compression bit are two of the three special cutters the author used for this project.

Computer Desk Exploded View

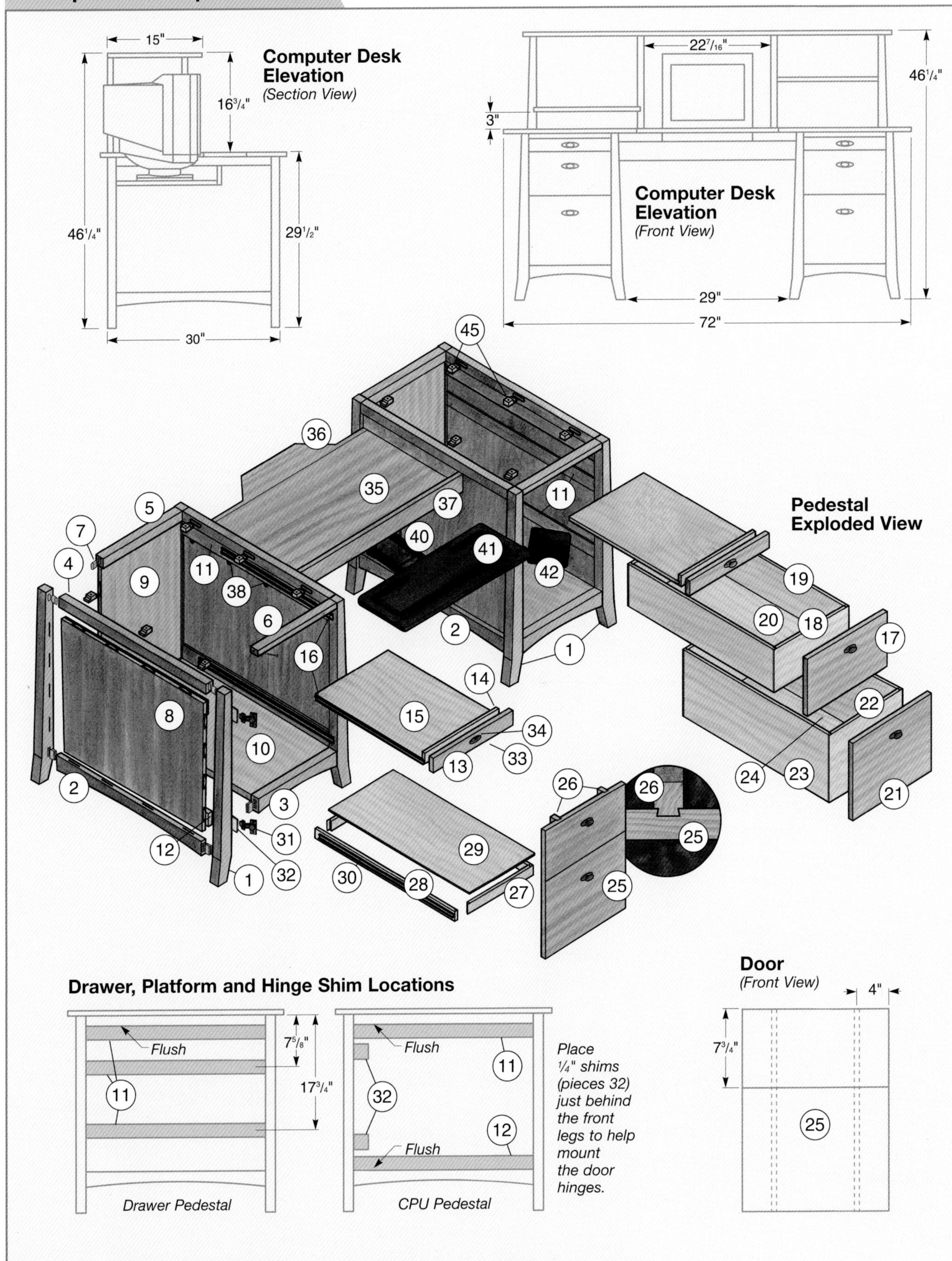

Material List – Pedestals & Drawers

		T x W x L
1	Legs (8)	1½" x 2 ½" x 28¾"
2	Bottom Side Rails (4)	1⅜" x 2¼" x 27"
3	Bottom Front and Back Rails (4)	1⅜" x 2¼" x 14½"
4	Top Side Rails (4)	1¼" x 1½" x 27"
5	Top Back Rails (2)	1⅜" x 1½" x 14½"
6	Top Front Rails (2)	⅞" x 1⅜" x 14¼"
7	Loose Tenons (44)	Hardwood
8	Side Panels (4)	¾" x 27" x 21¼"
9	Back Panels (2)	¾" x 14½" x 21¼"
10	Bottom Panels (2)	¾" x 14½" x 27"
11	Drawer Slide Shims (9)	¼" x 2" x 27"
12	CPU Slide Mount (1)	¾" x 2" x 26"
13	Pencil Drawer Faces (2)	¾" x 2¼" x 14½"
14	Tray Fronts (2)	½" x 1⅝" x 13½"
15	Tray Bases (2)	½" x 13½" x 20⁵⁄₁₆"
16	Pencil Drawer Units (2)	Slides, Plastic Trays
17	Drawer Face (1)	¾" x 7¾" x 14½"
18	Drawer Front and Back (2)	½" x 6½" x 13½"
19	Drawer Sides (2)	½" x 6½" x 26½"
20	Drawer Bottom (1)	¼" x 13" x 26⅜"
21	File Drawer Face (1)	¾" x 11⅞" x 14⅞"
22	File Drawer Front/back (2)	½" x 10¼" x 13½"
23	File Drawer Sides (2)	½" x 10¼" x 26½"
24	File Drawer Bottom (1)	¼" x 13" x 26⅜"
25	Door (1)	¾" x 14½" x 19½"
26	Cleats (2)	¾" x 1¼" x 19⅜"
27	Platform Front/back (2)	½" x 1½" x 12"
28	Platform Sides (2)	½" x 1½" x 25⅞"
29	Platform Base (1)	¾" x 11½" x 25½"
30	Drawer Slides (3 pair)	Accuride, 26"
31	Cup Hinges (1 pair)	120° Self-closing
32	Hinge Shims (2)	¼" x 2" x 3"
33	Pulls (6)	1⅜" Oval bronze
34	Backplates (6)	3" x ⅞" Bronze
35	Monitor Platform (1)	¾" x 16⅝" x 32"
36	Edge Brace (1)	¾" x 4⅞" x 32"
37	Apron (1)	¾" x 3¼" x 32"
38	Connector Bolts (6)	¼"-20 x 3"
39	Cross-dowels (6)	¼"-20 x ⅜" Dia. x ⅝"

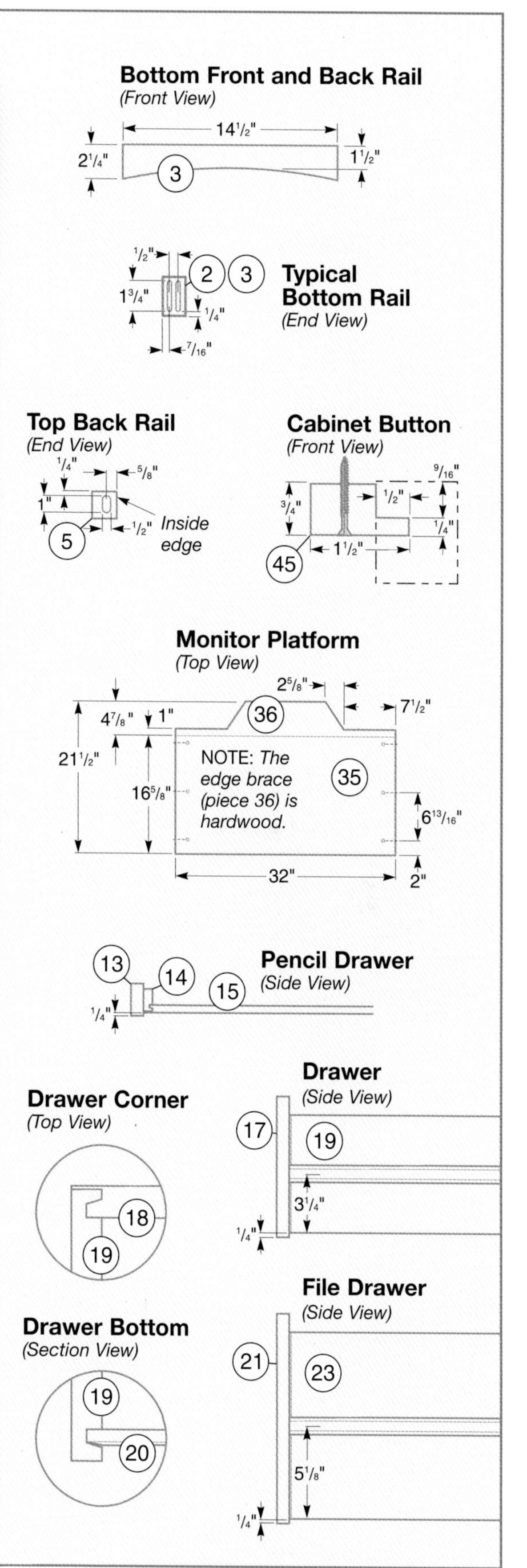

Technical Drawings

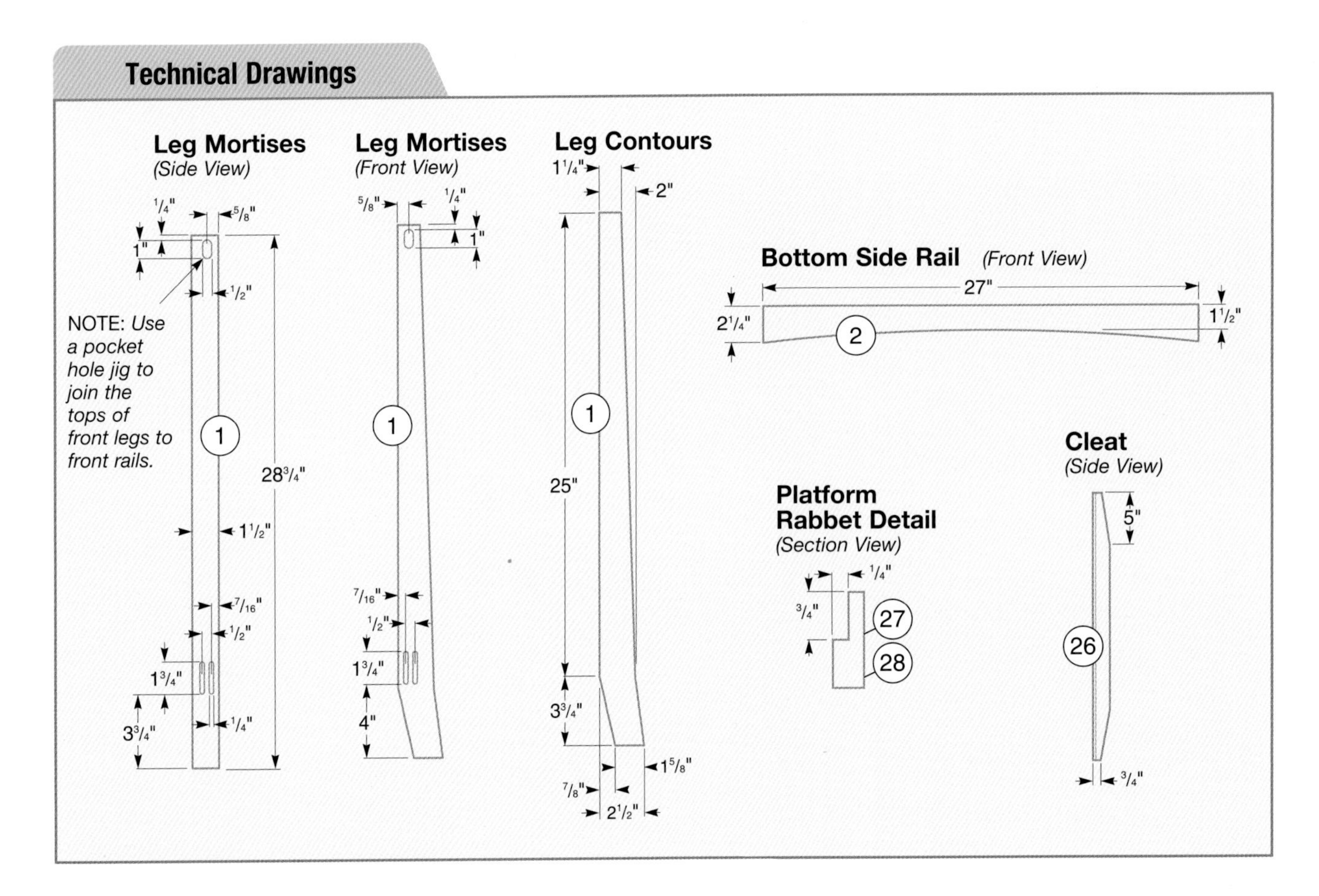

Identify and orient the front and back legs. Mark locations for the top rail mortises (except where the top front rails join the legs). The author chose pocket joints for that task.

Compression Bit: Cutting plywood in the home shop can be a challenge. The sheets are big, heavy and awkward to maneuver in tight quarters. Some of the desk's panels—like the desktop and the pedestal sides—exceeded the capacity of my biggest crosscut sled. In addition, the face veneers are fragile, and when you saw across their grain, they splinter and chip.

I dealt with these problems by using a router and compression bit to make critical cross-grain cuts. A compression bit has both up- and down-spiral cutting edges. It doesn't lift the wood fibers from either face, so the plywood is left with crisp, chip-free edges, even on those cross-grain cuts. Spun with a 2 horsepower router, it plows through ¾" thick plywood in a single pass.

To size the biggest panels, I set up a straightedge to guide the router, making sure it was absolutely square to the table-sawn reference edge. The routine isn't quick, but with patience and care, you can achieve excellent results. I also used the bit on a number of the primary template-guided cuts.

Even at $90, a compression bit is a lot cheaper than a panel saw. And it's more space efficient, too.

Drawer Lock Bit: I made all the drawers and the printer platform frame using the drawer lock joint. While it lacks the cachet of dovetails, it is effective and a lot easier to master. It works in plywood as well as solid wood. One bit is all you need. It even makes the groove to house the drawer bottom!

The Burgess Edge: Edge-banding panels cut from sheet goods—plywood, MDF, and the like—is pretty simple, but the results tend to vary. Tape is fast, but the adhesion, in my experience, can be iffy. Using ⅛" strips of hardwood often yields color and grain mismatches at the very margins of the panel's face.

The patented Burgess Edge is produced by a special pair of router bits. The doubled-bearing plywood bit follows the surface veneers as it excavates the inner plies of the plywood. The insert bit shapes a solid wood infill strip. Glue the insert in place, then trim it. Look at the edged panel,

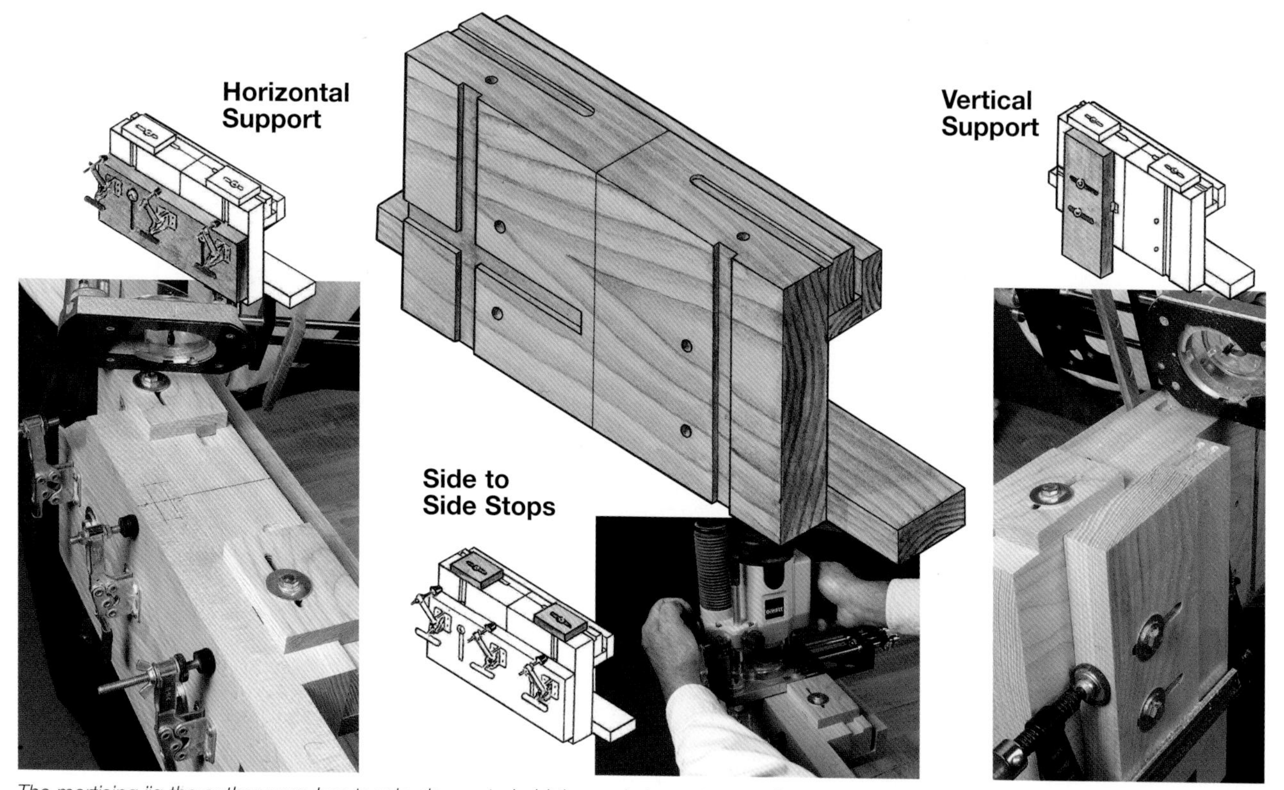

The mortising jig the author uses has toggle clamps to hold the workpiece, stops to limit the router's travel and a channel for the edge guide's wooden fence. The bit governs the mortise width, the plunge governs the mortise depth, and the edge guide positions the mortise on the workpiece. When routing the end of a piece, the author uses a separate clamp to secure the work.

and you see the solid wood and just a knife-edge of the surface veneers.

This was the first time I used this process, but I liked the results.

Build the Pedestals First

The construction of the pedestals (pieces 1 through 12, see Material List on page 43) is post and rail. The legs and rails are joined with mortise and loose tenon joints. Plywood panels are joined to the legs and rails with biscuits. The first task is to construct these basic units. (For all of these construction details, see the Drawings on pages (42 and 43.)

Begin by laying out the legs in sets of four, as shown in the photo on the previous page. Don't be concerned with the contours now—focus on the mortises, which are cut before shaping the legs. Select and identify the front and back legs. You don't want to be cutting mortises or slots on the wrong sides.

Twin mortises are used for the bottom rails and a single mortise for the top ones. Because you mortise adjacent faces of the legs, the mortises do intersect. The "outer" mortise of the twins can be deeper than the "inner" one. When you make the loose tenons, you simply bevel one end of each.

Before you begin the final pedestal glue-up, glue the loose tenons into the rail mortises. Be sure you orient the bevels properly.

Cut the mortises in both the legs and the rails. I used a plunge router with a good edge guide and a shop-made mortising jig for this operation (see photos and drawings above), but use whatever approach you are most comfortable with.

Once the mortises are completed and the tenons made and fitted, shape the legs and rails. The rails have an arched bottom edge. The legs have a reverse taper from top to ankle, and the foot section cants outward from that point. In the assembled pedestal, the inner surface of the leg is plumb.

To shape the legs, make a template and attach a fence and toggle clamps to it. This will allow you to band-saw the majority of the waste from the parts, then rout the final contour (see photos, next page) on the router table.

The foot's inner surface is the exception. On half the legs, the correct feed direction on the router table

Attach fences to the leg template, and mount a couple of toggle clamps on them to secure the leg blank. Band-saw off the majority of the waste, then template-rout the leg flush using a bearing-guided bit.

would require cutting against the grain, guaranteeing major tearout. To avoid this, make a tapering jig and saw this surface on the table saw (see photos, next page).

The panels are biscuited to the legs and rails. While they really aren't necessary for strength, the biscuits make it infinitely easier to assemble the parts and ensure that everything stays aligned. To get the appearance I wanted, the side and back panels are offset 1/4" from the inner edges of the legs and rails. Set up your biscuit joiner to position the slots on the legs and rails, and use a scrap of 1/4" MDF as a shim when cutting the slots in the panels. You can also use the shim when cutting the slots in the rails for the bottom (so it will be flush).

Now that I've glued-up this project, with lots of biscuits, loose tenons and parts, I'll tell you right now that it can get hectic. To simplify things, I recommend that you stage the work.

First, join the side panels to the side rails and the back panels to the back rails. Glue the loose tenons into the mortises in the rails. As you do this, make sure the bevels are correctly oriented, the longer tenon is in the correct mortise, and that you clean up any squeeze-out. Any of these goofs will thwart you in the next assembly stage.

In the second stage, join these subassemblies to the legs and bottom panel. The last little job—completing the basic pedestals—is to attach the 7/8"-thick top front rail with glue and a pair of screws in pockets.

Building the Drawers

The desk has two standard drawers, two pencil drawer trays and a sliding platform for the CPU (pieces 13 through 34). You'll find Elevation Drawings for the drawer construction on page 43. All but the CPU platform have maple "show" faces attached to the drawer's structural front with screws. The CPU platform is concealed behind a door. To clear the open door, this platform is narrower than the other drawers, and it is mounted differently (see Exploded Drawing).

The boxes for the two regular drawers are 1/2" Baltic birch plywood, assembled with routed drawer lock joints. The bottoms are 1/4" birch plywood.

The pencil drawers originated with dandy molded drawer side inserts packaged with a pair of slides. Because the inserts were not as wide as the pedestals, I made a Baltic birch plywood tray for each one, attached the slides to it, then fastened the insert to the tray.

These drawers are mounted in the pedestals with Accuride slides. Drill mounting screw holes along the centerlines of 1/4" MDF shims (which bring the mounting surface flush with the legs), then screw them to the side panels. Screw the case members of the slides in place next. Then screw the slides' drawer members to the drawer sides and install the drawers in the pedestals to wrap up.

The CPU platform is a 1 1/2"-high drawer frame (front, back and sides), with a 3/4" rabbet all the way around. The platform base drops into this rabbet.

Because it is narrower than the opening, a mounting point for a slide must be provided on the door-hinge side of the pedestal. This mount is simply a 2"-wide strip of plywood that's screwed to the pedestal bottom. Cut it about 1/2" longer than the slide, then position it against the pedestal back.

With the drawers in place, fit the "show" fronts to them next. The front to the CPU platform is, of course, a door. I made it to mimic the appearance of the fronts on the two full drawers in the opposite pedestal. After fitting the 19 1/2"-wide panel to the opening, kerf it to represent the gap between the drawers. To keep it flat, mount two cleats on the back with sliding dovetail joints. Then mount it to the pedestal. You'll need a 1/4" shim to mount the hinge plates to, as with the slides. Complete the drawers by mounting the pulls.

The monitor sits on a platform mounted between the pedestals, several inches below the desktop.

A keyboard slide and tray is screwed to its underside. When you pull it forward, the keyboard ends up in its cutout. The monitor platform (piece 35) is a plywood panel with hardwood brace (pieces 36) and an apron (piece 37). Follow the drawings on page 42 for its shape and construction details.

Use connector bolts and cross-dowels to attach it to the pedestals (pieces 38 and 39). The bolts penetrate the pedestal sides and extend into the edge of the platform. A blind hole for the cross-dowel, drilled into the underside of the platform, intersects the bolt hole. You don't see the fasteners, but you can remove them to dismantle the desk. Mount the keyboard slide, platform and swivel mousepad later (pieces 40, 41, and 42).

Making the Desktop

The desktop (piece 43) is, of course, the main working surface. Make two U-shaped cutouts in it (see the Elevation Drawings), one for the monitor, and the other for the keyboard. The desktop is plywood with hardwood edging (pieces 44). There are a number of ways you can edge the plywood, so use the one that works for you. With the patented Burgess Edge system that I used, doing the cutouts was a bit involved. Making cutouts in the desktop for the monitor and keyboard isn't difficult. But cutting them so they can be edged with the Burgess system is. To pull it off, I used a pair of templates, a maple frame assembled with half-lap joints, the right combination of template guides and straight bits, and, of course, the Burgess-Edge bits. The first template of each pair is critical, since it is used for three steps: the second template, the initial cutout, and final edge-trimming. To make this U-shaped template, drill out the inside corners

The drawer lock joint is a great way to join plywood drawer sides because it covers the plywood strata as shown in the drawing at left. The author also cut the groove for the drawer bottoms using the drawer lock bit.

Glue the rails to the panels and the loose tenons into the rails. When the clamps are off, glue the legs to the back rail and panel subassembly.

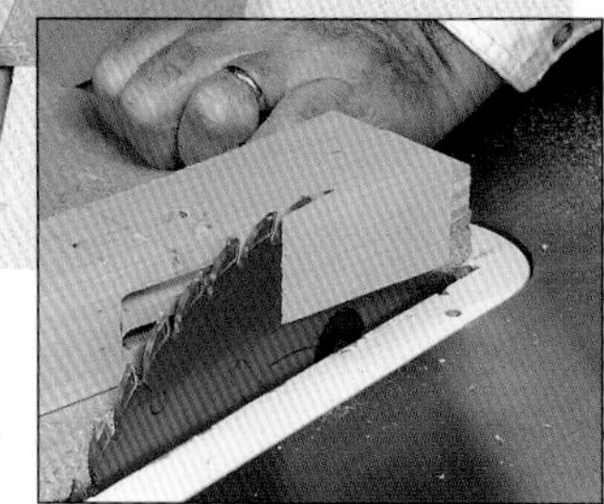

Saw the inside foot taper to avoid major tearout problems. Attach a couple of fences to a scrap panel to make the jig quickly. Recycle the screws and panel after the legs are cut.

Burgess Bit

With its center bearing and a little fine adjustment, this bit forms perfectly sized hardwood edging with plenty of glue surface.

The Burgess Edge plywood bit has two stacked, adjustable cutters that scoop out the panel edge, leaving a knife-edge of hardwood veneer.

with a Forstner bit, then cut from edge to hole, from hole to hole, and from hole to edge. Clamped to the desktop, this template will guide your router as you make the actual cutout, shown in the photo on the next page.

To make the second template, clamp the first to the blank, fit your router with the appropriate template guide and straight bit, and rout along the edge of the first template. Then screw this template to the hardwood frame and rout around the outside.

After contouring the frame, rout the cutout with the Burgess plywood bit and the frame's edge with the insert bit. Now the frame should fit perfectly into the desktop. Glue it in place and trim the excess with a jigsaw. Finally, use the original template to trim the cutout, leaving a crisp edge on the desktop.

The desktop is secured to the pedestals with cabinetmaker's buttons (pieces 45). I used a ¼" slot cutter to

*Quick*Tips

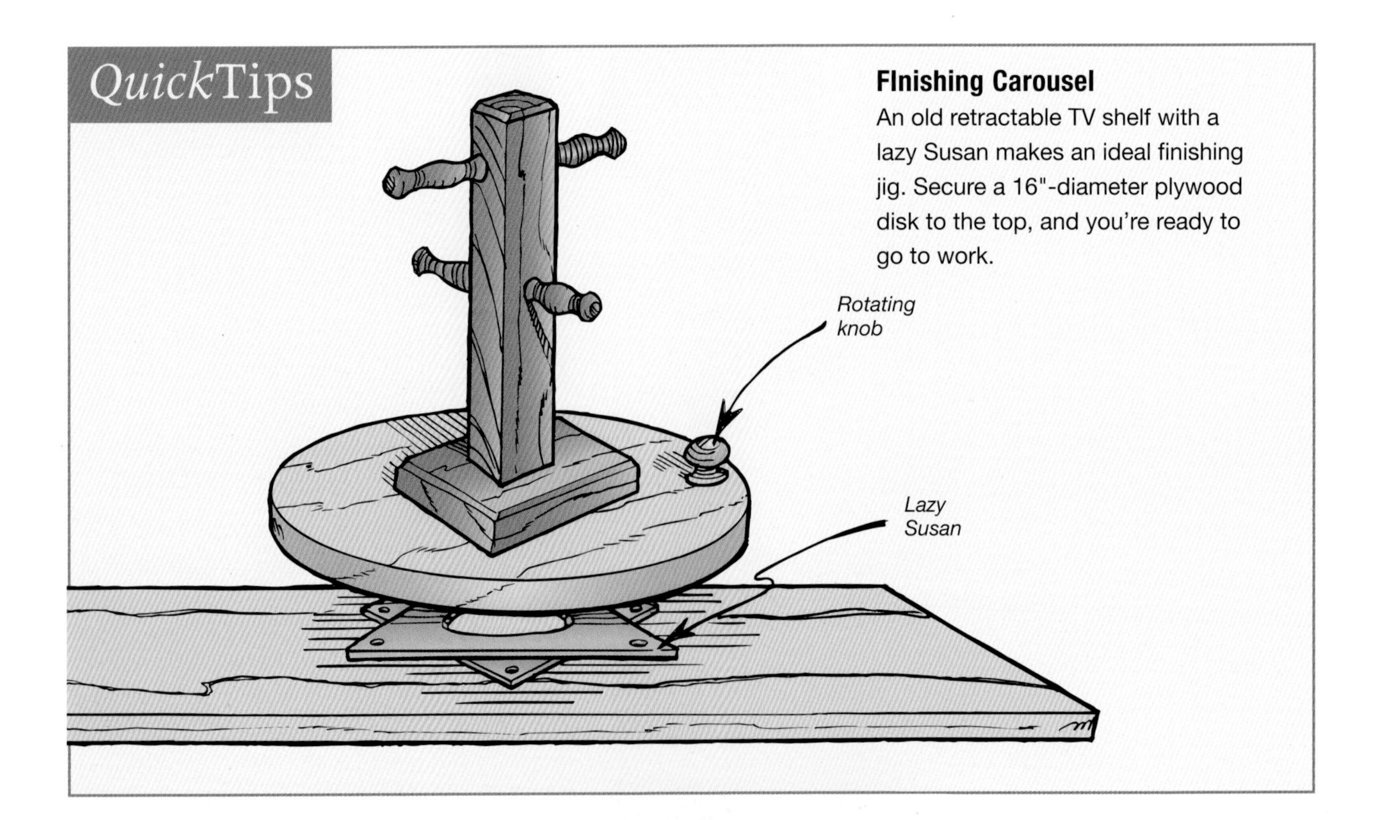

FInishing Carousel

An old retractable TV shelf with a lazy Susan makes an ideal finishing jig. Secure a 16"-diameter plywood disk to the top, and you're ready to go to work.

Use your master templates to form the cutouts in the desktop. The templates will guide a router fitted with a 3/4" template guide and 1/2" compression bit. Then, use the same templates to create secondary templates (left). For this step, clamp the master to your plywood and guide a router fitted with a 3/8" template guide and 1/4" straight bit along the edge.

rout three slots in each top side rail for both pedestals. With the pedestals upended on the overturned desktop, I aligned them and joined them with the monitor platform. Then I fitted a button in each slot and screwed it to the desktop. (Later, when it was time to apply a finish and move the desk to its home location, I dismantled it.)

Constructing the Gallery

Last to be constructed is the gallery (pieces 46 though 57). It features a long edge-banded plywood top, supported by two shelf units. One has a slightly elevated platform that could hold a small printer. Under it is a built-in power strip.

The shelf units consist of plywood panels and tapered posts (a taper that duplicates that of the pedestal legs; see the drawings on the next page). The

The secondary template was used to shape the edges of the infill frame that was assembled with half-lap joints. The template was screwed in place with about 1/2" of the frame exposed on three sides. Then it was a simple matter of routing around the template to trim the frame to exact size.

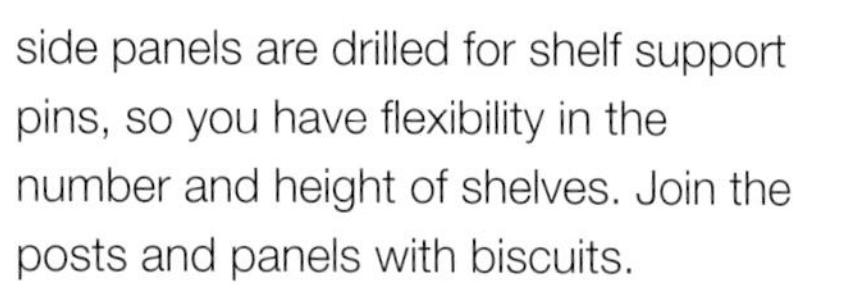

side panels are drilled for shelf support pins, so you have flexibility in the number and height of shelves. Join the posts and panels with biscuits.

Assemble the units, then lay out and cut biscuit slots in their top edges. Now position the units on the underside of the gallery top and transfer the slot locations to it. Then slot the top and glue up the subassembly.

The frame for the power strip is a drawer box with plywood sides and back and a hardwood front. Cut an opening in the front for the power strip. I incorporated a truncated bottom as a mounting point for the power strip bracket, but left most of the area open so I could cut a port in the desktop for cables. The gallery covers the hole, and a removable shelf covers the frame.

Rather than attach the gallery permanently to the desktop, gravity holds it down and a half-dozen dowels position it. Drill holes for them in the bottom edges of the gallery, then use dowel points to transfer their locations to the desktop.

When this is done, lay out and cut the cable port in the desktop. You should also determine the best locations for other essential cabling ports—in the pedestal side for the power cords and monitor, keyboard, and mouse cables,

Machine the desktop cutout with the Burgess Edge plywood bit and the newly shaped infill frame with the Burgess insert bit. Apply glue and slide the frame into the cutout.

The final, trimmed edge (on the inside of the three-sided infill frame) is produced using the master template and the same router, guide and bit combination that made the initial cutout.

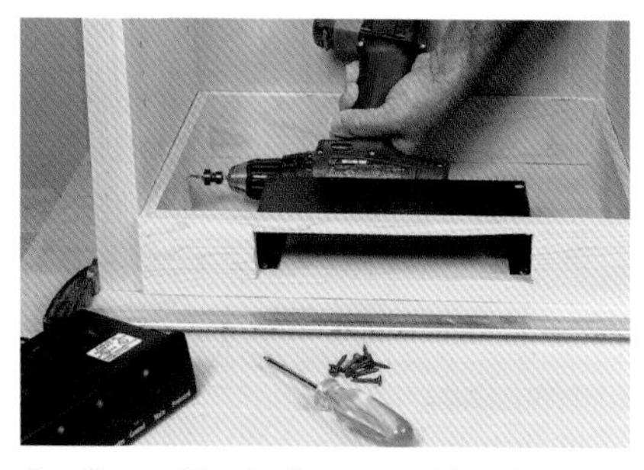

The Power Director is mounted in a frame at the bottom of one of the gallery towers. The frame is screwed to the side of the tower and a port is cut in the desktop for cables. A removable shelf hides wire clutter.

in the gallery for the print cables and for the power strip cord.

After completing all the parts and assembling the desk, dismantle it to apply the finish. I used multiple coats of Waterlox on the desk and a single coat of shellac on the drawers, pencil trays

Gallery Exploded View

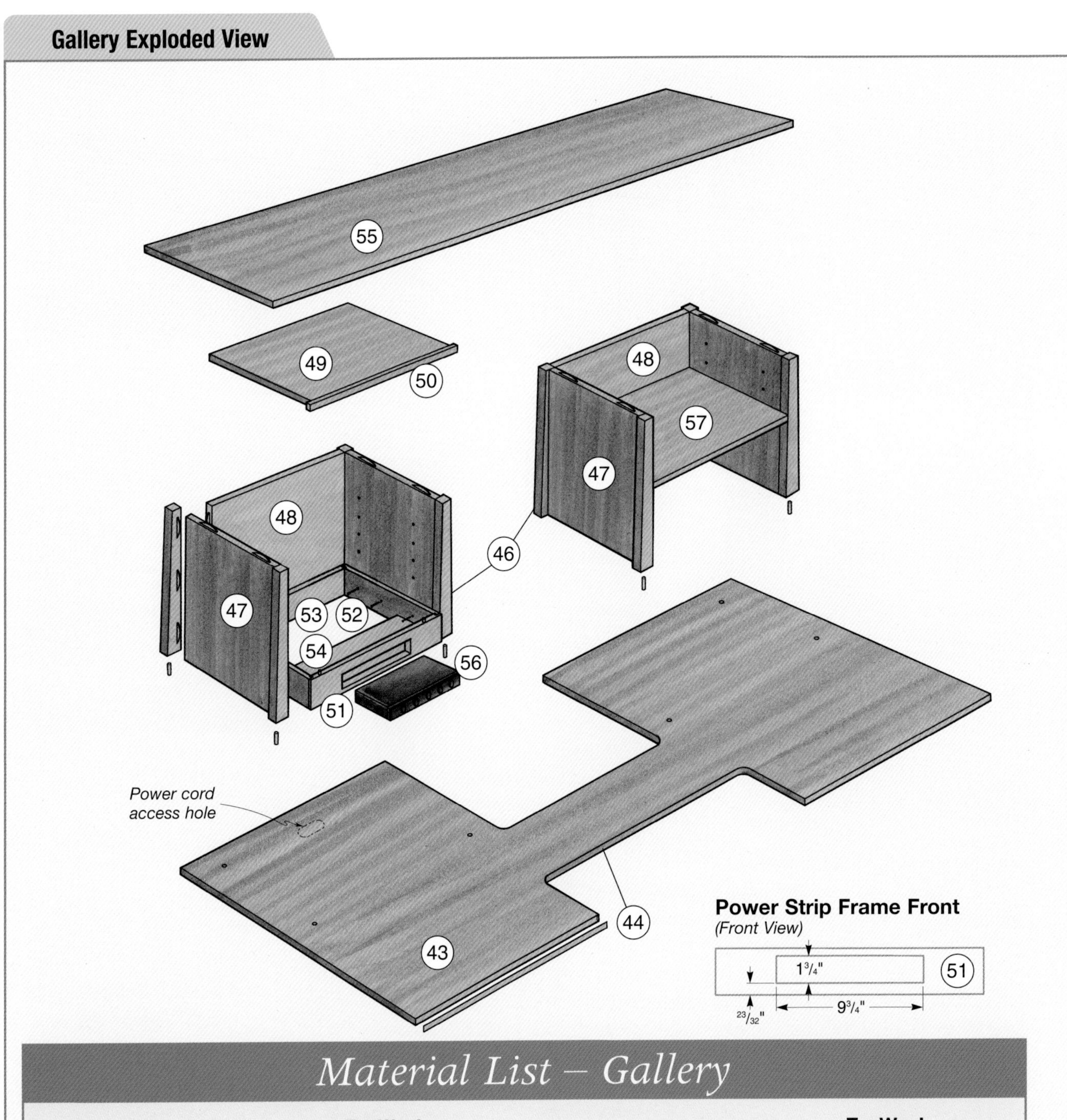

Material List – Gallery

	T x W x L
40 Premium Keyboard Slide (1)	Adjustable
41 Keyboard Platform (1)	Black
42 Mouse Pad (1)	Black
43 Desktop Panel (1)	¾" x 32½" x 72"
44 Edge Banding (1)	¾" x 1" x 300"
45 Cabinetmaker's Buttons (12)	¾" x 1" x 1½"
46 Posts (8)	1" x 1⅝" x 16"
47 Side Panels (4)	¾" x 12" x 16"
48 Back Panels (2)	¾" x 17¾" x 16"
49 Printer Platform (1)	¾" x 12⅞" x 17¾"
50 Edge Banding (1)	¾" x ½" x 18¾"
51 Power Strip Frame Front (1)	¾" x 3" x 17¾"
52 Power Strip Frame Sides (2)	½" x 3" x 13½"
53 Power Strip Frame Back (1)	½" x 3" x 17¾"
54 Power Strip Frame Bottom (1)	½" x 4" x 16¾"
55 Gallery Top Panel (1)	¾" x 15" x 65"
56 Power Manager (1)	Black
57 Adjustable Shelves (2)	¾" x 12" x 17¾"

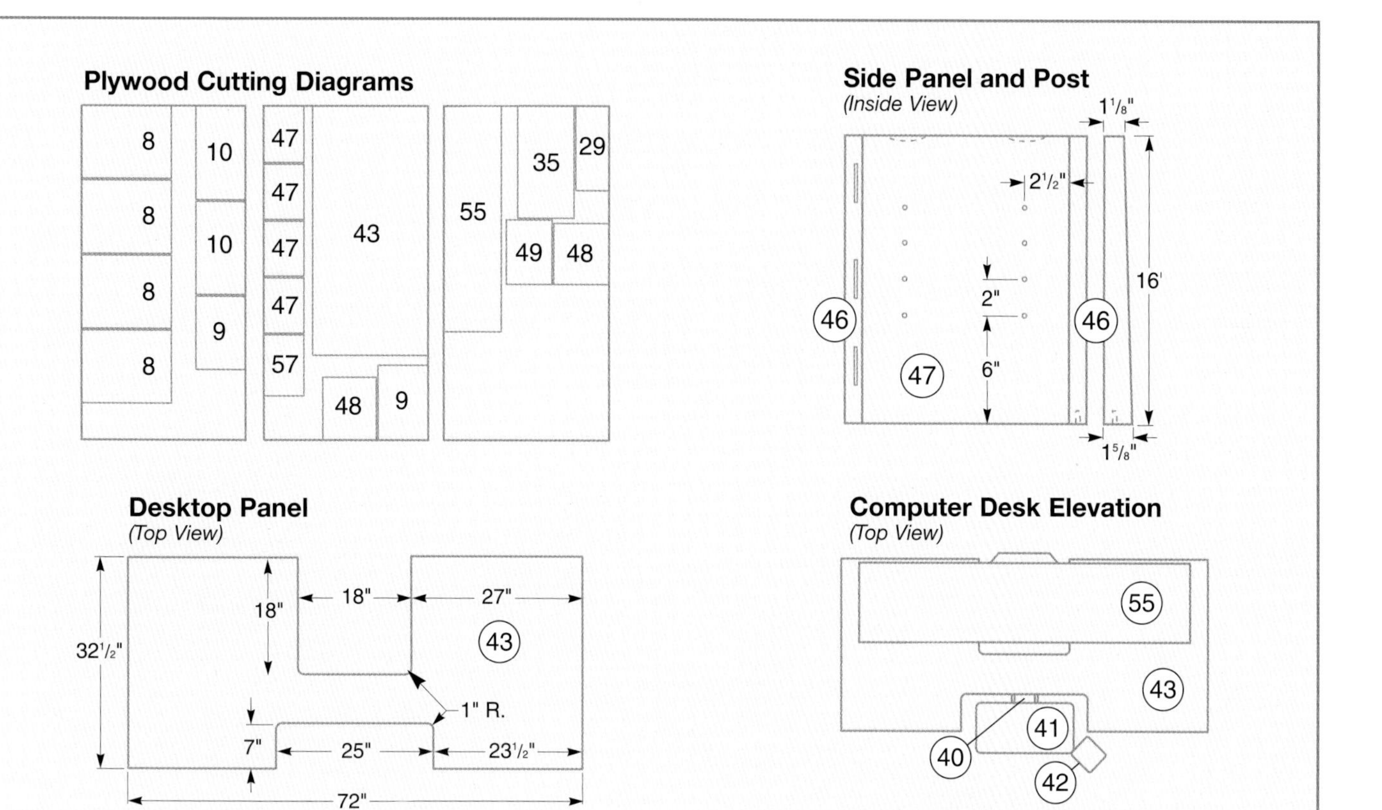

One of the last tasks is to drill for the dowels that secure the gallery to the desktop. It must be done with considerable care.

and CPU platform. The shellac merely seals the bare wood from accidental moisture and imparts a little color to the maple and birch plywood.

Once the finish dries thoroughly, reassemble your new desk, install your computer and cables and go to work. I sure did—writing this story!

With plenty of storage room and a place for your high-tech components, this computer desk cuts down on clutter and increases efficiency. And it looks great to boot!

Modular Computer Desk

These days, almost everyone owns a computer. Along with the CPU and monitor come a host of other desk-cluttering gadgets. And even if you do most of your work on screen, there are still notes to pen, bills to pay, and paraphernalia to keep organized on a desktop. Our four-piece modular desk gives you plenty of room for it all, and you can organize these components any way you like to suit your workspace.

by Rick White

The advantage of a modular desk is that you can arrange it many different ways to suit your work habits or room layout. The one constant with our design is the corner unit, which makes the most of this often unused space.

Whether your home office is the size of an average living room or as small as a closet, a modular computer desk gives you the ultimate flexibility for setting up a workspace that makes sense for your needs and environment.

You may choose to line up the desk pieces along one wall of a room or spread them apart to fit between windows and doorways, or to be near outlets and phone hook-ups.

Desk/Bookcase Exploded View

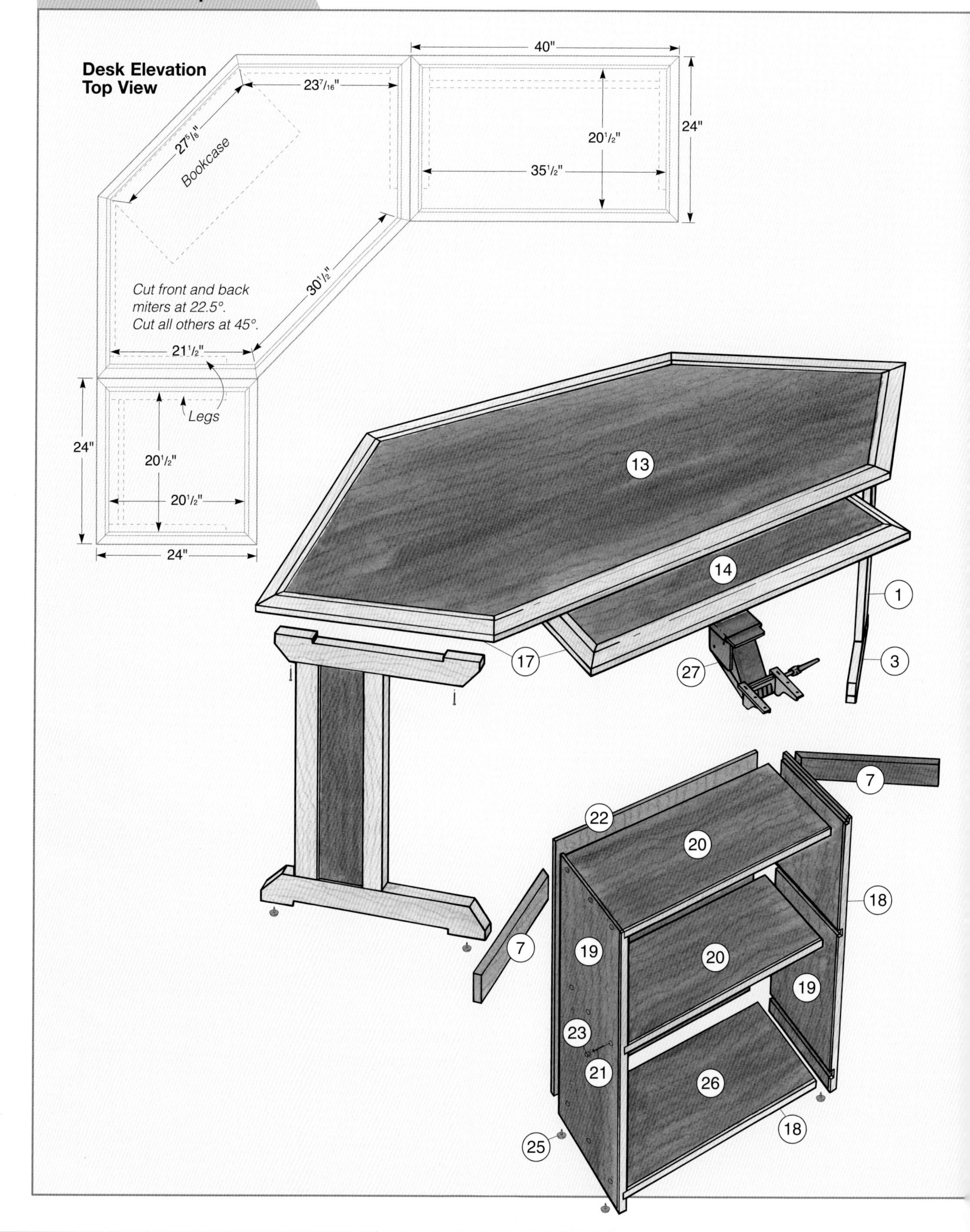

cut ½"-deep dadoes for housing the upper cross rails (pieces 6, 7 and 8). Remember, make two passes to get dadoes that fit the plywood cross rails snugly. After completing the dadoes, glue each leg assembly together.

Install a shelf (piece 9) in your printer stand for storing extra paper. To support the shelf, cut dadoes in the legs of the printer stand and drive screws through the joints. Lay out the dado locations on a pair of legs (see the Leg Detail on page 57), then cut them on your table saw with a miter gauge and your ½" dado blade raised ½". Next, drill counterbored pilot holes in the legs.

Drawer Exploded View

30

Material List

29	Drawer Front and Back (2)
30	Drawer Sides (2)
31	Drawer Bottom (1)
32	Drawer Face (1)

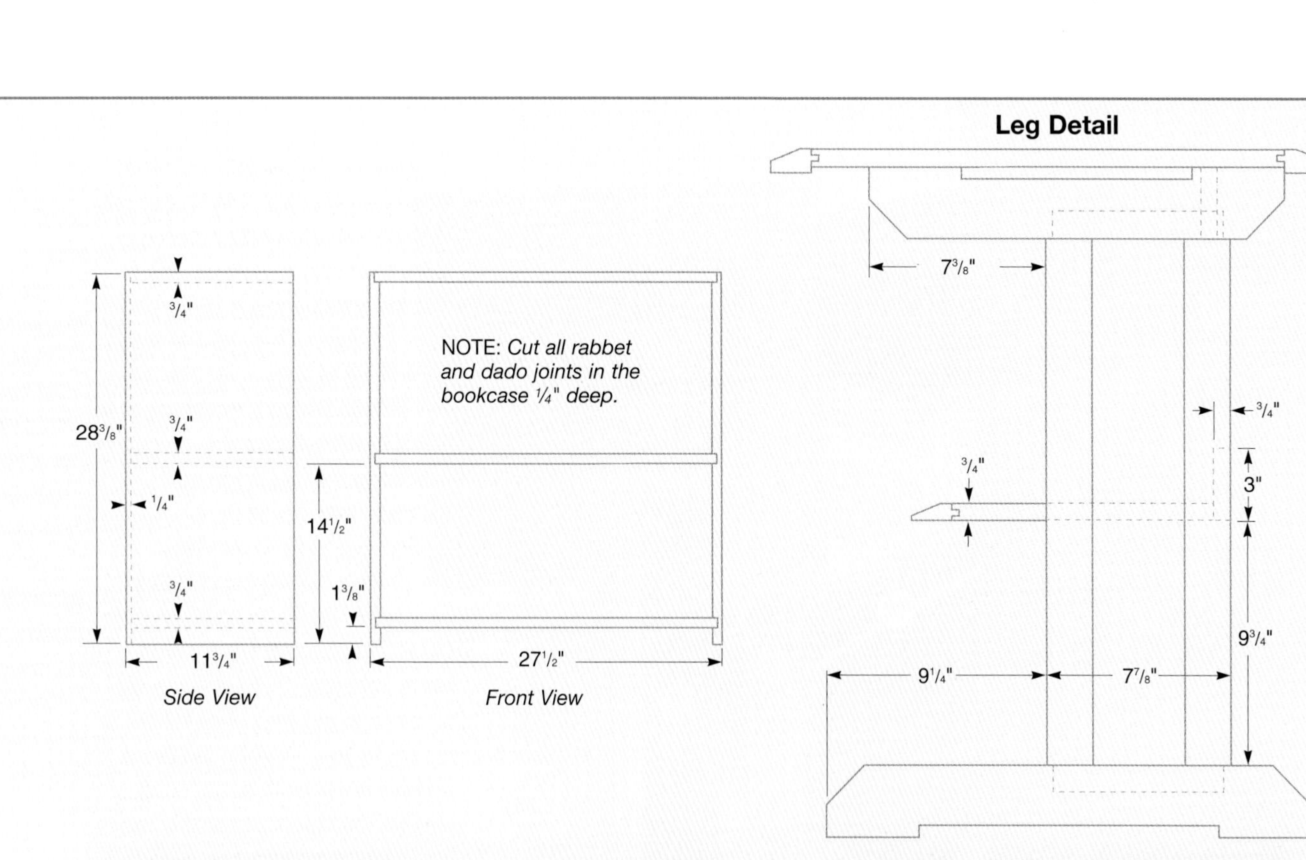

Material List

(Note: P.: Printer W.D: Writing Desk C.D.: Corner Desk)

		T x W x L			T x W x L
1	Leg Stiles (12)	1⅛" x 2" x 24¹⁄₁₆"	**11**	W.D. Lower Cross Rail (1)	¾" x 2¾" x 35³⁄₁₆"
2	Upper Rails (6)	1⅛" x 3" x 17½"	**12**	Printer Stand Top (1)	¾" x 20½" x 20½"
3	Lower Rails (6)	1⅛" x 3" x 21"	**13**	Writing Desktop (1)	¾" x 20½" x 36½"
4	Leg Panels (6)	¾" x 5" x 24¹⁄₁₆"	**14**	Keyboard Platform (1)	¾" x 11½" x 27½"
5	Hold Down Screws (16)	#8-1¼"	**15**	Corner Desktop (1)	¾" x 31¾" x 60¾"
6	P. Upper Cross Rail (1)	¾" x 3" x 19³⁄₁₆"	**16**	Cherry Edgebanding (1)	¹⁄₃₂" x 1" x 72"
7	W.D. Upper Cross Rail (1)	¾" x 3" x 35³⁄₁₆"	**17**	Edging (7)	1⅛" x 1¾" x 96"
8	C.D. Upper Cross Rails (2)	¾" x 3" x 21"	**18**	Banding (3)	¼" x ¾" 96"
9	Printer Shelf (1)	¾" x 11" x 19⅛"	**19**	Bookcase Sides (2)	¾" x 11¾" x 28⅜"
10	P. Lower Cross Rail (1)	¾" x 2" x 19³⁄₁₆"	**20**	Top, bottom and shelf (3)	¾" x 11" x 26½"

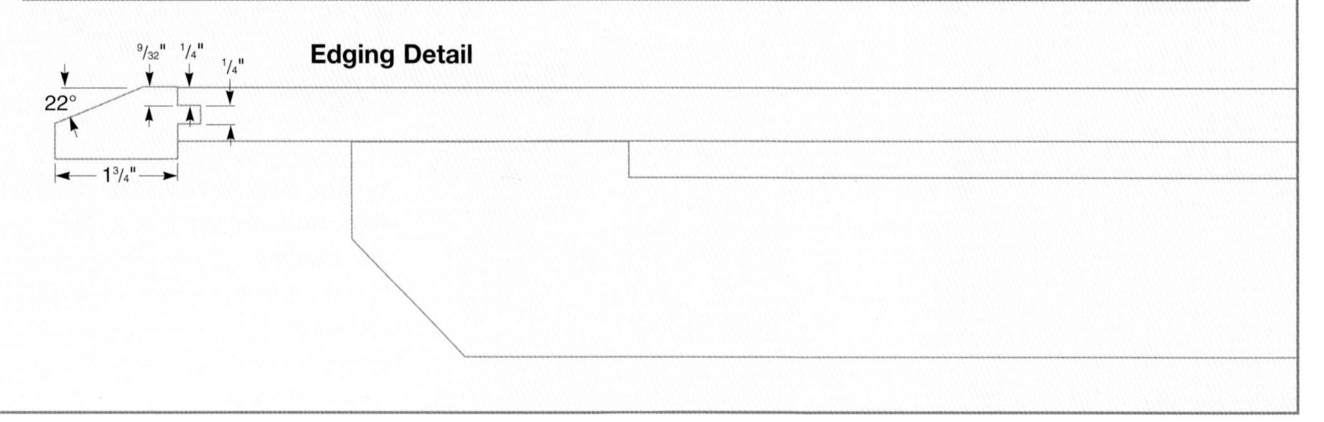

Printer Stand Exploded View

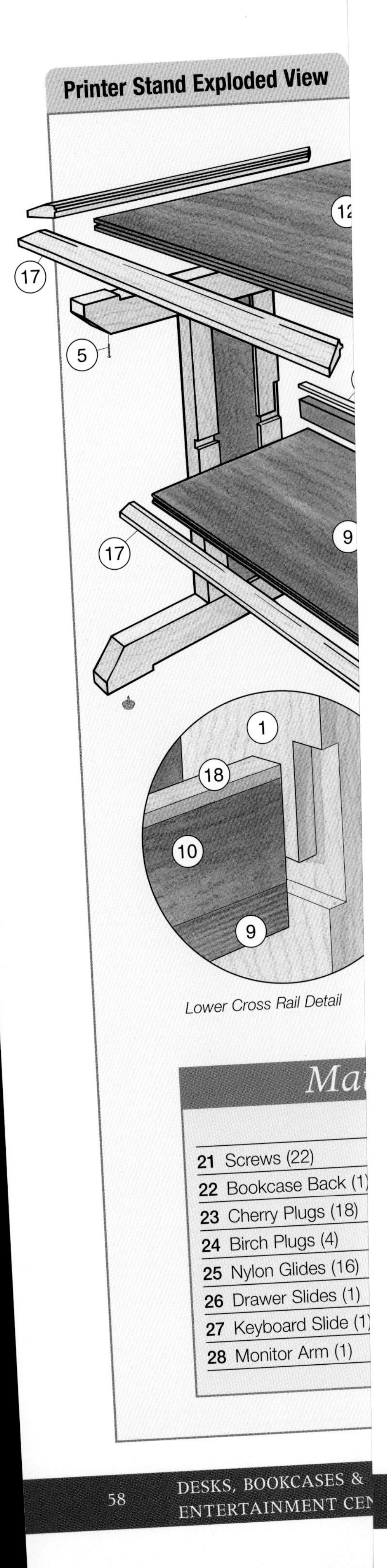

Lower Cross Rail Detail

Ma

- **21** Screws (22)
- **22** Bookcase Back (1)
- **23** Cherry Plugs (18)
- **24** Birch Plugs (4)
- **25** Nylon Glides (16)
- **26** Drawer Slides (1)
- **27** Keyboard Slide (1)
- **28** Monitor Arm (1)

Cabinet Exploded View

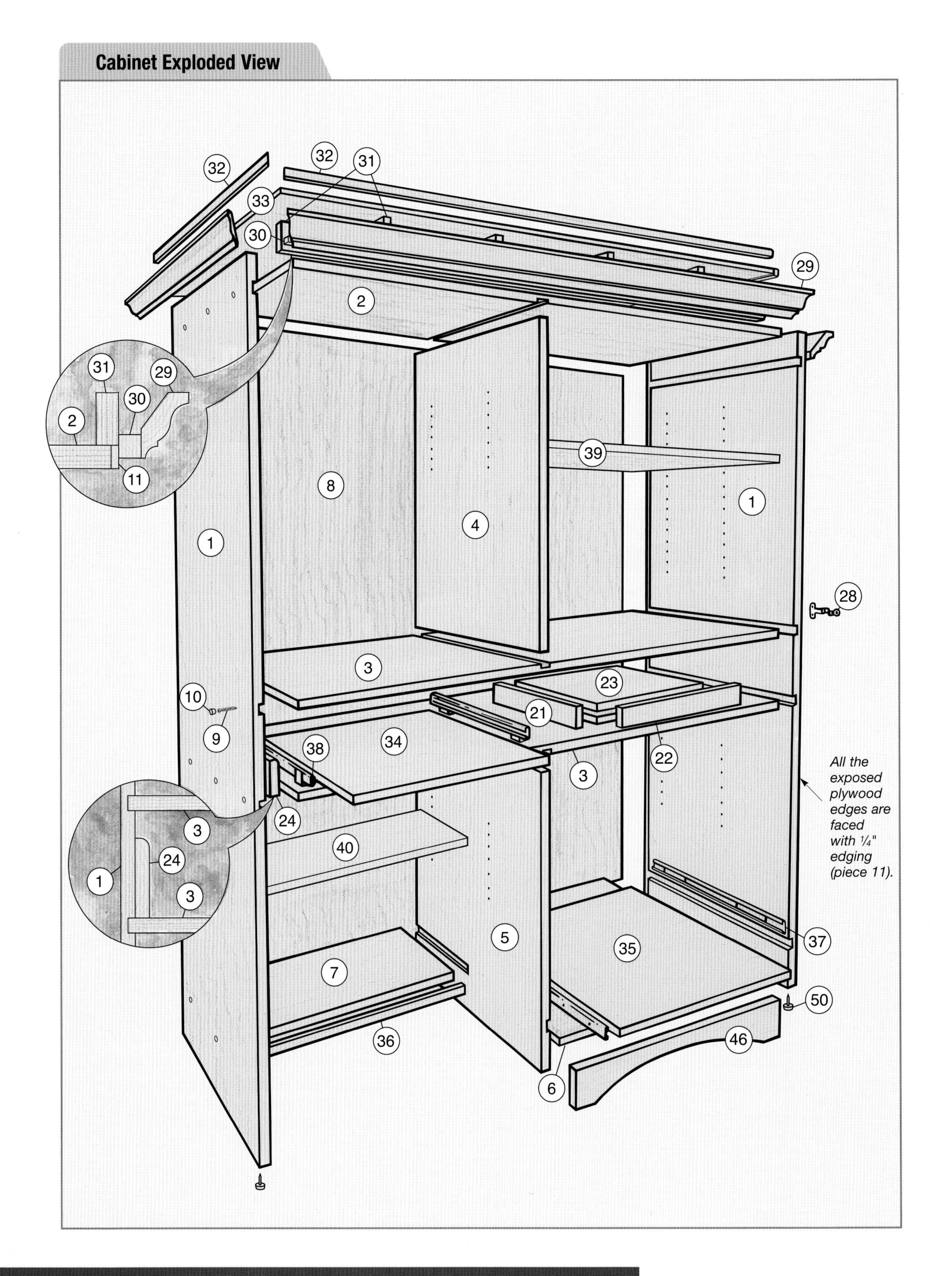

Worktop Exploded View

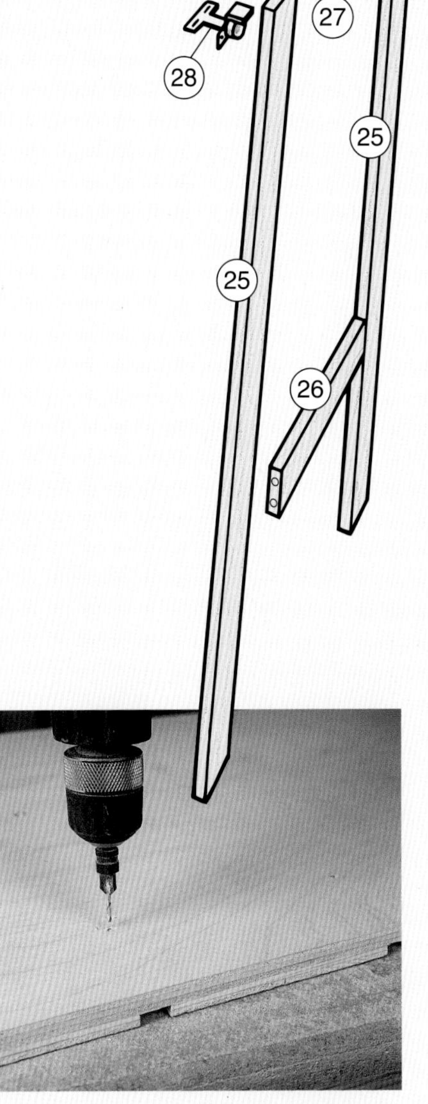

Material List – Computer Cabinet

	T x W x L
1 Sides (2)	¾" x 23½" x 70"
2 Top (1)	¾" x 23¼" x 47¼"
3 Fixed Shelves (2)	¾" x 23¼" x 47¼"
4 Upper Divider (1)	¾" x 23¼" x 34¾"
5 Lower Divider (1)	¾" x 23¼" x 27⅛"
6 Deep Bottom Panel (1)	¾" x 23¼" x 23⅝"
7 Shallow Bottom Panel (1)	¾" x 11½" x 23⅝"
8 Back (1)	¼" x 47³⁄₁₆" x 67"
9 Wood Screws (100)	#8 x 1⅝"
10 Hardwood plugs (50)	⅜" Dia.
11 Edging (4)	¼" x ¾" x 96
12 Worktop (1)	¾" x 17⅞" x 44⅝"
13 Drawer Front (1)	¾" x 6" x 47⅝"
14 Worktop Side Trim (1)	½" x 1½" x 17⅞"
15 ⅛" Worktop Edging (1)	⅛" x ¾" x 44⅝"
16 ¼" Worktop Edging (1)	¼" x ¾" x 18"
17 Short Cleats (2)	¾" x ¾" x 2½"
18 Long Cleat (1)	¾" x ¾" x 16"
19 TV Swivel Pullout (1)	360° x 130 lbs.
20 TV Swivel Screws (12)	#10 x ⅝ panhead
21 Pivot Deck Sides (2)	¾" x 1½" x 16⅜"
22 Pivot Deck Front & Back (2)	¾" x 1½" x 14⅝"
23 Pivot Decks (2)	¾" x13⅛" x 16⅜"
24 Worktop Stabilizer (1)	¾" x 4" x 23"
25 Worktop Legs (2)	¾" x 2" x 31⅜"
26 Worktop Leg Stretchers (2)	¾" x 2" x 9"
27 Worktop Leg Dowels (8)	⅜" x 1½"
28 Euro-style Hinges (5 pairs)	270°; ¾" offset
29 Crown Molding (1)	¾" x 2½" x 105"

(continues on page 68)

Figure 1: *Position the screws that hold the carcass together by drilling pilot holes in the dadoes, then counterbore them from the outside.*

Material List – Computer Cabinet

(continued from page 67)

		T x W x L
30	Crown Molding Cleat (1)	¾" x ¾" x 48"
31	Blocking (5)	¾" x 1¾" x 144"
32	Crown Shelf Edging (1)	⅜" x ¾" x 108"
33	Crown Shelf (1)	½" x 26⅛" x 51 3/
34	Keyboard Shelf (1)	¾" x 18" x 23¼"
35	Printer Shelf (1)	¾" x 21½" x 21 3/
36	Shelf Edging (1)	¼" x ¾" x 168"
37	Drawer slide	22" over travel
38	Keyboard slide	Accuride
39	Large Adjustable Shelves (4)	¾" x 20" x 22 13/1
40	Small Adjustable Shelf (1)	¾" x 11½"x 22 13/
41	Door Rails (8)	¾" x 2½" x 19⅞'
42	Upper Door Panels (2)	¼" x 19¾" x 30 3/
43	Lower Door Panels (2)	¼" x 19¾" x 22 3/
44	Upper Door Stiles (4)	¾" x 2½" x 34½'
45	Lower Door Stiles (4)	¾" x 2½" x 24"
46	Arched Toekicks (2)	¾" x 4" x 22¾"
47	Shelf Supports (20)	5mm. nickel
48	Handles (2)	Southwestern
49	Pulls (4)	Southwestern
50	Glides (4)	Nylon

and screwing them into dadoes. Some are stopped while others are plowed all the way across the sides and fixed shelves. Refer to the Technical Drawings on page 71 for the locations and dimensions of these dadoes as well as the dimensions of the rabbets that hold the back in place.

Chuck a straight bit in your portable router and run it against a long straightedge to plow the dadoes and rabbets. Note: All our dimensions assume that the plywood is actually ¾" thick, so check your stock to ensure that's true, or make adjustments accordingly. Before you set your router aside, plow two more dadoes, one in each side of the lower divider, to hold the bottom panels in place. One of these is stopped while the other goes all the way through (see the Technical Drawings).

We'll glue and screw the carcass together here. This method lets you build the entire carcass without using any clamps. There are two little tricks here that make this possible. First, you can get all the screw holes to line up properly by drilling pilot holes from the inside out, setting the point of your drill bit in the exact center of each dado (see Figure 1). Then drill pilot holes in the shelves half the diameter of your screws, but make the counterbored holes in the sides the same diameter as the screws. This lets the screw pull the two parts together tightly.

Assembling the Carcass

Find a level floor to lay out your main cabinet parts; this will help keep everything square. Begin assembling the carcass by attaching the dividers to the fixed shelves with glue and screws (pieces 9), making sure the lower divider is oriented correctly. Check for square before setting these assemblies aside to dry. Use the same glue-and-screw method to attach these two subassemblies to the sides, again making sure their orientations are correct. Fill all the holes with wood plugs (pieces 10).

Install the top and two bottom panels next, again checking that everything is square. Tack the back in place next with ¾" brads every 12", then rip the edging (pieces 11) to face the sides, shelves, dividers, bottoms and top. Apply this molding with glue and 4d nails spaced every 8 inches or so, pre-drilling for the nails to avoid splitting the molding.

Figure 2: *The hidden worktop is anchored to the cabinet by a TV swivel so it can easily pull out and swing into place when needed.*

Making a Pullout Worktop

Our computer cabinet's hidden worktop is built to look like a drawer in the center of the cabinet. It's actually a plywood shelf with a solid-birch front that swivels out on some hardware designed for TV sets in entertainment centers (see Figure 2). Cut the worktop (piece 12), drawer front (piece 13) and side trim (piece 14) to size, then move to your router table to create the profile on the outside face of the drawer front with a 1/4" roundover bit. Face one long edge of the worktop with 1/8"-thick solid-hardwood stock (piece 15), and cover one short edge with 1/4"-thick edging (piece 16). Cut the rabbet (see Technical Drawings) in the side trim and attach it to the remaining short worktop side.

The worktop is attached to the drawer front with two short cleats (pieces 17) and one long cleat (piece 18). Glue and screw these in place, pre-drilling for the wood screws and countersinking them (see the Technical Drawings for the screw locations and the position of the drawer front in relationship to the worktop edge).

The TV swivel (piece 19) is mounted with screws (pieces 20) directly to the bottom of the worktop (see Technical Drawings for location). The bottom of the TV swivel is essentially a pair of drawer slides. To attach them to the carcass, you need to build a small six-piece deck made up of two sides (pieces 21), a front and a back (pieces 22), and two decks (pieces 23). All six pieces can be cut from scrap 3/4" stock, since they won't be visible when the cabinet is completed. They're simply butt jointed, then glued and screwed together. Screw the TV swivel to this deck, then install the worktop/swivel subassembly with more wood screws driven up through the lower fixed shelf, as shown in the Technical Drawings.

Cut the worktop stabilizer (piece 24) next, and test-fit it against the left wall of the cabinet. This stabilizer supports the pivoting shelf in its closed position and keeps the drawer front aligned properly. Shape the inside edge of the piece with a 1/2" roundover bit in your router table, and attach it to the side with glue and screws.

Building the Leg Assembly

The leg assembly folds up and lies on top of the worktop when not in use. It's comprised of two legs (pieces 25) and a pair of stretchers (pieces 26), all cut from hardwood stock. Use glue and dowels (pieces 27) to join the legs to the stretchers (see Technical Drawings for dowel locations). After the glue cures, move to your router table and round over

Whitewash

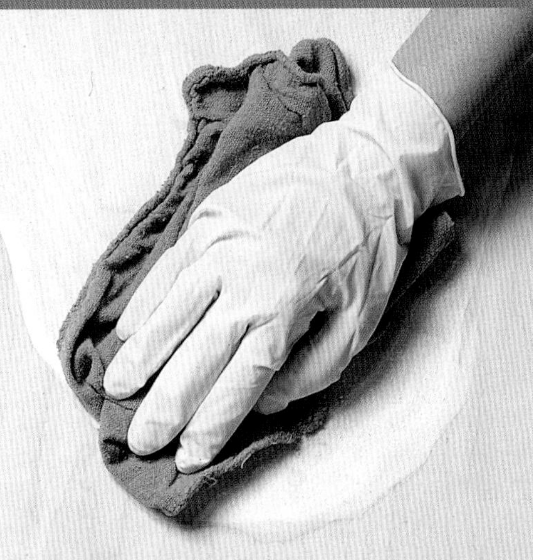

Sometimes when a piece of unfinished wood has been exposed to just the right amount of sun, wind and water, it attains a wonderful light colored patina. A whitewash finish is very similar to that rare, naturally occurring phenomenon.

There are several ways to achieve the light-colored treatment generally called a whitewash. One technique is to use a thinned white flat latex or oil paint. There are also spray-on stains that create the same effect. We used an oil-based stain that simply wipes onto the workpiece, followed by clear lacquer finish.

The challenge in each of these approaches is to keep the coverage even—to significantly lighten the tone of the wood without hiding the grain. In my test pieces, I experimented with a light undercoat of clear sealer to help keep the whitewash tone even. This proved to be a mistake. It was difficult to get a balanced finish using this technique because the sealer inhibited stain absorption.

As with any finishing operation, the best results will be achieved with proper surface preparation. Sand the project smooth and treat each surface exactly the same. Compare all the pieces and make adjustments for color as you work. Your efforts will be well rewarded.

Figure 3: *Install the Euro-style cup hinges by boring a couple of 35 mm holes, then screwing the hinges in place.*

Figure 4: *You can mill tenons on the ends of the door rails vertically by using a shop-made tenoning jig like this one.*

Figure 5: *Use 270° Euro-style hinges for full clearance. Accuride slides (inset) provide easy access to the printer and keyboard.*

all the edges. Then bore ½"-deep holes for the Euro-style hinges (pieces 28) using a standard 35 mm Forstner bit, as shown in Figure 3. (These sturdy, concealed hinges are a great piece of specialty hardware, with a full 270° swing and a ¾" offset.) Pre-drill for the screws that come with the hinges, then drive them home.

Making the Crown Assembly

The crown molding (piece 29) is mitered to fit across the front and sides of the cabinet, then nailed in place with a scrapwood cleat (piece 30) behind it for stability. We used stock crown molding from a local lumberyard, so the profile of yours may not match it exactly (see the Technical Drawing on page 72). Apply a little glue to the miters before installing the crown molding, then pre-drill it for 4d finish nails and set them after they're driven (this is a good time to set the nails in the edging throughout the cabinet, too). Fill the holes and sand them flush. Now glue the blocking (pieces 31) into the cavity in the top of the cabinet (see Technical Drawings for locations).

Shape the crown shelf edging (piece 32) with a ¼" roundover bit in your router, then miter and attach it to the front and sides of the crown shelf (piece 33). Secure this subassembly to the blocking with glue and screws, and move on to installing the hardware.

Adding Slides and Shelves

The front edges of both the keyboard and printer shelves (pieces 34 and 35) are faced with ¼"-thick hardwood stock (piece 36). Simply cut this molding to length and apply it with glue and 1" brads, setting and filling their heads. The printer shelf is mounted on a standard 22" over-travel slide as shown in the inset photo (above), while the keyboard shelf rides on an Accuride® keyboard slide (pieces 37 and 38). Use the rest of your ¼" molding to edge the four large and one small adjustable shelves (pieces 39 and 40), then move on to building the doors.

Assembling the Doors

The only difference between the upper and lower doors is that the lower doors are a bit shorter. Knowing that, you can cut all eight rails (pieces 41) to size, then mill a ½"-deep groove in one edge of each for the upper and lower door panels (pieces 42 and 43). Make these cuts with a ¼"-wide dado head in your table saw, then mill the same groove in each of the upper and lower door stiles (pieces 44 and 45). When you're done, lower the blade to ¼" and use a tenoning jig (see Figure 4) to cut a tenon on the ends of each rail (see the Technical Drawings).

Test-fit the components of each door and when everything fits just right, assemble the doors by gluing the corner joints only; the panels must float freely to allow for wood movement.

Cut the two decorative toekicks (piece 46) on your band saw, following the profile shown on the Technical Drawings. Sand the curves smooth, then install one toekick on the lower left door and one under the bottom of the main cabinet, trimmed to fit in the location shown on the Technical Drawings. Secure them with glue and wood screws through counterbored holes. (Note: the toekick on the door is attached from the inside.) Plug these holes with hardwood plugs and sand flush.

Wrapping Things Up

We used the same hinges to hang the doors as we used for the worktop legs (see Figure 5). These doors overlay the entire cabinet except the false drawer front that hides the worktop.

Install the hinges according to the instructions included (see Technical Drawings for locations), then adjust the doors for a perfect fit. Drill holes and temporarily install the shelf supports, door handles and drawer pulls (pieces 47, 48, and 49) at the locations shown on the Technical Drawings, then remove all the hardware and refer to the sidebar on the previous page for finishing instructions. When the finish is dry, reinstall your hardware and add some nylon glides (pieces 50) under the cabinet. Now load up the cabinet with your electronic hardware and go to work!

Technical Drawings

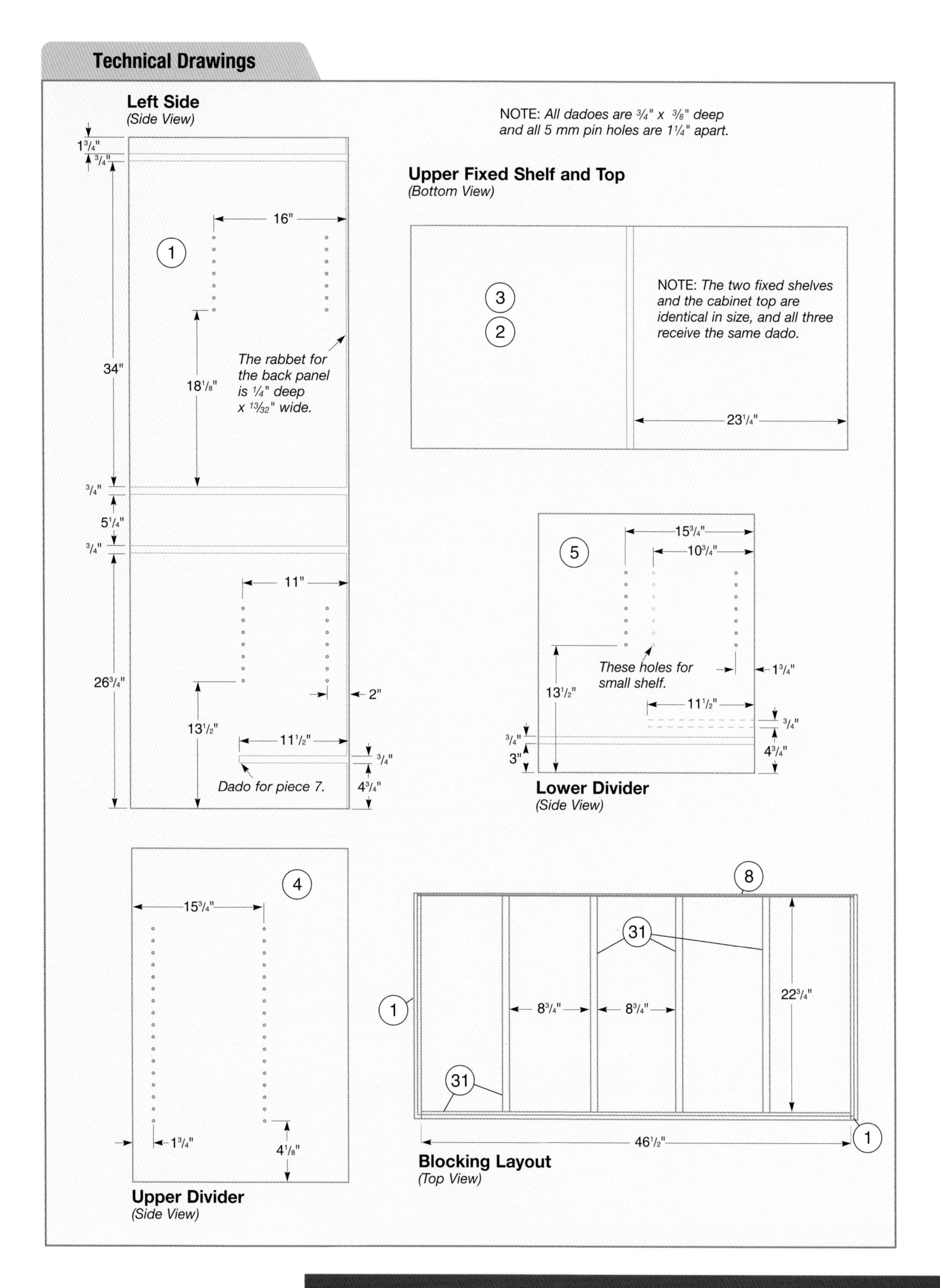

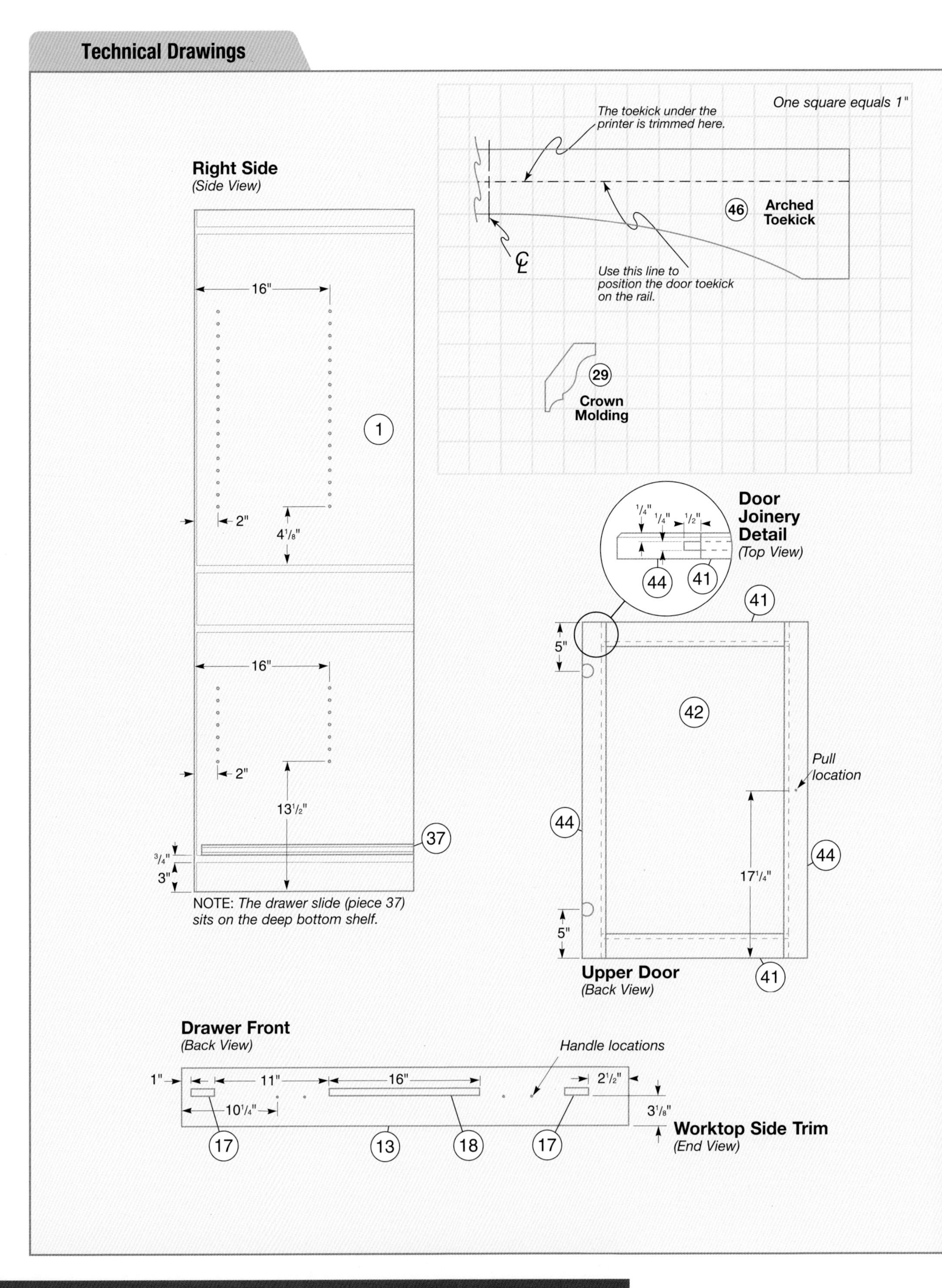
One square equals 1"
The toekick under the printer is trimmed here.
Right Side
(Side View)
46
Arched Toekick
Use this line to position the door toekick on the rail.
16"
29
Crown Molding
1
2"
4 1/8"
Door Joinery Detail
(Top View)
1/4"
1/4"
1/2"
44
41
41
5"
16"
42
2"
Pull location
13 1/2"
44
37
44
3/4"
3"
17 1/4"
NOTE: The drawer slide (piece 37) sits on the deep bottom shelf.
5"
Upper Door
(Back View)
41
Drawer Front
(Back View)
Handle locations
1"
11"
16"
2 1/2"
10 1/4"
3 1/8"
Worktop Side Trim
(End View)
17
13
18
17

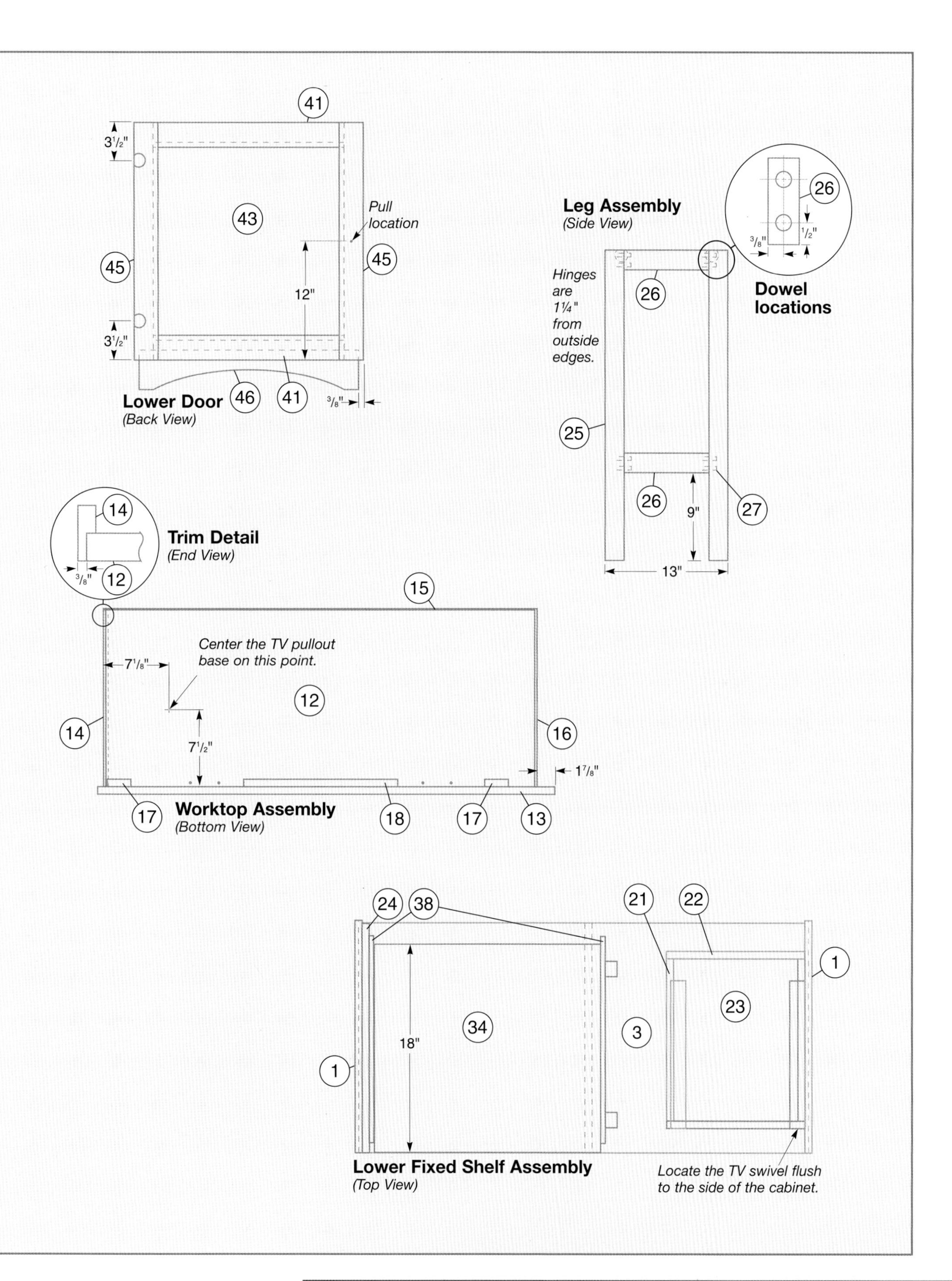
41
3½"
43
Pull location
45
45
12"
3½"
Lower Door
46
41
⅜"
(Back View)
Leg Assembly
(Side View)
26
½"
⅜"
Dowel locations
Hinges are 1¼" from outside edges.
26
25
26
9"
27
13"
14
Trim Detail
(End View)
⅜"
12
15
Center the TV pullout base on this point.
7⅛"
12
14
7½"
16
1⅞"
17
Worktop Assembly
(Bottom View)
18
17
13
24
38
21
22
1
23
34
18"
3
1
Lower Fixed Shelf Assembly
(Top View)
Locate the TV swivel flush to the side of the cabinet.

Introduction to Sociology
GENERAL PSYCHOLOGY
Cabinetmaking
WOODWORKER'S SOURCE BOOK
GARDEN FURNITURE
GEORGE BUCHANAN
THE HUMAN BRAIN
Minnesota's Geology
PHOTOGRAPHY
Anatomy
THIRD EDITION
Marieb
Human Anatomy and Physiology
LEGEND

Build a Knockdown Bookcase from One Sheet of Plywood

Here's proof that well-designed knockdown furniture can be sturdy and attractive, while still maintaining its most important features—easy disassembly and compact storage. This design is made with the frugal (or modestly budgeted) in mind: You'll only need one sheet of plywood, a little solid stock and a handful of Minifix knockdown connectors to hold the parts together.

by Chris Inman

The old woodworkers' saw about never having too many clamps can easily be applied to bookcases. There just never seems to be enough of these versatile pieces of furniture around to store everything.

You may have doubts about how well knockdown furniture will hold up, particularly when you see what's stocked at discount stores. But if you use quality knockdown (KD) hardware and design plenty of bracing into a project, KD furniture can be as stylish as its conventionally built counterparts and survive many years of hard use.

The bookcase featured here comes apart with a few turns of a screwdriver and all the pieces can be stacked in a neat pile less than 7" tall. In addition to its knockdown capabilities, this project comes with another outstanding advantage: it can be completed in a single weekend using just one sheet of ¾" red oak plywood and a few feet of solid stock.

Cutting Your Plywood

Lay out the bookcase panels on your plywood, as shown in the Cutting Diagram on page 76, and cut the oversized pieces from the sheet. Now you can cut the individual pieces to their finished sizes with more control and accuracy.

Next, use the Technical Drawings on pages 77and 79 to make hardboard templates for the sides, apron, shelves, and back stops (pieces 1 through 7).

When it's time to move, this knockdown-style bookcase comes apart in minutes and will stack neatly into a pile less than 7" tall.

Bookshelf Exploded View

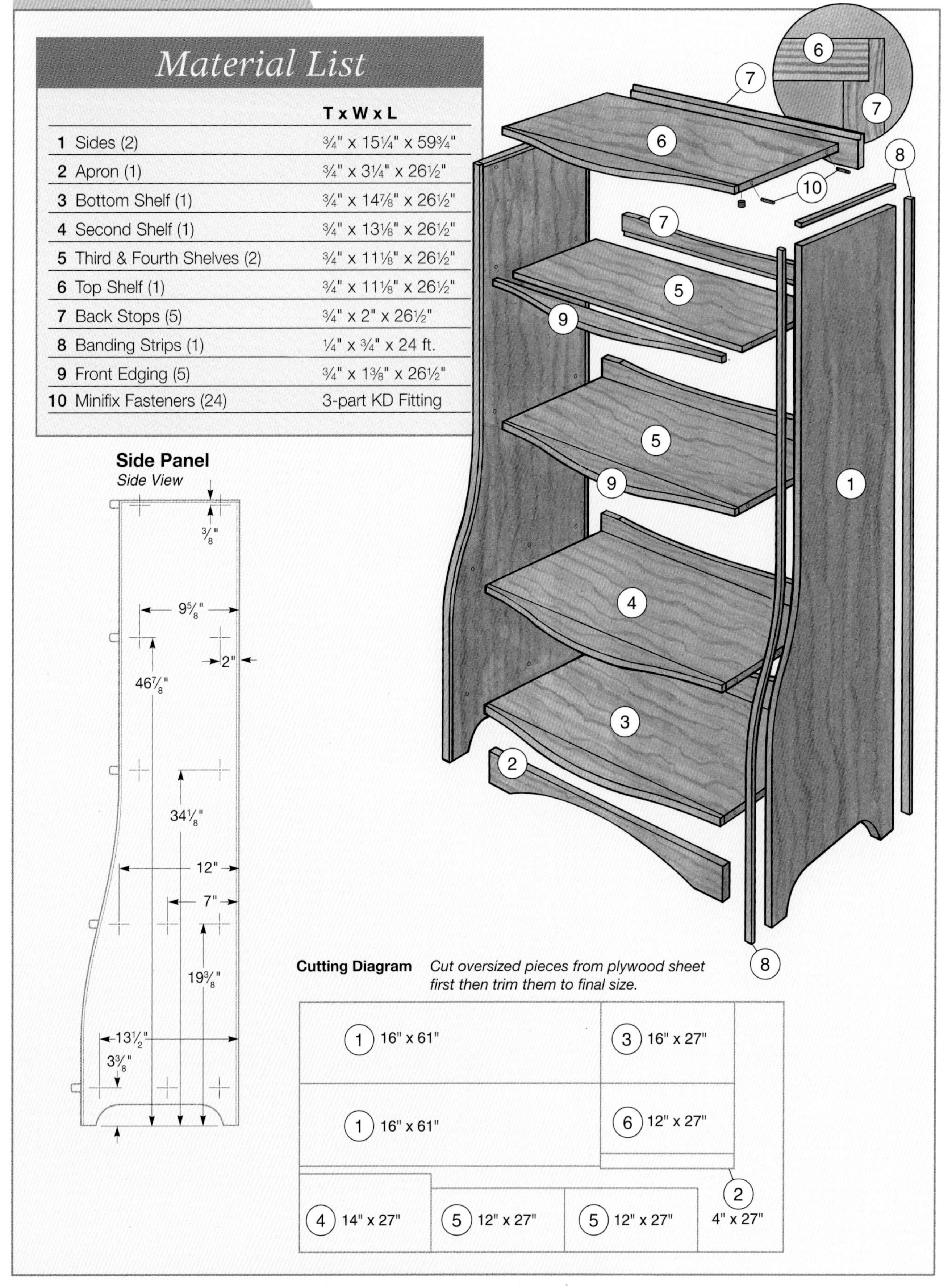

Material List

		T x W x L
1	Sides (2)	¾" x 15¼" x 59¾"
2	Apron (1)	¾" x 3¼" x 26½"
3	Bottom Shelf (1)	¾" x 14⅞" x 26½"
4	Second Shelf (1)	¾" x 13⅛" x 26½"
5	Third & Fourth Shelves (2)	¾" x 11⅛" x 26½"
6	Top Shelf (1)	¾" x 11⅛" x 26½"
7	Back Stops (5)	¾" x 2" x 26½"
8	Banding Strips (1)	¼" x ¾" x 24 ft.
9	Front Edging (5)	¾" x 1⅜" x 26½"
10	Minifix Fasteners (24)	3-part KD Fitting

Cut the templates to size, then bandsaw the curved edges staying just a hair outside the lines. Finish up by sanding right to the layout lines with a drum sander chucked in your drill press. Remember, your templates are the key to getting accurate plywood panels.

Now chuck a template-routing straight bit in your router and clamp the side and apron templates to the plywood. Rout the curved edges on each of these pieces, but hold off routing the shelves until you've glued on the front edging.

Banding the Edges

To protect the side panels and to improve their appearance, glue solid-wood banding (pieces 8) to the edges. Begin by ripping ¼"-thick strips and adhering them first to the top edge of each side, then to the front and back edges. Be sure to use plenty of clamps to pull the banding tight against the curved front edge of the sides (see Figure 1, right).

The shelf back stops provide two important functions. They keep books and knickknacks from falling off the shelves and provide the essential bracing the bookcase needs to prevent racking, which would likely occur without any permanent joinery or a back panel to stiffen the assembly. Cut the back stops to size and plow a rabbet in each piece, as shown in the back stop detail in the top right corner of the drawings on the facing page.

Now rout the back stops to shape using the template you made earlier. Glue the stops to each shelf, then cut stock for the front edging (pieces 9). Once all the edging is glued to the shelves, sand the joints flush and use your template and router to trim the front edging of each shelf to shape.

Figure 1: *The ¼" banding will easily conform to the front edge of the sides, but use as many clamps as necessary to get a seamless joint.*

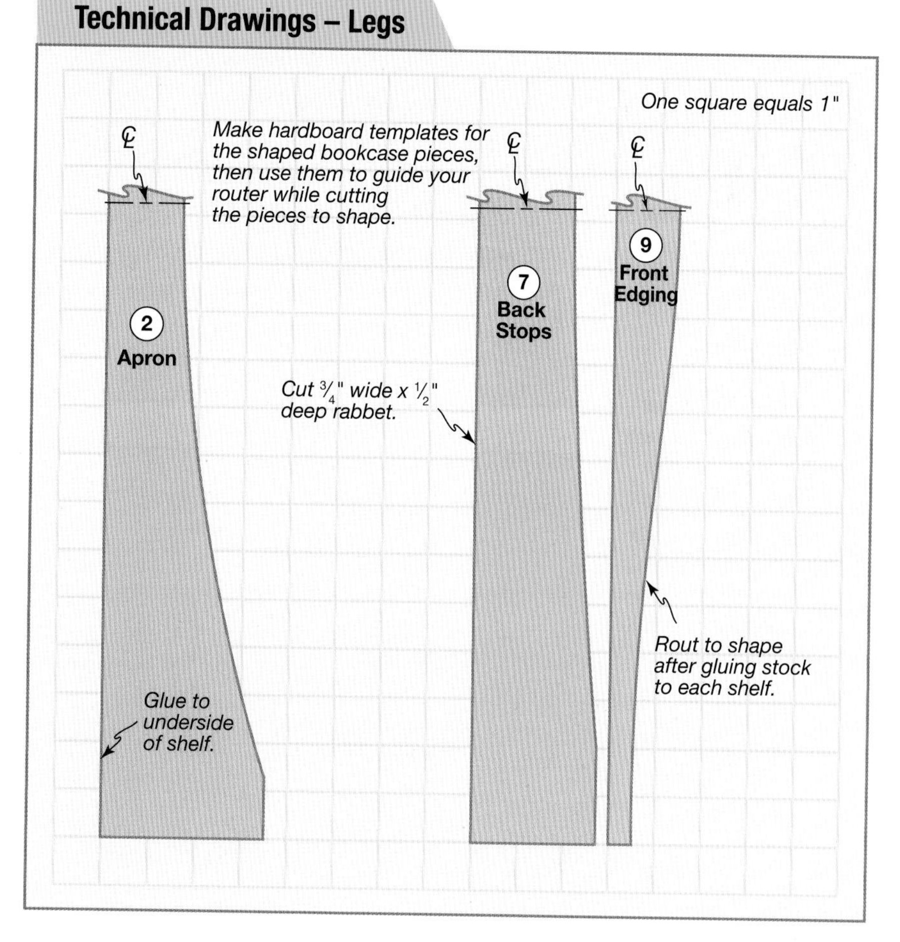

a rabbet to cut along the back edge of each glued-up panel (for the back). Glue the slide support rails (pieces 4) in place, but hold off on installing the door support hardware (pieces 10).

The bottom is next. Its sides have a tongue (trimmed to fit the stopped grooves you just made in the side rails), and its back edge has a rabbet to accommodate the back. The front edge is trimmed with a strip of hardwood edging (piece 8) that receives a 35° bevel along its inside bottom edge.

The top features two trimmed tongues on its sides, a back rabbet and some trim along its front edge. This trim (piece 7), shown on page 82, is milled oversized and a cove is formed on its bottom. After the cove is shaped, the edging is ripped to width, exposing a portion of the cove.

After the unit is assembled, the cove on the top edging and the bevel on the bottom edging meet to form an arc, which accommodates the opening and closing of the door. (Note: if you stack more than two cases, screw them together for safety.)

With the side panels assembled and milled and the edging added to the top and bottom, bring the cases together with clamps and glue. You can test-fit the back, but don't install it yet—that has to be done later.

Making the Top Subassembly

As with the case, start on the top by cutting your parts (pieces 11 through 14) to size. Once again, however, there's an exception: The top's side rails (pieces 11) are a glued-up subassembly designed to carry the appearance of stiles and rails all the way to the top. To make these side rails, glue up a blank of horizontal pieces, trim and joint its edges and add two vertical "stiles," one along each edge. When the glue dries, rip off each top side rail (with "stile-ized" ends). These pieces receive a stopped groove (see Drawings) for the top platform, which has a trimmed-off tongue along each edge, just like the case top.

Move on to making the top's front and back rails, which also require a little shaping (see Drawings).

As you can see in the inset photo on page 85, a template is handy for drawing cloud lift shapes on the top's sides and back (as well as the base's sides and front). With all of the pieces cut and machined, you can glue and clamp the top together.

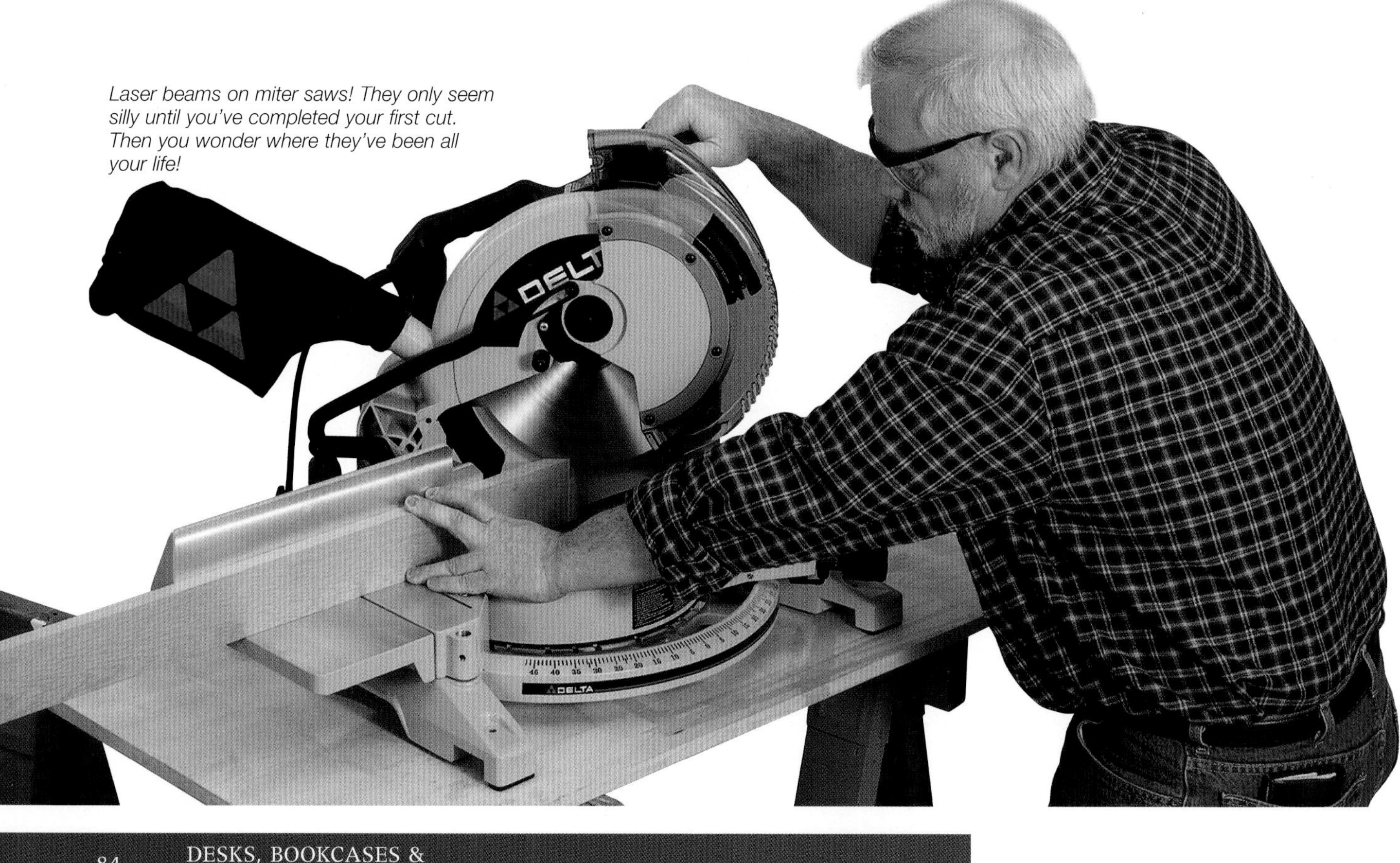

Laser beams on miter saws! They only seem silly until you've completed your first cut. Then you wonder where they've been all your life!

A cope and stick router bit set makes fast work of the door frames. After sticking the rails and stiles (above), the ends of the rails are coped, as shown at right. Then use your table saw to cut the glass retainer strips free.

Making the Base Subassembly

The base subassembly (pieces 15 through 19) is different from the case and top in that it has no rabbets or tongues. Use your miter saw to miter-cut the corners, then turn to your table saw to make two "drop" cuts on the front rail and one each on the other three rails. The upper drop cut on the front rail helps form the notch (see Drawings). The other three help form the shaped cutout on each piece. (Be sure to use a start and stop line on your fence for these cuts.) Use the template to draw the cloud lift shape, but this time you can turn to your drill press to actually mill their shape. As for the top notch, we recommend gluing up the base pieces (including the cleats and glue blocks) before you use your hand saw to finish cutting out the notch (see Drawings). It's a delicate part of the project, so take your time here. You'll notice that the base platform sits a little proud of its rails (just like the case top sits proud of its rails). This is how the pieces interlock.

Making the Door Subassembly

The doors are so easy to make it's a little scary. The secret is to use a cope and stick router bit set. With these two bits, you can make doors all day long! Get started by milling the rails and stiles (pieces 20 and 21) to overall size. [This would seem to be the right time to order your glass (piece 22), but it's a good idea to wait until your frames are completed.] Now simply insert your "stick" bit and mill the inside edges of the frame pieces from end to end. Switch to the "cope" bit and mill the ends of the rails. Now turn back to the table saw and remove the retainer strips, which have magically appeared on the inside edge of each piece you've machined. The bits account for the kerf you're about to make, and the pieces you trim off become your perfectly sized glass retainer strips (pieces 23)—just miter them to length!

Now things move quickly. Measure for your glass, install it with the retainer strips and brads and, with the case on its front, position your slides for installation. Cut 2" off the back of these nylon slides so they'll fit the boxes. Doing so will not present any problems for installation.

Once the doors are working in concert with the case, lay out and drill a ¼" hole on the inside of the case (see Drawings). This hole is for a short length of dowel that serves as a doorstop. With the hardware and stop in place, install the back with small brads.

Finishing Up

Sand through 220 grit, add the sash knobs (pieces 24) and select your finish. We went with a coat of Watco® Medium Walnut Oil followed by a coat of wipe-on polyurethane for these white oak cabinets.

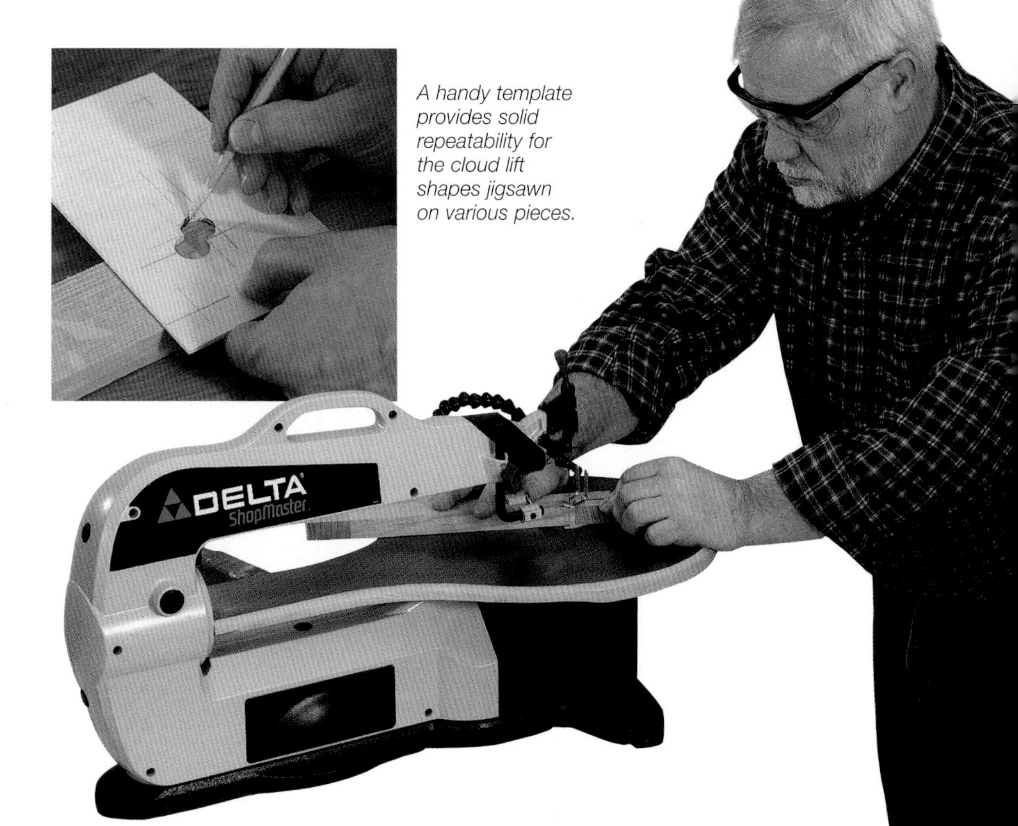

A handy template provides solid repeatability for the cloud lift shapes jigsawn on various pieces.

perform on the bottom before it can be installed: Following the dimensions on the Technical Drawings pages 96 and 97, use the band saw to cut a notch that houses the two subframes (pieces 3). These subframes each receive two rabbets (see Technical Drawings) that can be milled at this time using the same dado setup in your table saw.

The assembly cleats (pieces 4, 5 and 6) are already cut to size, so start putting your base unit together by doweling and gluing this subassembly together, as shown in the Technical Drawings. Remember that the front cleat is centered on the side cleats so there's only room for one dowel at each front corner. Clamp the cleats together until just snug. Overtightening is a common mistake, one that usually results in a weaker joint because most of the glue gets squeezed out. Check for squareness and lay the cleats aside.

While they're drying, glue and clamp the two subframes (pieces 3) to the sides. When the pieces dry, you're ready to assemble the bottom carcass. Start by gluing the bottom into the side dadoes, keeping a damp cloth handy to wipe off excess glue. Now glue the cleat subassembly flush with the tops of the sides and clamp the base together. Since the back (piece 7) is cut to size, dry-fit it in place. This will help square up the assembly, but don't nail it in place quite yet.

Upper Carcass Exploded View

Material List – Upper Unit

	T x W x L
15 Bottom Panel (1)	1" x 14" x 36"
16 Sides (2)	¾" x 11⅜" x 40¼"
17 Top (1)	¾" x 14½" x 36"
18 Back (1)	¼" x 34½" x 41"
19 Shelf Standards (4)	½" x 1⅛" x 39½"
20 Shelf Supports (6)	¾" x ½" x 10⅜"
21 Shelves (2 or 3)	¾" x 11⅛" x 33¾"
22 Upper Face Frame Rail (1)	¾" x 4¾" x 36"
23 Upper Face Frame Stiles (2)	½" x 1⅝" x 40⅜"
24 Top Braces (2)	¾" x 1⅛" x 33¾"

Figure 1: *Creating the edge of the top piece is a two-step process. Start with a roundover bit on the router table (right) and add the rabbet on the table saw (above).*

Making the Face Frame and Shelves

Following traditional procedures, the face frame is built as a separate subassembly, then applied in one step to the carcass. The top and bottom rails (pieces 8 and 9) are attached to the two frame stiles (pieces 10) with hidden lap joints (see the Technical Drawings for dimensions). The laps on the rails are created on a table saw using a dado head, while the stopped laps on the stiles (see Lap Joint Detail on page 88) are formed on a router table. Clamp a stop to your fence to limit the cut, and remove most of the waste with a straight bit. Follow up by squaring the corners with a sharp chisel. You'll notice that the top rail and the stiles are made of ½"-thick stock, a subtle deviation from standard dimensioning that lends a little lightness and elegance to the design.

Before moving on, chuck a ⅜" straight bit in the router table and make the groove in the bottom rail for the bricking molding, as shown on the Technical Drawings. Assemble the face frame with glue and clamps and set it aside to dry.

The base shelf standards (pieces 11) are cut from ½"-thick stock and feature triangular reliefs notched at 4"-intervals along one edge. Shelf

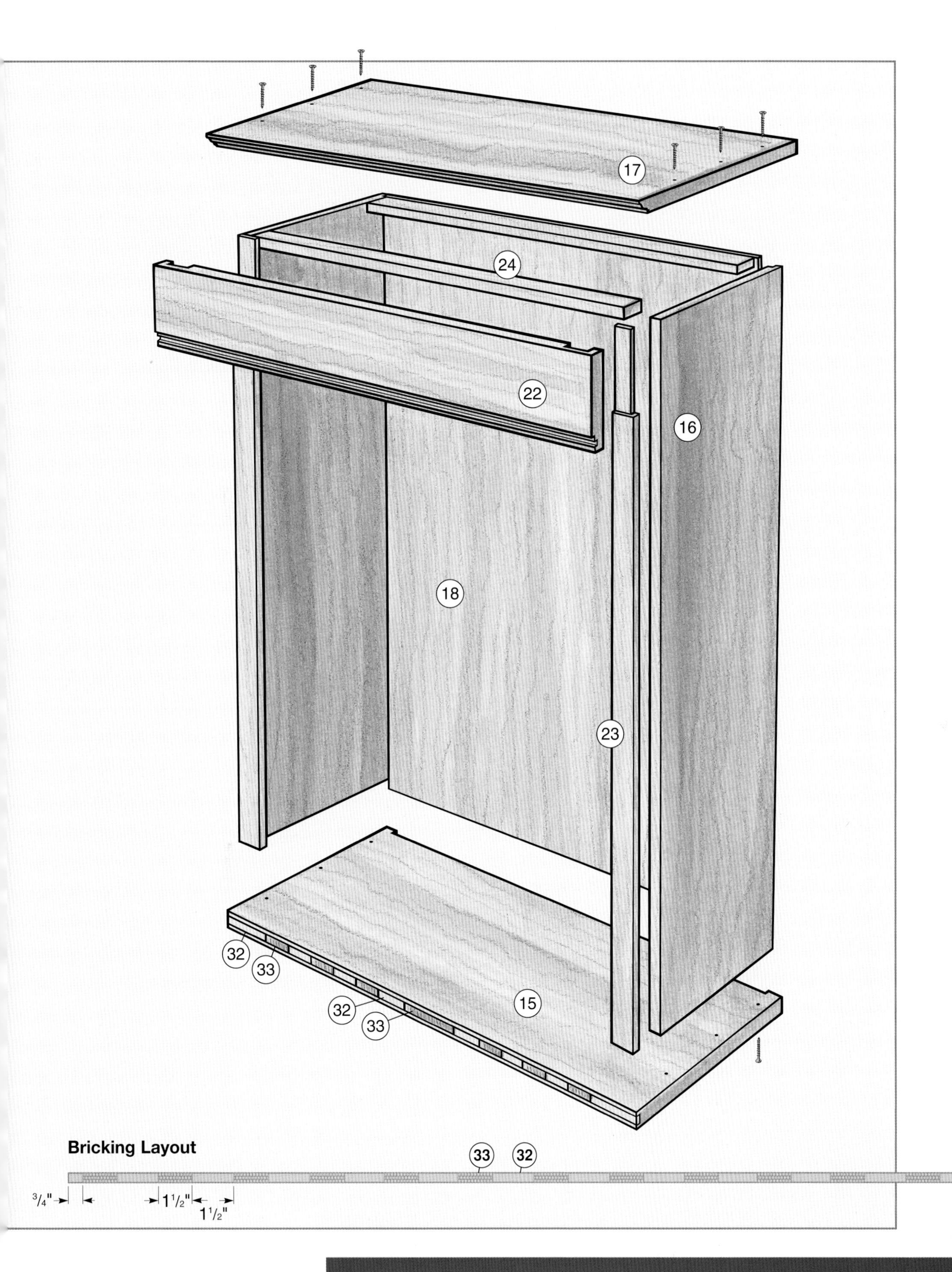
17
24
22
16
18
23
32
33
32
33
15
Bricking Layout
33
32
3/4"
1 1/2"
1 1/2"

Crown Molding Exploded View

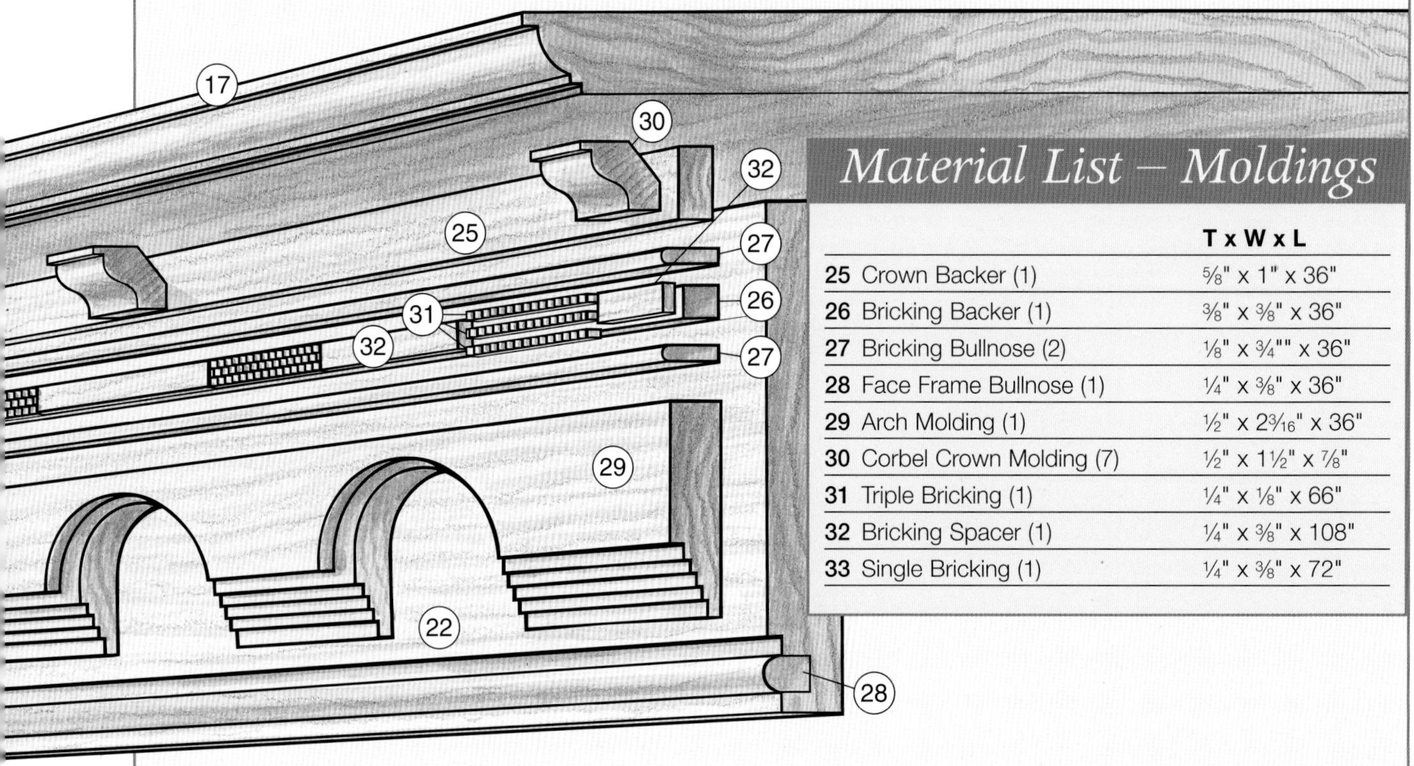

Material List – Moldings

	T x W x L
25 Crown Backer (1)	5/8" x 1" x 36"
26 Bricking Backer (1)	3/8" x 3/8" x 36"
27 Bricking Bullnose (2)	1/8" x 3/4"" x 36"
28 Face Frame Bullnose (1)	1/4" x 3/8" x 36"
29 Arch Molding (1)	1/2" x 2 3/16" x 36"
30 Corbel Crown Molding (7)	1/2" x 1 1/2" x 7/8"
31 Triple Bricking (1)	1/4" x 1/8" x 66"
32 Bricking Spacer (1)	1/4" x 3/8" x 108"
33 Single Bricking (1)	1/4" x 3/8" x 72"

supports (pieces 12) rest in these cutouts, their ends mitered to fit. The supports hold one or two shelves (pieces 13) that are notched at the corners to fit around the standards (see Technical Drawings). Cut these notches on your band saw, but to make the notches in the standards and the miters on the supports, switch over to the table saw.

We clamped four pieces together and made the angled relief cuts on the standards and the miter cuts on the supports first, and then made the 90° relief cuts. Once everything is milled, install the face frame subassembly (which should be dry by now) with glue and clamps. If you have enough clamps, go ahead and glue the shelf standards in place while you're at it. When everything dries, remove your clamps and tack the back in place. Use 1" brads and nail every six inches along the perimeter, checking for squareness early on in this process.

Before dropping the shelves in place, lay the base on its back and install four cabinet levelers (pieces 14). Since the bottom rail on this bookcase is 6" high, you should be able to adjust the levelers without drilling access holes for the Allen wrench. That takes care of the base for a while.

Building the Upper Unit's Carcass

As with the base, the first construction step on the upper unit is to cut all the pieces to overall size. Begin milling the parts by creating the bricking groove on the front edge of the bottom panel (piece 15). To house the back, cut the rabbets on the bottom panel and the sides (pieces 16). Use your table saw for the rabbets on the sides, but switch to a router for the stopped rabbet on the bottom, as shown on the Technical Drawings.

With the rabbets formed, attach the bottom to the sides. Since they're hidden, countersink screws for this operation, driving them up through the bottom. Glue these joints, and make the holes in the bottom slightly larger than the diameter of the screws to allow each fastener to pull the joint snug as it is tightened.

The next step is to shape the leading edge of the top (piece 17). Begin on the router table (see Figure 1), using a 3/8"-radius roundover bit set to leave 1/8" square at the top of the cut, as shown on the Technical Drawings. Switch to the table saw to cut the rabbet along the bottom (see Figure 1 inset). Set the blade for a 1/8"-deep cut and take a few passes to nibble the waste away. You can now glue and screw the top to the sides, counterboring your holes. They won't be visible, but hide the heads with plugs anyway.

If you were building a standard cabinet, this would be the logical time to install the back (piece 18). Hold off on that step to make it easier to clamp the shelf standards in place. For the upper unit's standards, supports and shelves, (pieces 19, 20, and 21), just follow the same steps you used earlier on the base, wrapping up by gluing the shelf standards in place on the sides.

Now you're ready to machine and install the upper face frame rail and stiles (pieces 22 and 23) and the top braces (pieces 24). Follow the Technical Drawings to complete the tongues on the tops of the stiles and the dadoes on the inside of the face frame rail.

You'll also find details for the rabbet and groove along the bottom of the face frame rail. This groove is cut with a 1/4" dado blade to house a piece of bullnose trim that will be formed during the next step. Complete your top carcass by gluing the top braces and face frame pieces in position and tacking on the back. Now you're ready to bring this piece to life with the crown molding details.

Crown Molding Backers and Bullnoses

A series of small moldings are combined at the top of the bookcase to create the effect of a corbel and brick building facade. The first pieces to mill are the crown and bricking backers (pieces 25 and 26) that back up the corbels and bricking. Cut these to size on your table saw. The next two elements in the assembly are small bullnoses (pieces 27 and 28) that serve to offset the bricking details at the top of the crown and create a beaded look at the bottom.

Make the cuts on a router table using 1/16"- and 1/8"-radius roundover bits. To prevent these small pieces from being pulled into the router table clearance holes, clamp a piece of melamine to the fence and table so that only the bit is exposed. Be sure to make these cuts on wider stock, ripping the finished moldings off after you complete the routing.

*Quick*Tips

Knee-activated Safety Switch

This simple addition to your table saw requires less than $10 in materials and takes about 30 minutes to complete. It allows you to safely hit the OFF switch with your knee or shin without having to grope blindly while your hands are still holding the stock. A light tap anywhere on the 1/2" PVC frame does the trick, and the large open frame doesn't obstruct access to the ON switch or the blade height crank.

If the wood binds, this jig allows you to keep your hands on the workpiece while shutting off the saw

Figure 2: *Get started on the arch molding by drilling a series of 1/8"-deep holes with a 2" Forstner bit. To create the stepped appearance, follow up with a 1 1/2" bit centered in the first hole.*

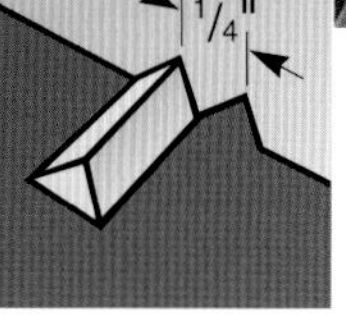

Figure 3: *To mill your bricking, set the dado head at 45°, insert an indexing pin in your auxiliary miter gauge fence (see inset) and cut a series of peaks 1/4" apart. Cutting with the grain will create a much cleaner brick.*

Once the bullnoses are trimmed to length and width, glue pieces 25 through 28 to the face frame rail.

Creating the Arches and Corbels

Though it looks a little daunting, making the arch molding (piece 29) is actually a lot easier than you might think. The 11 arches are cut on a drill press using two Forstner bits in series, and the key to success is proper preparation and setup.

Begin by using the Technical Drawings to mark the center of each of the arches on your raw stock. With a 2"-diameter Forstner bit chucked in your drill press (don't forget to slow down the speed to avoid burning your bits), use a piece of scrap lumber the same thickness as the workpiece to set your depth of cut to ⅛". Drill the larger arches, then switch to a 1½" Forstner bit and repeat the operation, this time going all the way through (see Figure 2).

To convert the holes to arches, use a try square to draw lines from the bottom of the rail to the outside edge of each hole, then make the short cuts with a sharp dovetail saw.

The steps below the arches are formed in five passes on the table saw. The first cut is ⅛" wide (to match the depth of the 2" arches) while the remaining four cuts are 1⁄16". With each pass, drop the blade 3⁄16" to create the steps. The Technical Drawings offer complete dimensions to help you create the shape.

The corbel crown moldings (pieces 30) are simply short pieces of commercially available molding cut to length and applied with glue.

Adding the Bricking Moldings

The bricking details (pieces 31, 32, and 33) that accent this project are based on a bricklaying technique that was widely used on the facades of commercial buildings in the latter part of the nineteenth-century. To add texture and depth to an otherwise plain facade, the architect would insert single or triple rows of bricks set at 45° angles to form a sawtooth pattern. These rows often ran both horizontally across the building and vertically down the sides, where they helped break up windowless walls of brick.

Like the arch molding, the process for making the bricking is easy with the right setup. In this case a simple miter gauge jig (see Figure 3), does the trick. Use this jig to form the bricking on the face of the board and then turn to the bandsaw to cut your pieces to thickness and length. You can now glue your three different sized piece in place, alternating bricking (pieces 31 or 33) with spacers (pieces 32), as shown on the Technical Drawings. Press these into place without clamps to avoid crushing the fragile detail.

Finishing Up

Wrap up this project by first sanding methodically through the grits up to 180. Since pine tends to blotch under a stained finish, we suggest applying a clear topcoat to this project and allowing the natural grain and wood tone show through. Satin polyurethane is an excellent choice here. Use the wipe-on formulations or aerosol spray so you can control varnish in the nooks and crannies of the moldings.

One of the crowning details on this piece is the seemingly intricate bricking. Actually, it's simple to make. After milling your bricking stock (see Figure 3 at left), create the triple bricking by offsetting ⅛"-wide strips, as shown above. The single bricking (below) is simply ⅜"-wide strips cut to length.

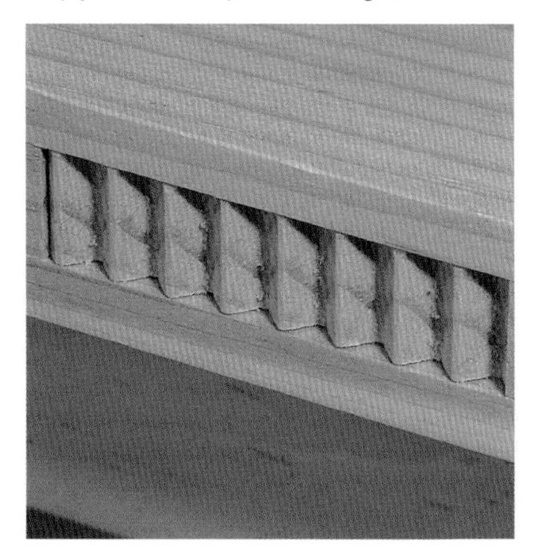

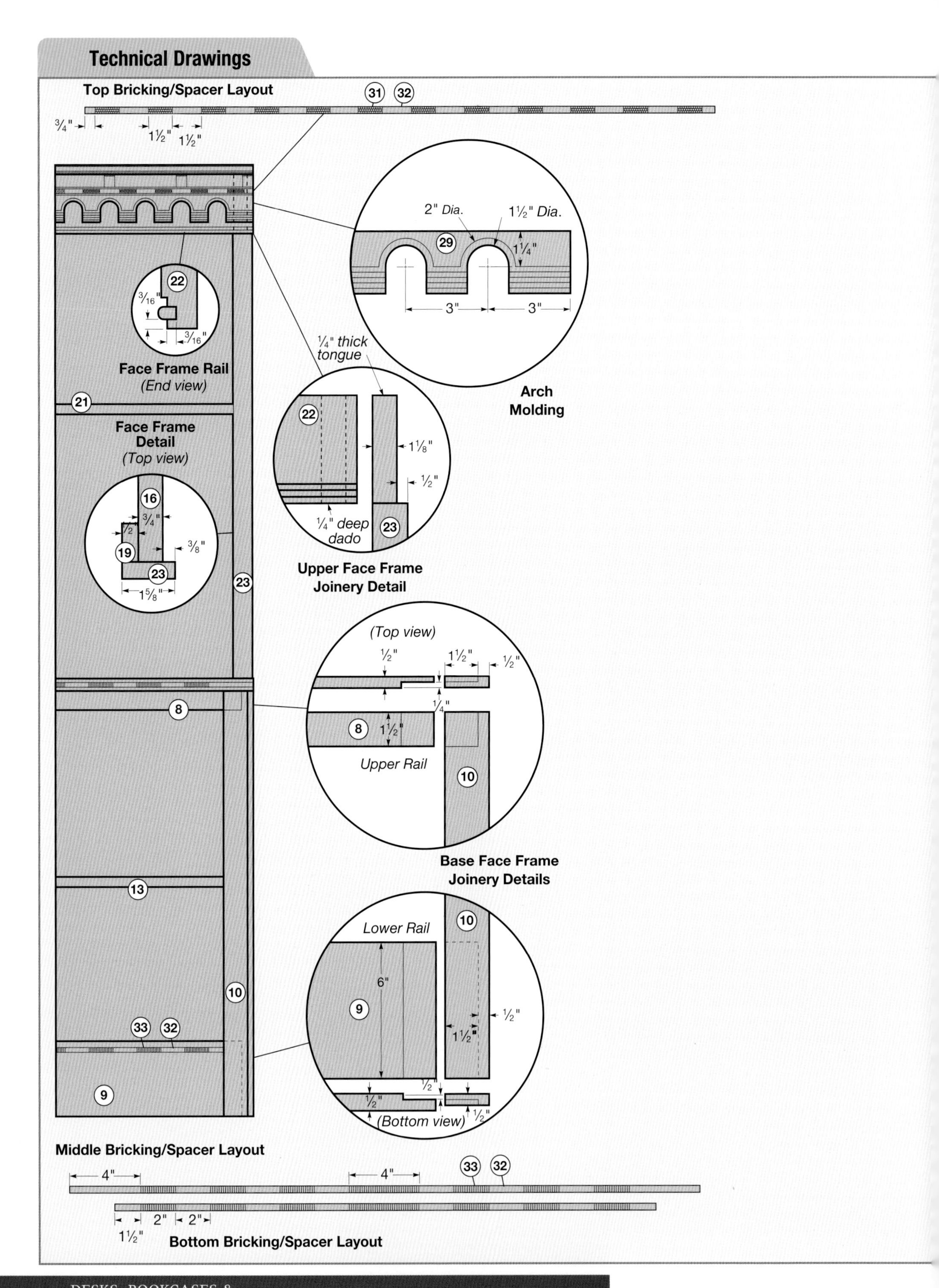
Top Bricking/Spacer Layout
31
32
¾"
1½"
1½"
2" Dia.
1½" Dia.
29
1¼"
3"
3"
Arch Molding
22
3/16"
3/16"
Face Frame Rail
(End view)
21
Face Frame Detail
(Top view)
16
¾"
½
3/8"
19
23
1⅝"
¼" thick tongue
22
1⅛"
½"
¼" deep dado
23
Upper Face Frame Joinery Detail
23
(Top view)
½"
1½"
½"
¼"
8
1½"
Upper Rail
10
Base Face Frame Joinery Details
8
13
Lower Rail
10
6"
9
½"
1½"
½"
½"
½"
(Bottom view)
10
33
32
9
Middle Bricking/Spacer Layout
4"
4"
33
32
2"
2"
1½"
Bottom Bricking/Spacer Layout

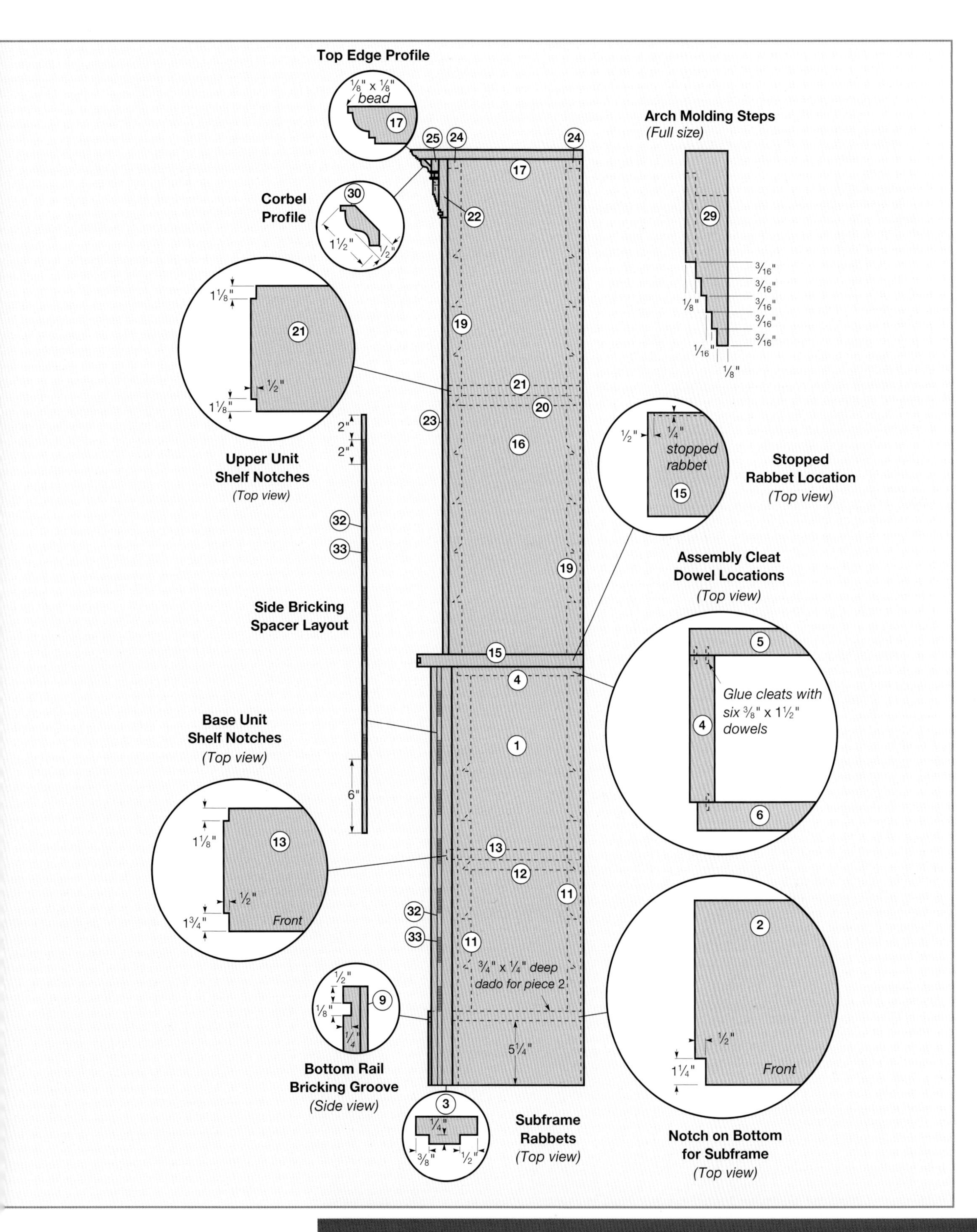
Top Edge Profile
1/8" x 1/8" bead
Corbel Profile
1 1/2"
1/2"
Arch Molding Steps
(Full size)
3/16"
3/16"
3/16"
3/16"
3/16"
1/8"
1/16"
1/8"
1 1/8"
1/2"
1 1/8"
Upper Unit Shelf Notches
(Top view)
2"
2"
6"
Side Bricking Spacer Layout
1/2"
1/4"
stopped rabbet
Stopped Rabbet Location
(Top view)
Assembly Cleat Dowel Locations
(Top view)
Glue cleats with six 3/8" x 1 1/2" dowels
Base Unit Shelf Notches
(Top view)
1 1/8"
1/2"
1 3/4"
Front
3/4" x 1/4" deep dado for piece 2
5 1/4"
1/2"
1/8"
1/4"
Bottom Rail Bricking Groove
(Side view)
1/4"
3/8"
1/2"
Subframe Rabbets
(Top view)
1/2"
1 1/4"
Front
Notch on Bottom for Subframe
(Top view)

LAKE WOBEGON DAYS
ECO
FOUCAULT'S PENDULUM
TAD WILLIAMS
OTHERLAND
SAM MALOOF WOODWORKER
The HANDPLANE Book
Hand Tools
Encyclopaedia Britannica

Heirloom Bookcase

With its bowed front, fluted accents and mahogany veneers, this classic bookcase design will expand your woodworking skills and deliver a project worthy of the ages. If you haven't yet invested in a vacuum press for veneering, now would be a good time to get one—you're going to need it.

by Rick White

Wouldn't it be great to know something you build today will be around generations from now? That's the kind of notion that tends to keep you going when you tackle a big project like this bookcase. Although there's a lot of work tied up in a piece of casework like this, it's definitely got heirloom potential.

As different as the various sections of the bookcase look, all the lumber used here is farm-raised Honduras mahogany in various guises. Solid mahogany stock is attractive, stable, and a joy to work. The shelves and back of the case are built from mahogany plywood, but the distinctive beauty of the piece is created by contrasting mahogany crotch and ribbon veneers.

Flattening the Veneer

You'll need to address the crotch veneers up front because it takes a little time for them to become workable. They're taken from the part of a tree where two large branches create a "Y," so it's their nature to have erratic grain, making them wavy and brittle. By clamping them in a press now, you can straighten them while you build the bookcase base. That way, they'll be available when you get ready to make the sides.

A nice trick is to take a large piece of paper and cut a rectangular hole in it the same size as the veneer you require. Use it as a moving window to view and select just the right areas of dramatic grain pattern from larger sheets of veneer. Trim these about an inch oversize before you flatten them.

Create the simple, shop-made veneer flattening press shown in the illustration on page 100. Soak the wavy veneer in a commercially available glycerine-based softener, following the manufacturer's instructions. Then lay it between two layers of window screen (to allow a little air movement). Place this assembly between several sheets of brown kraft paper—the type used to make grocery bags—to soak up the excess moisture. Use a scrap of 3/4" plywood on the top and bottom to ensure flatness, then weigh the whole thing down with a concrete block or two. After the veneer has dried, quickly apply it to its plywood substrate and put it under pressure. Crotch veneer has a memory, and its wavy nature will reappear if it

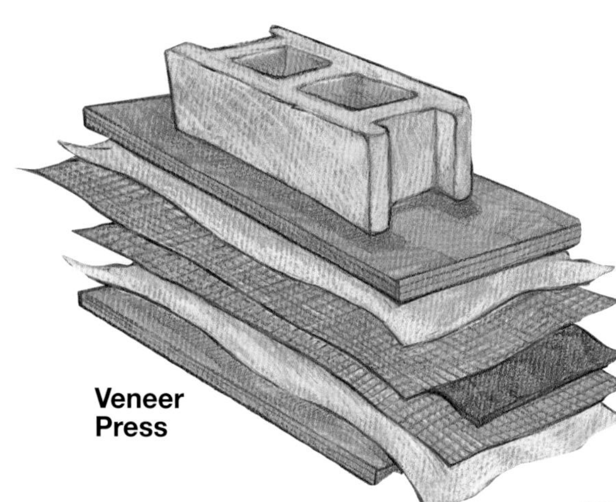

Nothing fancy to a simple veneer press like this—it's just a couple of scraps of plywood, layers of kraft paper, and window screen weighed down with a cinder block or two. The veneer is centered between the layers of this sandwich.

is not quickly glued and clamped in place. While the veneer is drying, start working on the base.

Building from the Bottom Up

We'll order the rest of the construction process so you build the bookcase from the ground up. Make the four feet (pieces 1) from a 24"-long, glued-up block of mahogany measuring 2½" x 3¼". Crosscut the stock to length and chamfer the two back feet as shown in the drawing on page 101. Chop a stopped mortise and a corresponding large rabbet into the back and inside faces of the legs. See the Technical Drawings on pages 110–111 for dimensions and locations of the construction details.

Cut the base front, back and sides (pieces 2 and 3) to size. Use a cove bit and a straightedge to create the stopped flutes in the outside faces of the sides, following the dimensions shown on the Technical Drawings.

Make the fluted foot plinth blocks (pieces 4) by following the guidelines in the sidebar on page 104. Next, cut the two curved plywood supports (pieces 5) to size and shape. Screw and glue these supports to the base front, then rip the 1/4" plywood backer (piece 6) to size. Secure the backer to the curved supports with glue and brads, then refer to the sidebar below to apply ribbon veneer (pieces 7) to the backer. After the glue dries, trim the veneer flush with the edges all round using a sharp knife, sandpaper and a file.

Finish off the base by adding ¼"-thick moldings (pieces 8 through 10) at the locations shown on the Exploded View on page 101. Shape both front edges (the bullnoses) of each of these pieces on the router table with a ⅛" roundover bit and a fence. Note that the bullnosed moldings are of various widths and that the top pieces are mitered where they meet. After dry-fitting these pieces to the base assembly, secure them with glue and

Use a Vacuum Press for Curved Shapes

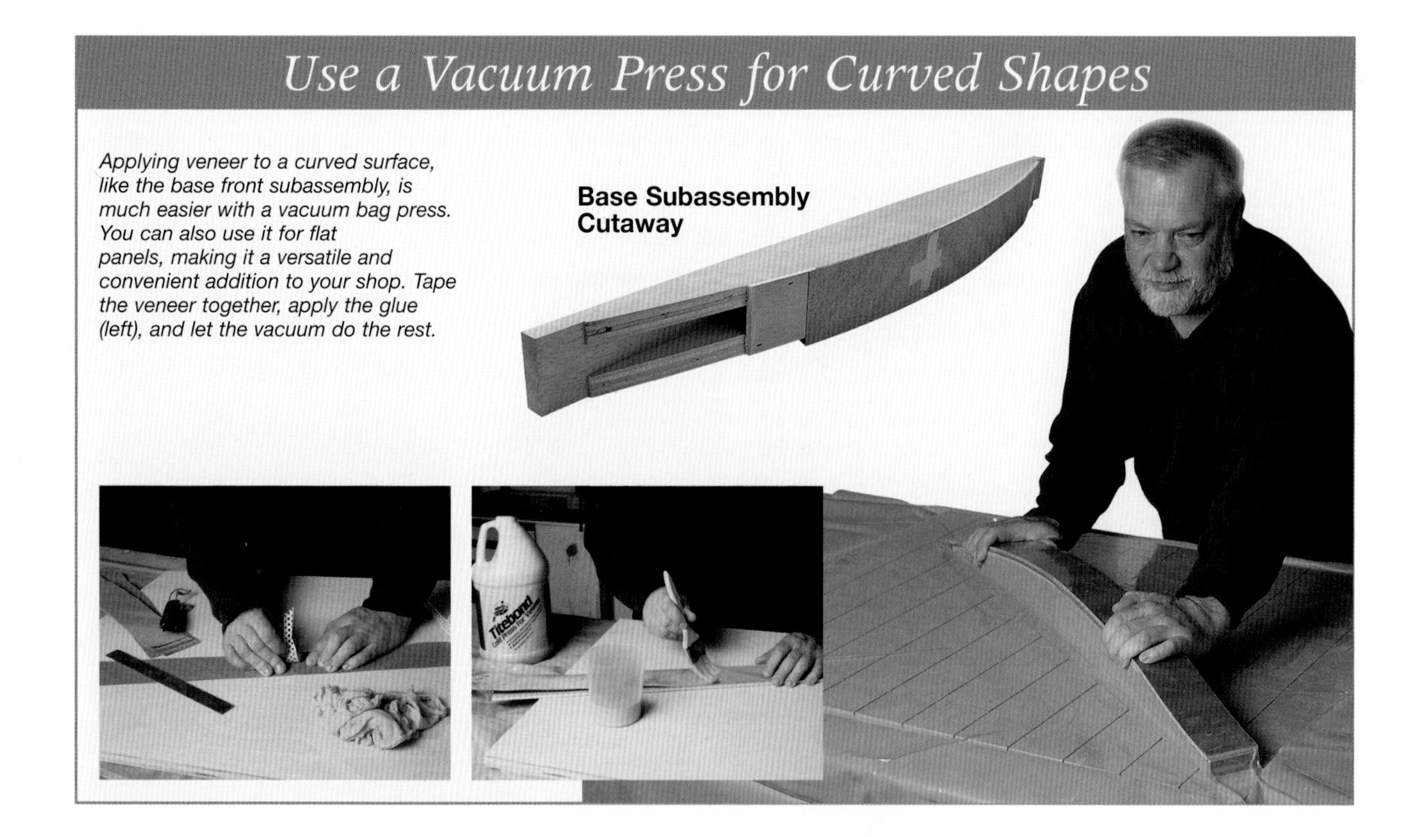

Applying veneer to a curved surface, like the base front subassembly, is much easier with a vacuum bag press. You can also use it for flat panels, making it a versatile and convenient addition to your shop. Tape the veneer together, apply the glue (left), and let the vacuum do the rest.

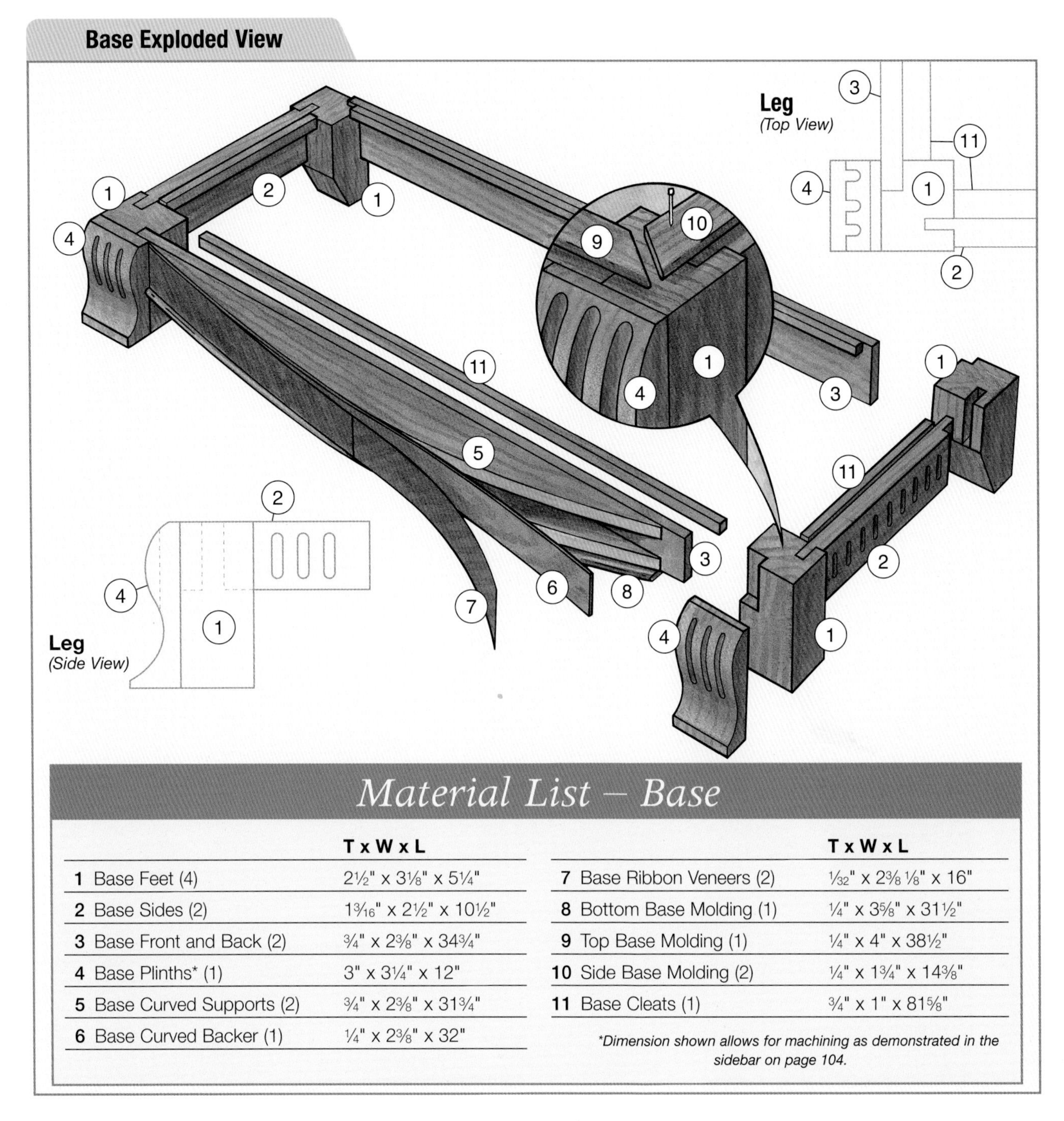

Material List – Base

	T x W x L
1 Base Feet (4)	2½" x 3⅛" x 5¼"
2 Base Sides (2)	1⁹⁄₁₆" x 2½" x 10½"
3 Base Front and Back (2)	¾" x 2⅜" x 34¾"
4 Base Plinths* (1)	3" x 3¼" x 12"
5 Base Curved Supports (2)	¾" x 2⅜" x 31¾"
6 Base Curved Backer (1)	¼" x 2⅜" x 32"
7 Base Ribbon Veneers (2)	¹⁄₃₂" x 2⅜ ⅛" x 16"
8 Bottom Base Molding (1)	¼" x 3⅝" x 31½"
9 Top Base Molding (1)	¼" x 4" x 38½"
10 Side Base Molding (2)	¼" x 1¾" x 14⅜"
11 Base Cleats (1)	¾" x 1" x 81⅝"

*Dimension shown allows for machining as demonstrated in the sidebar on page 104.

clamps. Cut, fit, and attach the base cleats (pieces 11) to the inside faces of the base sides, front and back.

Building the Carcass Sides

The bookcase is built around two ¾" plywood sides (pieces 12), to which the shelves and the stile and rail subassemblies are attached. Before ripping them to width, locate and plow five dadoes and a rabbet on the inside face (check the Technical Drawings for locations). By doing this before you separate the panels, you ensure the dadoes and rabbet will line up perfectly.

The outside faces of these plywood sides are covered with stile and rail subassemblies. Each is comprised of two vertical hardwood stiles (pieces 13 and 14) and four horizontal rails (pieces 15, 16, and 17). After ripping them to size, use a ¼" dado head to plow a groove down the center of one edge of each stile. Make a matching groove in one long edge of each top and bottom rail and in both long edges of the middle rails. Then form two rabbets on each end of the rails, producing a tongue. Dry-assemble the stiles and rails to check their fit, then disassemble before moving on to the six panels.

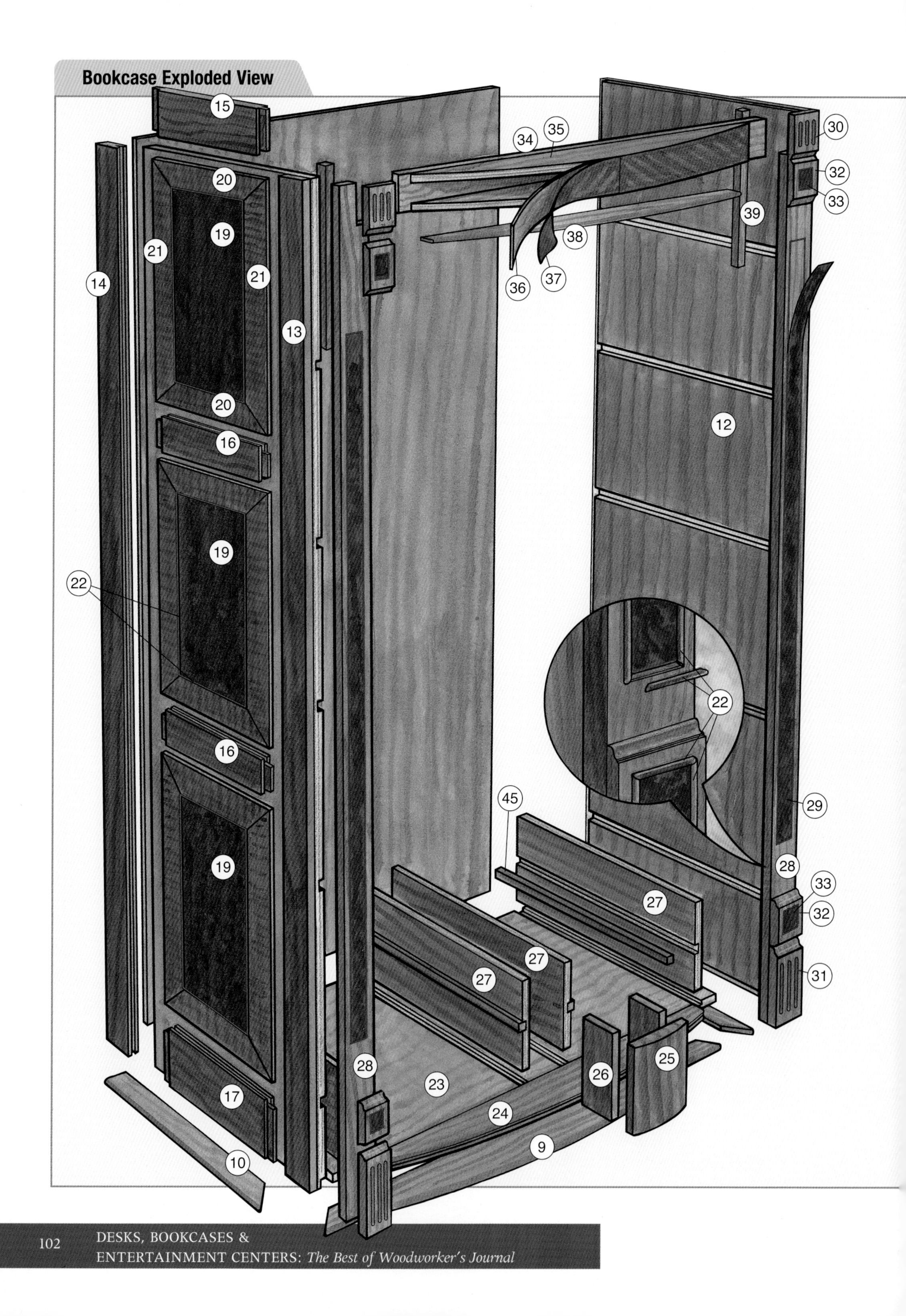
Bookcase Exploded View
15
34
35
30
32
33
39
20
19
21
21
14
38
36
37
13
20
16
12
19
22
19
16
22
45
29
19
28
33
27
32
27
27
31
28
25
26
23
24
17
9
10

Material List – Carcass

	T x W x L
12 Carcass Sides (2)	¾" x 12½" x 73⅜"
13 Front Stiles (2)	¾" x 1¾" x 73⅜"
14 Back Stiles (2)	¾" x 2⅜" x 73⅜"
15 Top Rails (2)	¾" x 4" x 9"
16 Middle Rails (4)	¾" x 2½" x 9"
17 Bottom Rails (2)	¾" x 5¾" x 9"
18 Side Panels (6)	¼" x 8$^{15}/_{16}$" x 19$^{15}/_{16}$"
19 Crotch Veneers (6)	$^{1}/_{32}$" x 4$^{15}/_{16}$" x 16$^{1}/_{16}$"
20 Horizontal Ribbon Veneers (12)	$^{1}/_{32}$" x 2½" x 9"
21 Vertical Ribbon Veneers (12)	$^{1}/_{32}$" x 2½" x 20"
22 Bullnose Molding Strips (1)	⅛" x ¼" x 525"
23 Shelves (6)	¾" x 12½" x 35¾"
24 Shelf Edging (6)	¾" x 3⅜" x 31¾"
25 Drawer Divider (1)	⅞" x 2½" x 4½"
26 Drawer Returns (2)	¾" x 2⅜" x 4½"
27 Drawer Walls (4)	¾" x 5¼" x 12½"
28 Decorative Front Stiles (2)	¾" x 3⅛" x 73⅜"
29 Front Stile Burl Veneers (2)	$^{1}/_{32}$" x 2" x 48"
30 Top Fluted Plinths (2)	¾" x 3⅛" x 4"
31 Bottom Fluted Plinths (2)	¾" x 3⅛" x 6"
32 Veneered Plinths (4)	½" x 3⅛" x 4⅛"
33 Plinth Burl Veneers (4)	$^{1}/_{32}$" x 2¼" x 2¼"
34 Apron Backer (1)	¾" x 3⅞" x 33¾"
35 Apron Horizontal Supports (2)	¾" x 2⅜" x 31¾"
36 Apron Front (1)	¾" x 3⅞" x 32"
37 Apron Veneers (2)	$^{1}/_{32}$" x 4½" x 17"
38 Apron Bottom Trim (1)	⅛" x 2⅞" x 31¾"
39 Glue Blocks (2)	1" x 1" x 11⅜"

*Quick*Tips

Small Stock Storage

Heavy cardboard carpet tubes (usually available at no cost from a carpet layer or store) can be cut to any length and bundled together with cord. Use them to separate different dowel scraps and leftover hardwood moldings. This way you can check your inventory at a glance. Mount the tubes on a plywood base to keep the ends of the contents off the floor.

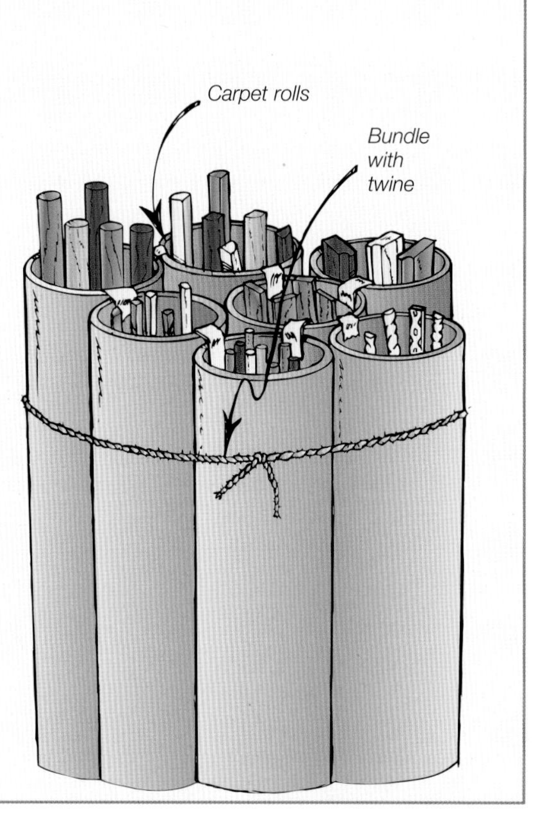

Creating the Veneered Panels

Each stile and rail framework houses three plywood panels (pieces 18), which are veneered on their outside faces (with pieces 19, 20, and 21). Follow the guidelines on page 105 to lay up the panels.

Remove the panels from the press and use a ⅛" veining bit to plow stopped grooves, as shown in the bottom photos on page 107. These grooves straddle the joint between the ribbon and crotch veneers and house the bullnose molding strips (piece 22), which help create the 3-D effect of a raised panel. Miter the molding to fit, then glue and clamp it in place.

Once the panels are well sanded, assemble the two frames and panels. Glue and clamp the frames together, checking for squareness and flatness as you go. Don't glue the panels in their grooves: they should be allowed to float freely. Sand the frames after the glue dries, then set them aside for a while.

Fluting on the Router Table

The front feet are adorned with curved and fluted plinth blocks, which are fluted before being cut apart. Band-saw the curved shape, then use a 3⁄8" core box bit in your router table to create the three flutes in each block. Crosscut them into two blocks on the table saw, then sand them before attaching them to the front feet with glue and clamps.

Step 1: *Start by band-sawing the curved shape onto the front face of each plinth block while they are both still part of the same piece of raw stock.*

Step 2: *Use a core box bit to plow three flutes in both pieces at the same time (see full-size pattern for shape). As you can see, the flute cut will be deeper at the center of the curve.*

Making the Shelves and Starting the Assembly Process

This bookcase is built around a carcass that takes shape when you attach the two dadoed sides you made earlier to a series of six fixed shelves. The lowest shelf is covered by a pair of drawers. All six shelves are mahogany plywood rectangles (pieces 23), faced with curved, solid-wood edging (pieces 24).

After cutting the shelves to size, band-saw the front faces of the edging to shape. This can be done in groups of threes by taping the stock together, as shown on page 106. Keep the waste pieces and use them as clamping blocks when gluing on the edging.

Sand the curves, then mill a triple bead in them with a beading bit chucked in the table router. To keep things lined up, cut biscuit slots in the shelves and edging before applying glue and biscuits. Make use of the curved waste pieces when clamping the edging in place, as shown on page 106.

After the glue has dried, sand the shelves smooth. Cut the drawer divider (piece 25) to shape. Cut the drawer returns (pieces 26) from hardwood stock and the drawer walls (27) from plywood. Now machine the grooves in the drawer walls (for the drawer runners) and the grooves on the lower and second shelves (for the walls). Screw and glue the shelves into the carcass dadoes. Apply glue to the grooves in the bottom two shelves and slide the four drawer walls in place. Moving fast, glue the divider and returns to the interior drawer walls and clamp these pieces in place between the two bottom shelves. Now screw and glue the completed base assembly in place. Finally, glue and clamp the stile and rail assemblies to the outside of the carcass.

Forming the Decorative Stiles

The front facade of the bookcase features two hardwood stiles (pieces 28) that are embellished with plinth blocks and veneered panels. Note the notched cutout shape at the top of each, creating a right and left stile. Start on these pieces by trimming two long strips of burl veneer (pieces 29) to size, then gluing these to the stiles at the locations shown. If these pieces are too long to fit into your vacuum bag system, use yellow glue and a clamping caul (a strip of melamine-covered MDF) to provide ample pressure for veneering. Use a veining bit to plow stopped dadoes around the edges of the veneer strips (like you did earlier on the side panels), then use up more of the 1/8" bullnose trim you made earlier. Miter this molding to fit into the dadoes and glue it in place.

Cut the top and bottom fluted plinth blocks (pieces 30 and 31) to size, then use a core box bit to plow flutes in their front faces. On such small pieces, make several router passes to reduce the tool's drag and preserve your grip (not to mention your fingers). After fluting, chuck an ogee bit in the table router to mill a classic profile on the top edge of the bottom plinth and the bottom edge of the top one. Sand them free of machining marks, then glue and clamp them to the decorative stiles.

The last two elements on each stile are smaller veneered plinths (pieces 32) with an ogee cut along their top and bottom edges. Glue a small rectangle of burl veneer (piece 33) to each block.

Veneering the Side Panels

Cut the veneer segments to size and carefully join them with veneer tape. Apply glue and sandwich them between thicker stock to ensure that you'll get even pressure.

Each of the six veneered side panels is laid up on a 1/4"-thick plywood base. The center of each panel is a piece of mahogany crotch veneer, and this is surrounded by a 2"-wide mitered frame of ribbon veneer (shown at left). Trim the pieces to their proper shape with a sharp knife and steel straightedge, then use veneer tape (on the faces that will be exposed) to assemble the five pieces. The tape will be sanded off later. Spread the glue and apply even pressure with your veneer press to flatten and bond the veneer to the plywood.

Drawer Exploded View

Drawer Assembly
(Top View)

Material List – Drawers

	T x W x L		T x W x L
45 Drawer Runners (4)	½" x ¾" x 12½"	**49** Drawer Backs (2)	¾" x 4⅜" x 13½"
46 Drawer Fronts (2)	3½" x 4⅜ x 14⅜"	**50** Drawer Bottoms (2)	¼" x 13½" x 12⅜"
47 Drawer Veneer (2)	1/32" x 4⅝" x 15"	**51** Drawer Pulls (2)	Antique Brass
48 Drawer Sides (4)	¾" x 4⅜" x 13"		

carcass, trim as needed to improve the fit, then cut the hardwood trim (piece 38) that will face the bottom of the apron.

Make minor adjustments for a perfect fit, bullnose the front edge of the trim, then glue and clamp it in place. Now glue the decorative stile and apron assembly in place on the carcass with the help of a couple of hidden glue blocks (pieces 39), as shown in the Exploded View Drawing on page 102.

Assembling the Top

To achieve the proper sense of proportion, the top of the bookcase is made from two sheets of ¾" mahogany plywood (pieces 40) face-glued together. And to stay in keeping with the rest of the design, the top is edged on the front and sides with hardwood (pieces 41, 42, and 43). This molding is glued on in its sticked-up form. Band-saw the gently curved shapes after the top has been glued up.

Chop a few biscuit slots in the top and the moldings, then assemble the parts. Exert equal pressure all the way around with a band clamp, as shown in the photo on page 107. After the glue dries, band-saw the edging to shape and bead the fresh edges.

Secure the top to the case with counterbored screws driven down through the top into pilot holes drilled in the top rails and apron. Cover the screws with mahogany plugs and sand them flush.

Installing the Back

With the top assembly in place, you can close up the bookcase by attaching the back (piece 44). Chuck a small rabbeting bit in your portable router to mill a ¼" rabbet in the top and carcass sides to inset the back panel, then square the corners with a chisel. Cut the back to fit with about 1/16" of play. Make sure the cabinet is perfectly square before you secure the back panel with 1" panel pins. Pin the back to the shelves, too.

Making the Drawers

The drawers slide on hardwood runners (pieces 45) that are cut to size and installed into the grooves you plowed earlier.

Band-saw the drawer fronts (pieces 46) from a glued-up solid piece of mahogany and create the locking rabbets on either side with a dado head in the table saw. Sand the curved fronts. Again, select book-matched crotch veneer (pieces 47) and glue it to the drawer fronts, then trim it flush all around. Cut the sides (pieces 48) to size, then use the dado head to plow a groove in each of them for the drawer slides. Stay with the dado head to cut matching locking dadoes to secure them to the front and the drawer backs (pieces 49), then change the cutterhead to ¼" width to mill grooves in the fronts, sides and backs for the drawer bottoms (pieces 50). Drill a hole in each front for a pull (piece 51): this will have to be counterbored from the back, as the screw won't be long enough.

Temporarily clamp each drawer together and test-fit it in its opening. When everything appears right, assemble the drawers permanently with glue and clamps.

Finishing Up

Sand the entire project through the grits up to 220. We used a light walnut General Finishes stain on the bookcase to good effect. It brought out the various grain patterns and veneer pieces well. Follow that with three coats of semi-gloss polyurethane to bring out the rich depths of the mahogany veneers and to protect the shelves from scratches. Now you've got a long-lasting finish to complete a long-standing bookcase.

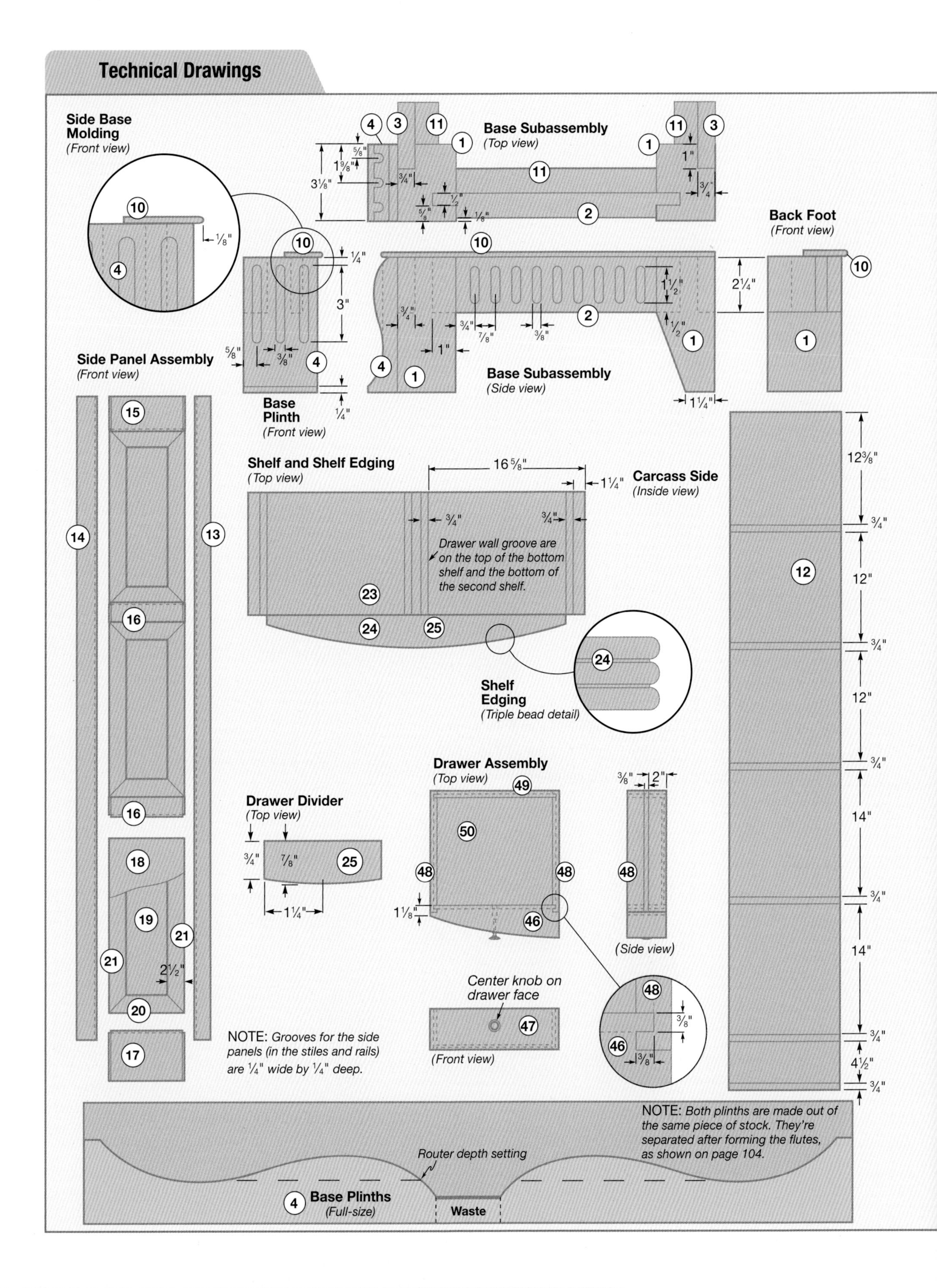
Technical Drawings
Side Base Molding
(Front view)
Base Subassembly
(Top view)
1"
3/4"
3 1/8"
1 9/8"
5/8"
1/2"
1/8"
Back Foot
(Front view)
1/4"
3"
1 1/2"
2 1/4"
3/4"
7/8"
3/8"
1"
5/8"
Side Panel Assembly
(Front view)
Base Plinth
(Front view)
Base Subassembly
(Side view)
1 1/4"
Shelf and Shelf Edging
(Top view)
16 5/8"
Carcass Side
(Inside view)
12 3/8"
Drawer wall groove are on the top of the bottom shelf and the bottom of the second shelf.
Shelf Edging
(Triple bead detail)
12"
14"
4 1/2"
Drawer Assembly
(Top view)
Drawer Divider
(Top view)
2 1/2"
1 1/8"
(Side view)
Center knob on drawer face
(Front view)
NOTE: Grooves for the side panels (in the stiles and rails) are 1/4" wide by 1/4" deep.
NOTE: Both plinths are made out of the same piece of stock. They're separated after forming the flutes, as shown on page 104.
Router depth setting
Base Plinths
(Full-size)
Waste

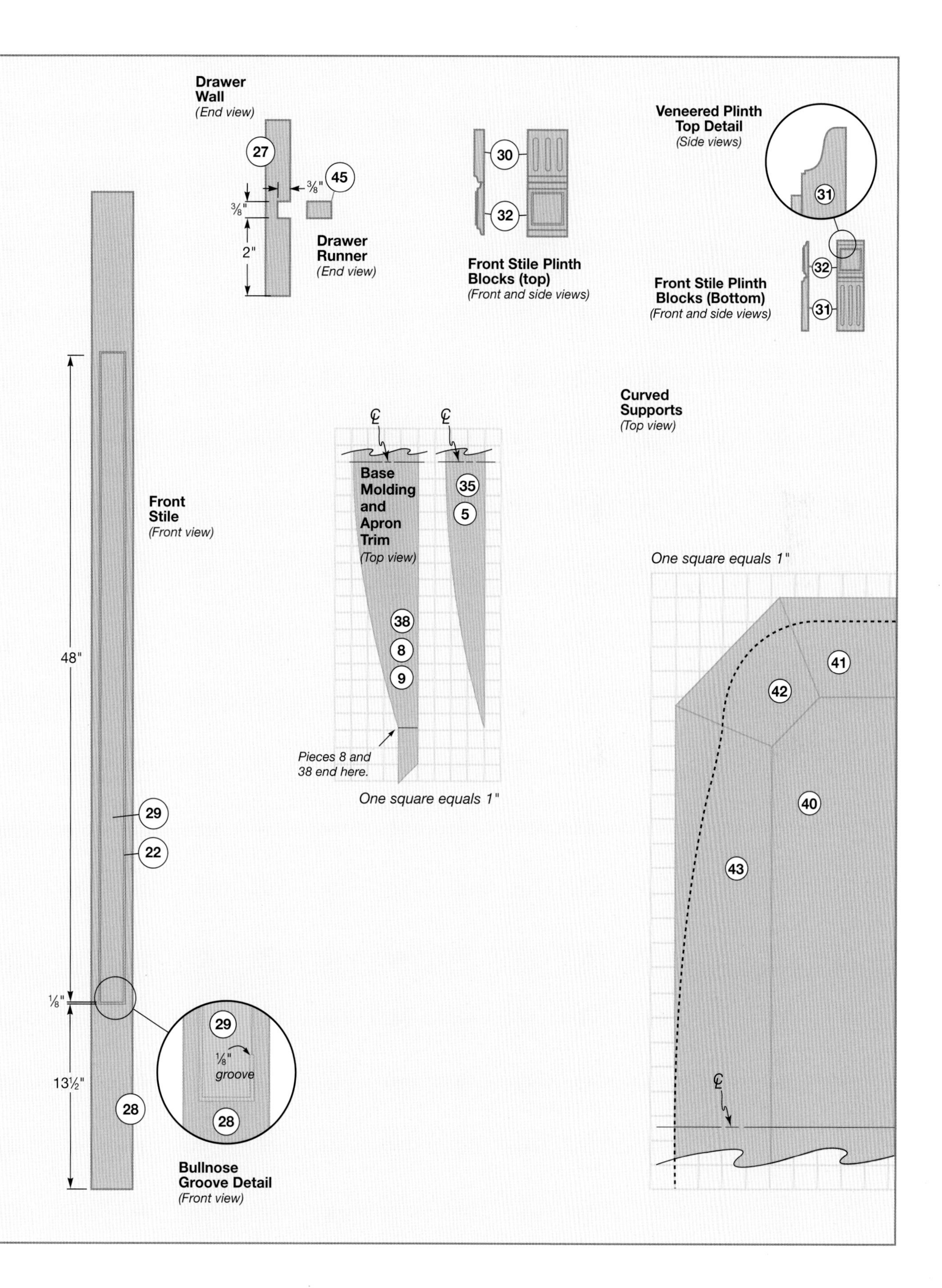
Drawer
Wall
(End view)
27
3/8"
45
3/8"
2"
Drawer
Runner
(End view)
30
32
Front Stile Plinth
Blocks (top)
(Front and side views)
Veneered Plinth
Top Detail
(Side views)
31
32
31
Front Stile Plinth
Blocks (Bottom)
(Front and side views)
Curved
Supports
(Top view)
Front
Stile
(Front view)
48"
Base
Molding
and
Apron
Trim
(Top view)
35
5
38
8
9
Pieces 8 and
38 end here.
One square equals 1"
One square equals 1"
41
42
40
43
29
22
1/8"
13½"
28
29
1/8"
groove
28
Bullnose
Groove Detail
(Front view)

WORLD BOOK
Britannica

Walnut Library Bookcase

You'll add a touch of elegant formality to your den or study when this handsome bookcase adorns a wall. Its built-up crown, fluted styles, and rosette accents include all of the classic elements. Choose some figured or burled walnut plywood to complete the package. Though it may look difficult to build, appearances are deceiving here. This is actually a straightforward casework project requiring only moderate skills.

by Rick White

Figure 1: *The number one safety rule in making rosettes is to make sure the workpiece is absolutely secure.*

Good woodworking doesn't have to be complicated. When my wife suggested I build a classic walnut library bookcase, I had visions of spending several months' worth of weekends in the shop. The word "classic" suggested intricate details and ornate accents—Chippendale swirls and Adams carvings came to mind. But the more I thought about it, the more I realized that wasn't really the case. A couple of fluted stiles, a pair of rosettes, and a handful of simple moldings were all that was required to capture the essence of a great tradition. Add some solid-walnut stock and a strip of burl veneer, and you have the quintessential American bookcase.

Beginning with the Carcass

Like any bookcase, our library unit is essentially a dressed-up box made of two sides (pieces 1), a top (piece 2), and a bottom (piece 3). You can begin construction by cutting all of these parts to size (see the Material List on pages 114 and 115), then choose the best face of each side to show. Lay one of the sides on a clean surface with the good face down. Make sure the plywood stock you use for the top and bottom is actually a full 3/4" thick, then chuck a 3/4" straight bit in your portable router. Clamp a straightedge to the workpiece and cut two 3/8"-deep dadoes across each side—one for the top and another for the bottom (see the Side Elevation Drawing on page 115 or 119 for the locations of these cuts).

Repeat this process on the second side, then switch to a 1/4" bit to cut the groove down each side for the back panel (piece 4). This groove is 1/2" in from the back of the cabinet to allow for the shelf support strip (piece 5) that will be attached to the center of the back panel. When both grooves have been cut, switch to a 3/8" straight bit to cut the three 1/16" dadoes across each outside face for the bullnosed moldings See the Side (Outside View) Elevation Drawing on page 119 to locate these shallow dadoes. Dry-assemble the carcass and, if everything fits well, disassemble and glue the top and bottom into the

Material List

	T x W x L
1 Sides (2)	¾" x 14¾" x 79
2 Top (1)	¾" x 14" x 37¼"
3 Bottom (1)	¾" x 14" x 37¼"
4 Back (1)	¼" x 37¼" x 71¼"
5 Shelf Support Strip (1)	½" x ¾" x 71¾"
6 Stiles (2)	¾" x 3½" x 70"
7 Upper Side and Lower Bullnoses (1)	⅜" x ⅜" x 76"
8 Front Bullnose (1)	⅜" x 1¼" x 80"
9 Crown Bullnose (1)	⅜" x 1¾" x 72"
10 Baseboard Side Bullnose (1)	⅜" x ⅝" x 34"
11 Baseboard (1)	¾" x 4¾" x 72½"
12 Base Blocking - Front (1)	¾" x 4⅜" x 38"
13 Base Blocking - Sides (2)	¾" x 4⅜" x 14"

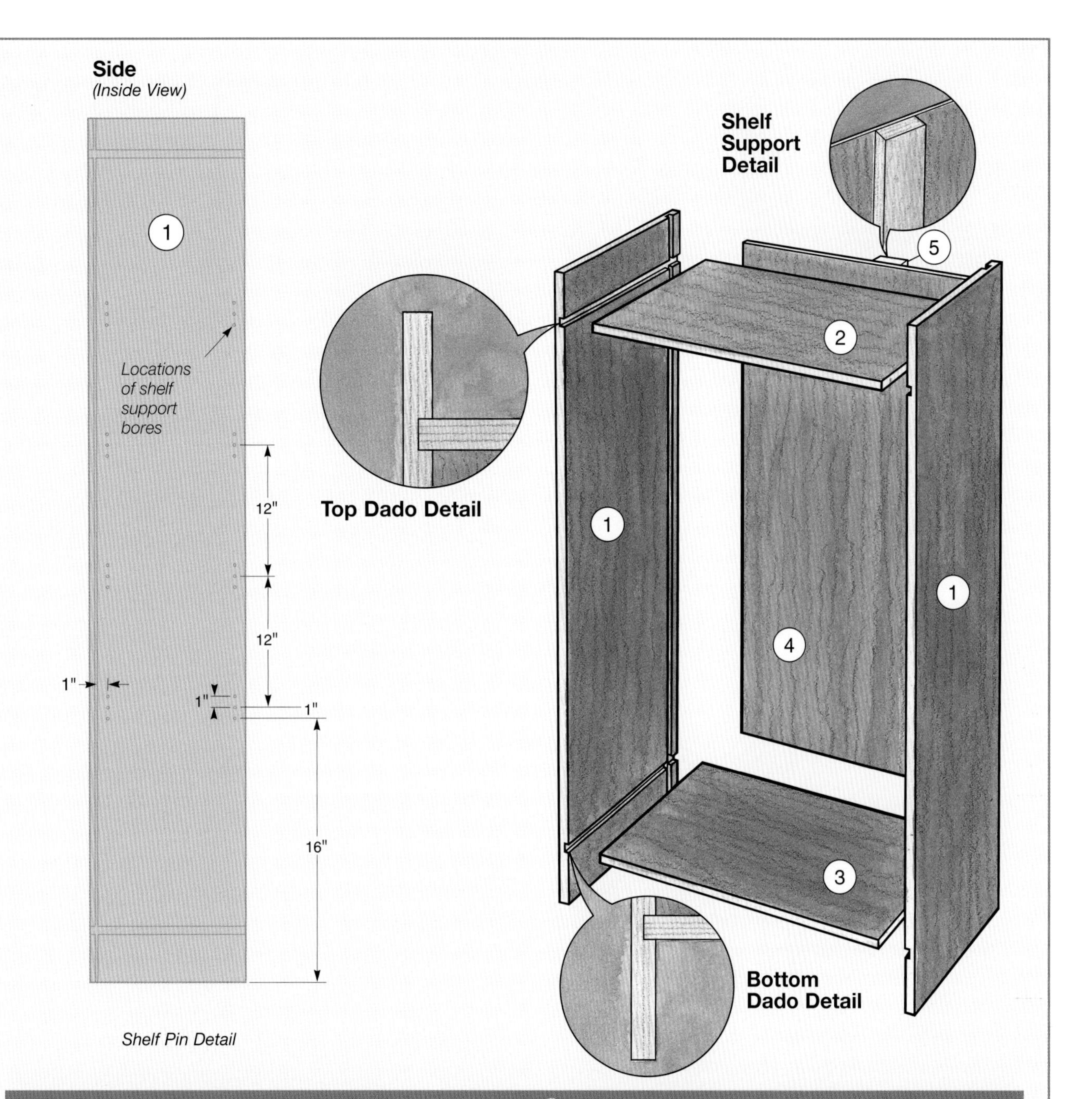

Material List

	T x W x L
14 Burl Veneer - Sides (2)	1⁄32" x 3½" x 14¾"
15 Burl Veneer - Front (1)	1⁄32" x 3½" x 31 1⁄16"
16 Top Rail (1)	½" x 3½" x 31"
17 Crown Blocking - Front (1)	¾" x 3" x 36½"
18 Crown Blocking - Sides (2)	¾" x 3" x 13⅜"
19 Rosettes (2)	¾" x 3½" x 3½"
20 Biscuits (2)	#0
21 Cove Molding (1)	¾" x 3" x 76"

	T x W x L
22 Ogee Molding (1)	¾" x 2 5⁄16" x 76"
23 Shelves (4)	¾" x 13 15⁄16 " x 36½"
24 Shelf Edging (4)	11⁄16" x 1¼" x 30 15⁄16"
25 Shelf Supports (20)	5mm Solid Brass
26 Lights (2)	20-Watt Halogen Puck
27 Transformer (1)	12 Volt
28 Switch (1)	Dimmer System
29 Cabinet Levelors (2)	Adjustable

sides, and clamp them. Slide the back in place, then check the carcass for squareness. Tack the back panel in place along its top and bottom edges with ¾" brads.

Figure 2: *The flutes in the stiles are cut with a core box bit. Stop these cuts by lining up pencil marks on the workpiece and router table fence.*

Shaping the Rosettes

Rick used a specialty bit to create the rosettes on this piece. If you don't have one, they're available for about $90 from catalog suppliers. A 3"-diameter bit (see Figure 1) fits any drill press with at least a ⅜" chuck. Like most rosette cutterheads, the profile knife can be removed from the head and replaced with a different profile.

Run your drill press at a low speed (about 300 rpm) and clamp the workpiece securely to the table. One clamp just wouldn't do the trick, so we recommend building a simple jig like the one shown in the photo to trap the workpiece. There's tremendous lateral force on the workpiece, so go slowly and be prepared to throw away a few setup pieces before you get the knack. To avoid burning, ease into the wood, then release the pressure, repeating this process until the cut is complete.

Making the Front Stiles

To maintain the classical authenticity of our bookcase, the front stiles (pieces 6) are fluted in the tradition of Greek columns. These are topped off with the rosettes. The fluting is done

*Quick*Tips

Butt Hinge Aids in Layout

Do you have need to draw a line around a corner? This might come up when you're laying out a table leg design—or when you're making mortise and tenon joints.

A heavy-duty hinge, such as you might use to hang a door, can help accomplish this task quickly and accurately. Simply turn the hinge backward to provide a sharp angle, then lay it on the work and mark along the edge with your pencil as shown. It's an easy way to make your markings turn the corner!

Treating and Applying Burl Veneer

Before the crown molding assembly can be installed, a ribbon of walnut burl veneer (pieces 14 and 15) is applied to the top of the bookcase. On the sides, this is simply cut to size and glued in place. However, burl veneer is often too wrinkly or wavy to glue and clamp, so the pros like to treat it with a glycerine-based veneer treatment. Simply brush on the treatment, then sandwich the veneer in a homemade drying press like the one shown here. It's made with two squares of mesh bug screen (to allow a little air circulation), some folded sheets of newspaper (to absorb the water in the glycerine compound) and a couple of pieces of scrap plywood to keep everything flat. Lay a cement block or similar weight on top of your makeshift press and let the veneer dry for a couple of days. Once dry it's critical the veneer be applied within hours or it may start reverting to its former unworkable shape. Glue and clamp slightly oversized pieces of veneer to the plywood top rail (piece 16) and the sides of the case. (Note: We used two pieces for the front, bookmatching them in the middle.) Make sure pressure from your clamps is applied evenly over the whole surface, beginning at the center and working to the outside. When the glue dries, trim the veneer—a veneer trimmer works best, but a sharp knife and a straightedge works fine too.

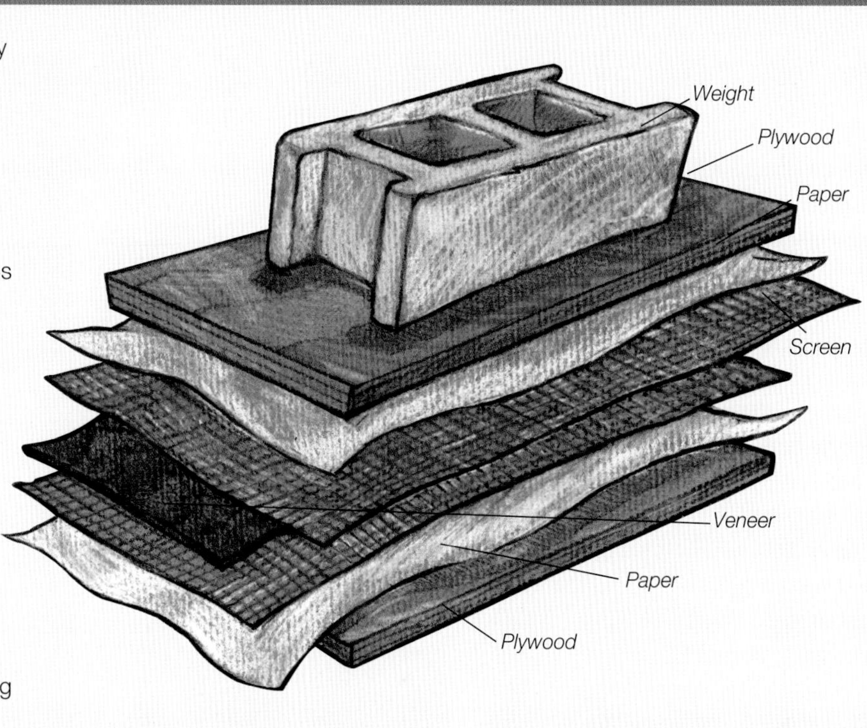

with a ¼" core box bit on a router table. It's important to test the setup for each cut on scrap before milling the actual workpiece, as any error will be quite obvious.

Check the two Stile Detail Drawings on page 114 for the locations and dimensions of these flutes. They can be started and stopped at the appropriate locations by matching up pencil lines on your router table and workpiece (see Figure 2 on page 116). You can achieve cleaner flutes if you take multiple passes and pare the ends with a chisel. Once you've completed the flutes, dry-fit the stiles to the bookcase carcass—the bottom of each stile must line up exactly with the top surface of the bottom panel. Now locate the ⅜" dadoes you cut earlier on the outside faces of the sides. Use a pencil to extend these lines across the fronts of the stiles. Remove the stiles and use a fine-tooth blade in your table saw to nibble the dadoes that will house the bullnose strips. (Note: These dadoes go across the face and two edges; see the Stile Elevation on page 120.) Glue and clamp the stiles in place.

Making Bullnose Moldings

The only difference between the bullnose moldings in this project is their width. (Note: When everything is milled to length you'll have 15 pieces.) All four moldings are ⅜" thick with identical profiles, so you can make them with a single router setup. The widest molding is 1¾"; we recommend starting with this width and then ripping the smaller ones to size later. Rip four six-foot lengths of ⅜" x 1¾" stock, enough to make the upper side and lower bullnoses, the front bullnoses, the crown bullnoses and the baseboard

Technical Drawings

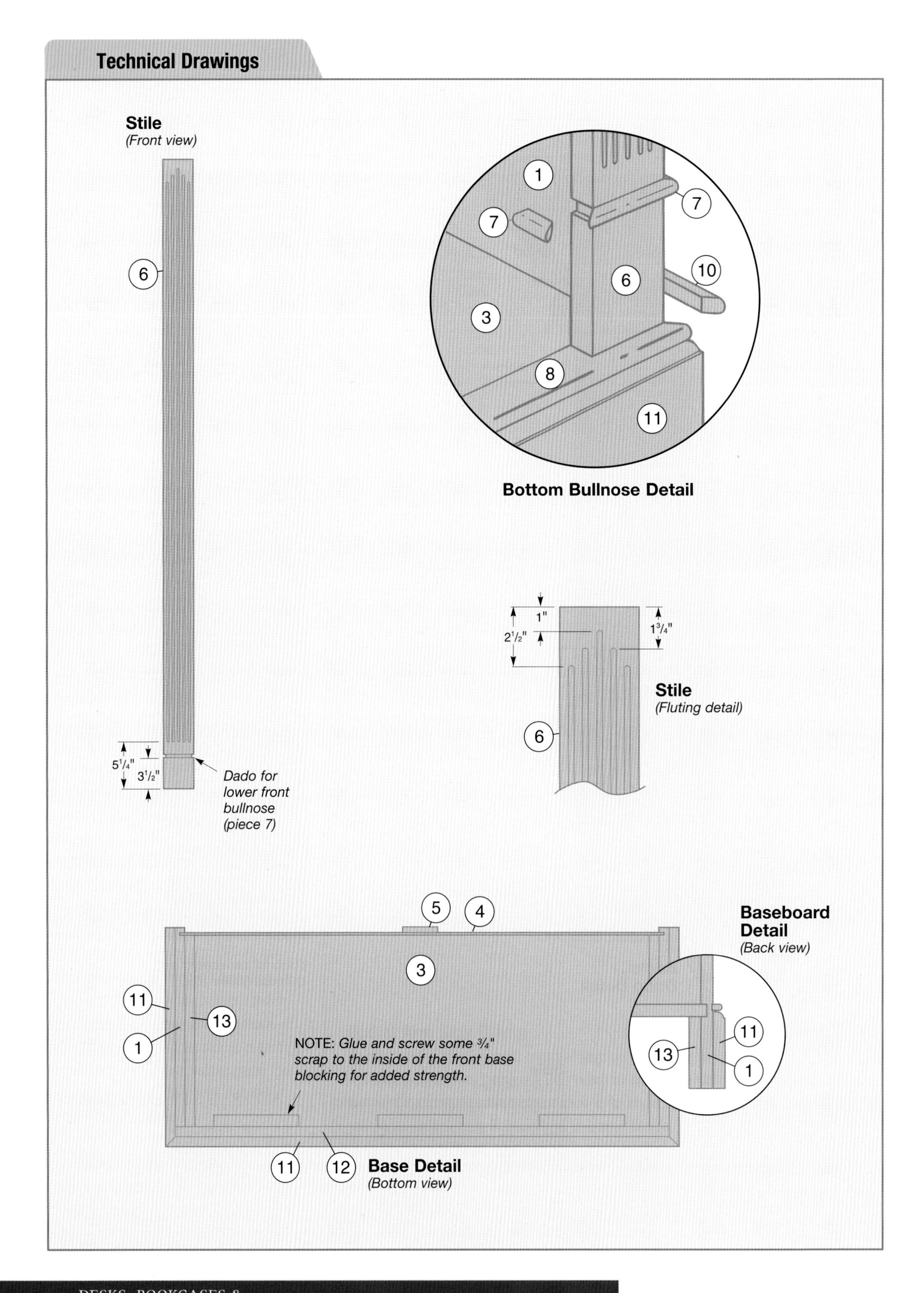

of the top rail with biscuits (pieces 20) and glue. When the glue dries, miter the upper side bullnoses (pieces 7) and the front bullnose (piece 8) to length and dry-fit them, along with the top rail subassembly. When everything fits, secure the pieces with glue and clamps. Now follow the same procedure with the crown bullnoses (pieces 9).

The last two pieces of the crown assembly are the cove molding and ogee molding (pieces 21 and 22). These are made with a 1/4"-radius Roman ogee bit and a 1/2"-radius cove bit. For the latter, set your fence and bit depth to leave the 1/4" reveal shown in the Crown Top Detail Drawing on page 118. Now miter both of these moldings to fit, and glue them in place.

Figure 3: *All the project's bullnose moldings can be machined at once, then ripped to width and mitered to fit.*

Completing the Shelves and Applying Finish

There's not a lot to making the shelves (pieces 23). Just cut them to size and add the shelf edging (pieces 24) to the front edge. This molding (see the Exploded View Drawing on page 114) is cut with a beading bit on the router table in four passes: Cut the bottom half of the profile, then flip the workpiece to cut the top half. Raise the bit and repeat the process with two more passes to complete the shape. Now glue and clamp the edging in position.

The finish Rick used on the bookcase requires a little more work. After thoroughly sanding everything down to 280 grit, apply a poly/oil finish in four coats. After each of the first three coats dries, rub the surfaces down with 400-grit wet/dry paper, then wipe with a tack cloth to clean off the dust. Add a fourth coat to produce a deep, warm finish that will enrich the walnut's natural color with a satin glow.

After the finish dries, drill holes for the shelf supports (pieces 25). See the Side Elevation Drawings on page 115 or 119 to locate the shelf pin spacing. You don't want to do this any earlier because these small 5mm holes may get clogged with finish, and you'll just end up drilling them twice.

Figure 4: *Form the top edge of the baseboard with a 1/4"-radius beading bit as shown in the illustration here.*

Installing Halogen Puck Lighting

The top shelf in our bookcase makes a perfect illuminated display space if you add a couple of fixed-beam puck lights (pieces 26). Bore two 2 1/8 "-diameter holes with a hole saw, and insert the friction-fit units (see Figure 5).

The lights plug into a transformer (piece 27) and a switch (piece 28). Conceal both pieces of hardware behind the crown. Train the switch wires down behind one of the stiles. Touching this wire dims or brightens the lights. With that done, screw two cabinet levelors (pieces 29) in place behind the baseboard, level the unit, and tuck your favorite books into their new home.

Figure 5: *After drilling holes, the halogen lights are pushed in place for a friction fit, then plugged into their transformer and switch.*

IMPRESSIONISMUS
GULLIVER'S TRAVELS

Entertainment Center for Two

If you'd like to build a substantial display piece for the den or family room, this entertainment center offers the best of two worlds: With its unique sliding doors in their closed position, the cabinet displays your family's favorite collectibles. When the doors are open, the cabinet reveals a sleek layout of electronic components.

by Rick White

Why is this called an entertainment center for two? Simple—it evolved from two separate projects. On the one hand, I wanted a high-tech looking entertainment center for television and stereo components. On the other hand, large cabinets are also logical places to display family photos, collectibles, and favorite books. Most modern cabinets lean too much toward one function or the other. Here's a design that provides the best of both worlds. In short, it serves both as an entertainment center and a large display case. If it weren't for some unique door slide hardware, this project would probably have to remain two separate projects.

The sliding door hardware (see tint box, page 129) allows the raised panel doors to ride on almost invisible rollers in an inconspicuous plastic track. Best of all, this hardware is easy to install and inexpensive to boot. After the door challenges were solved, I concentrated on the drawers and shelves. The drawers alongside the VCR/DVD player compartment are sized to hold CDs, and the bottom drawers add lots of storage space for videos, DVDs, and audio tapes. All but one of the shelves in each side unit are adjustable for displaying books, photos, or virtually any collectible that fits on a shelf.

The entertainment center is very sturdy. If you've priced units of this quality, you know they go for as much as $3,000. Well, that's a lot of money, but thankfully for woodworkers we can pare that down to the cost of materials, which in this case top out at around $800. If this is still too steep, consider some shop-made drawer slide alternatives. By cutting out the drawer slides you can trim the material cost down by another $200 or so.

The entertainment center takes about 50 hours to build and requires 5 sheets of ¾"-thick plain-sawn oak veneer plywood, 2 sheets of ¼" oak plywood and one-half sheet of ½"

Cabinet Exploded View

Material List – Cabinet Carcass

	T x W x L
1 Sides (2)	¾" x 23¾" x 76"
2 Top (1)	¾" x 23¾" x 76"
3 Bottom (1)	¾" x 23¾" x 76"
4 Middle Platform (1)	¾" x 23½" x 76"
5 Upper Dividers (2)	¾" x 22¾" x 63½"
6 Lower Dividers (2)	¾" x 23½" x 8¾"
7 TV Shelf (1)	¾" x 22½" x 34¾"
8 TV Shelf Supports (2)	¾" x 22½" x 7"
9 Fixed Shelves (2)	¾" x 22½" x 20⅞"
10 Shelf Pins	¼"
11 Side Stiles (2)	¾" x 2" x 76"
12 Upper Divider Stiles (2)	¾" x 2" x 63"
13 Top Rail (1)	¾" x 3¼" x 73"
14 Middle Rail (1)	¾" x 2½" x 73"
15 Bottom Rail (1)	¾" x 3¼" x 73"

	T x W x L
16 Lower Divider Stiles (2)	¾" x 2" x 6½"
17 Back (2)	¼" x 20½" x 72¾"
18 Back (1)	¼" x 35" x 72¾"
19 Dowels (1 bag)	⅜" x 2"
20 Door Track (2)	Brown plastic
21 Banding (6)	¼" x ¾" x 54"
22 Small Shelves (6)	¾" x 22½" x 19⅞"
23 Large Shelves (3)	¾" x 22½" x 34¼"
24 Drawer Filler Strips (8)	⅝" x 6½" x 22¾"
25 Base Supports (6)	¾" x 2½" x 23¾"
26 Baseboard Moulding (1)	¾" x 3" x 135"
27 Middle Moulding (1)	½" x 2" x 135"
28 Crown Moulding (1)	3" x 1⅝" x 135"
29 Leveler Glides (6)	Heavy-duty

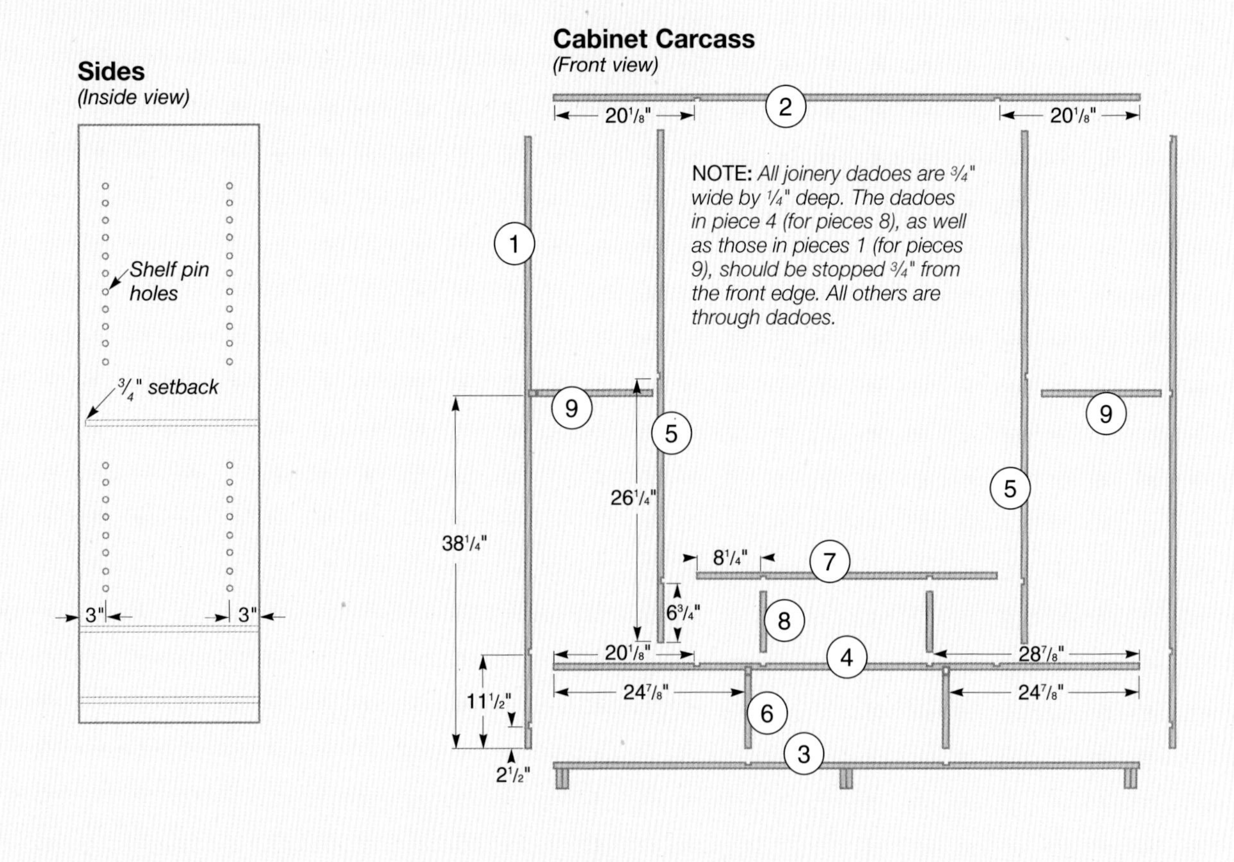

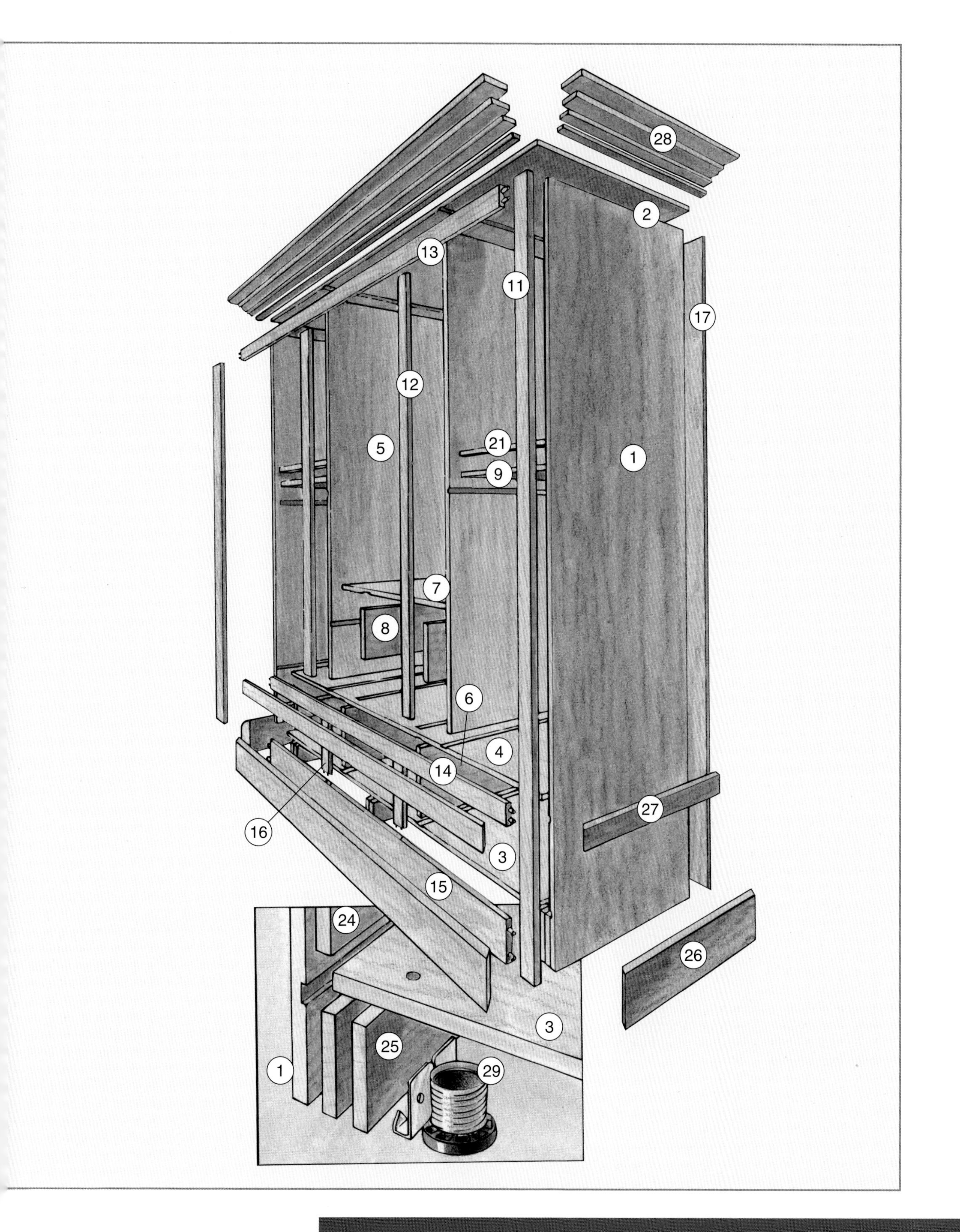
28
2
13
11
17
12
5
21
9
1
7
8
6
4
14
27
16
3
15
24
26
3
25
1
29

Box Joints Revisited

Step 1: *Install a ½" dado blade in your table saw and screw a tall fence to your miter gauge. Make sure the gauge is square to the blade. With the blade raised 9⁄16", make one pass.*

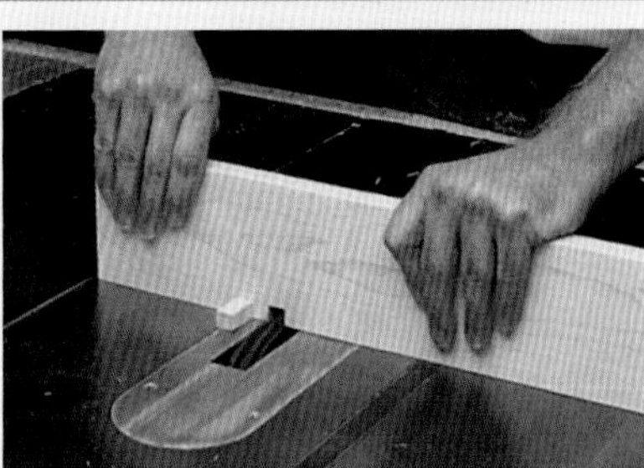

Step 2: *Glue a ½" x 9⁄16" x 2" piece of scrap in the dado and reposition the fence 1" further to the right on the miter gauge. Make a another pass, which should leave a ½" gap between the cuts.*

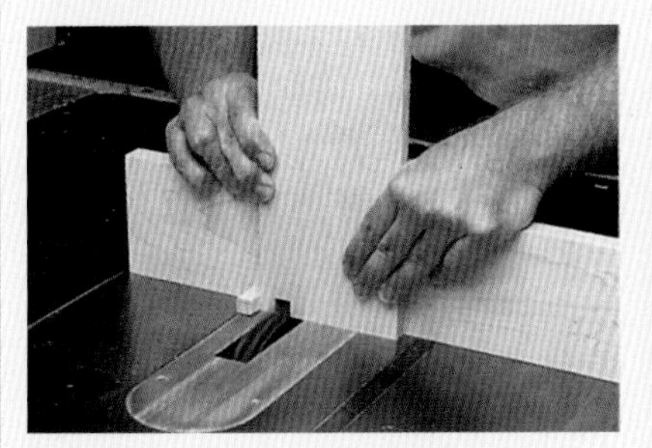

Step 3: *Position your drawer front against the fence and slide it against the scrap to make your first cut. Next, slip the dado in the stock onto the scrap and make the second cut. Repeat the process.*

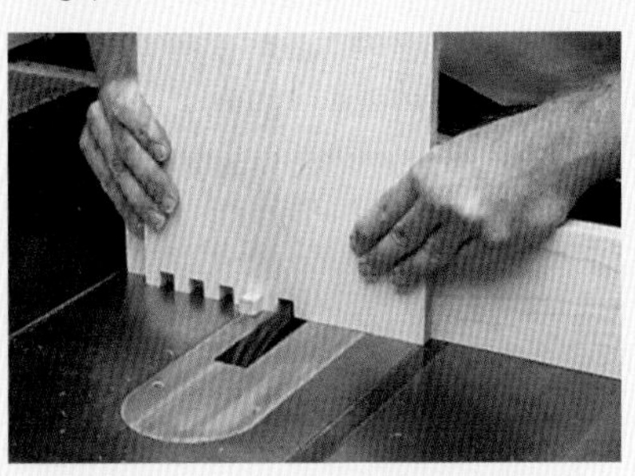

Step 4: *After making the last cut in the drawer front, set the mating drawer side into place tightly against it and cut the pins and slots on this second piece. Work around each drawer in this fashion.*

Fence

Platform

Figure 1: *This simple two-piece router jig makes routing the dadoes an easy task.*

Baltic birch. You'll also need 55 board feet of solid ¾" oak and 20 board feet of rift-sawn stock for the door and drawer panels. A few scraps came in handy for the hidden cabinet parts.

Cutting Your Plywood Panels

Unless you have a large shop with auxiliary table saw supports, cutting plywood is best done as a two-person job. Get a friend to help you cut all the large panels to size (pieces 1 through 9) from four sheets of ¾" oak plywood. Once all of the plywood is cut to size, begin laying out the dadoes as shown in the Elevation Drawings on page 122.

Cutting dadoes in plywood panels is a perfect task for a router and a straightedge jig. The jig shown in Figure1 takes just a few minutes to make and will save you lots of time. Make the basic jig, then chuck a ¾" straight bit in your router. Next, run the router along the jig fence to trim the platform to width. Now you have a precise edge for aligning the jig with your dado layouts. For each dado, align the platform edge with your layout line and rout ¼" deep.

Next, use a rabbeting bit to rout ⅜" x ¼" rabbets along the inside back edge of the sides, top and bottom panels so that later you can install the back panels (pieces 17 and 18).

All the dado joints in the sides, top and bottom, as well as the dadoes for securing the upper dividers and the shelf supports to the middle platform, are reinforced with screws. This helps eliminate the need for lots of long bar clamps during the assembly and improves the cabinet's resistance to racking. Use a ⅛" bit to drill five pilot holes evenly spaced along each dado, then turn the panels over and drill ⅜"-diameter by ¼"-deep counterbores at each pilot hole. Switch to a ¼" bit to drill rows of shelf pin holes in the sides. A piece of perforated hardboard makes a handy drilling jig for this task.

Assembling the Carcass

The key to successfully assembling a big project like this is careful organization. If you have all the parts, tools, glue and clamps ready to go, you're halfway home. When a few pieces of the assembly puzzle are missing, it can ruin your whole day.

The best way to approach this assembly is to work in sections. First glue the upper dividers to the TV shelf and top in one section, then join the middle platform and bottom to the

Technical Drawings

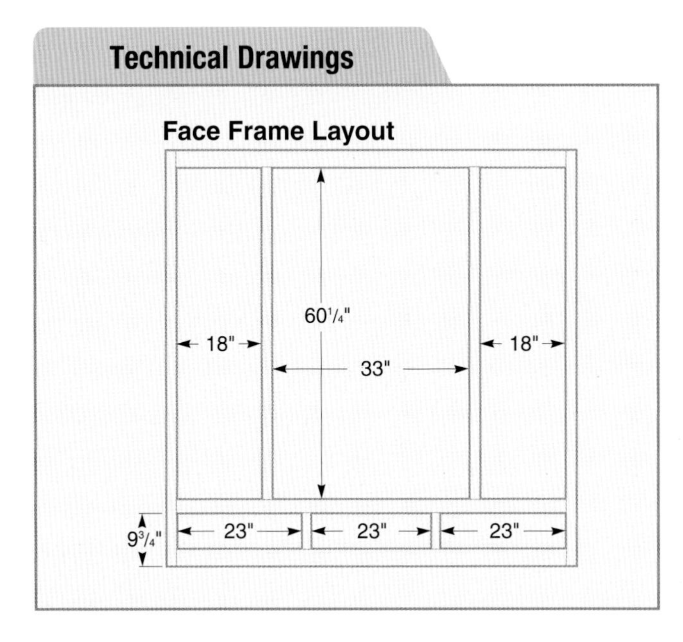

lower dividers. Be sure to check these subassemblies for squareness by measuring diagonally from corner to corner—if the measurements match, the unit is square. Spread glue in the dadoes and drive screws in the pilot holes as you proceed through the assembly, then combine the subassemblies with the sides, the fixed shelves and the TV shelf supports. Fill the counterbores in the sides with ⅜" oak face-grain plugs.

Next, install heavy-duty levelers (pieces 29) with access holes through the bottom panel so you can adjust the levelers from above. (After all, nobody's floors are perfectly flat.) First install the base supports (pieces 25) then drill ⅜" access holes through the bottom panel (see Exploded View Detail). Now install the levelers directly below the access holes.

Making the Face Frame

Screws and dado joints are perfect for joining the plywood panels of the entertainment center together, but they don't completely prevent the carcass from racking or leaning to one side. The way to overcome this grim possibility is by attaching a rigid face frame. Go ahead and cut your face frame stock (pieces 11 through 16) from ¾"-thick oak, and pull out your doweling equipment for the next joinery step.

Doweling is about the easiest method of joinery for the frame, and a Dowl-It Jig makes drilling perfectly straight holes a breeze. Butt the frame pieces together as shown in the Elevation Drawing above and make two marks about 1" apart that span each joint line. Use the Dowl-It to drill ⅜"-diameter by 1¹⁄₁₆"-deep holes into each member at the marks.

Because the upper divider stiles (pieces 12) aren't part of the main face frame, you can go ahead and glue them directly to the front edge of the upper divider panels. One more preliminary step before assembling the frame is to cut the grooves in the top and middle rails for the Hafele door track hardware (piece 20) following the manufacturer's instructions.

Once the dowel holes are drilled and the track grooves are cut, begin assembling the face frame. Squirt glue in the dowel holes and spread a little on each fluted dowel (pieces 19), then pull the assembly together with pipe clamps. Be sure to wipe off any glue squeeze-out with a damp cloth.

When the glue dries, sand or scrape the joints flush and glue the frame to the carcass. Gluing a large frame like this to the carcass can be a challenge, especially if you don't have enough clamps. Here's a unique way to use the scraps from your plywood cuttings to press the frame down on the carcass (see Figure 2). By wedging the strips between the project and the ceiling, you can create an effective clamping system. Put the project up on sawhorses first. This way you'll only need four clamps to hold the frame at each corner.

Cover the remaining exposed plywood edges on the TV shelf, the supports, and the fixed shelves with solid-wood banding (pieces 21). Cut the banding to length for each edge and, when the clamps are free from the frame assembly, glue the strips to the exposed plywood edges.

A belt sander makes quick work of sanding the banding flush with the plywood, but be careful not to sand too far and go right through the thin veneer on the surface. One way to avoid doing this is to scribble a pencil line back and forth along the joints, then belt-sand the solid wood until you begin to erase the lines on the plywood. That way,

Figure 2: *Once the pieces are cut and the dowel holes are drilled, assemble the face frame. Gluing the frame to the carcass can be a challenge, but with a little ingenuity (and a solid ceiling!) you can get by with just a few clamps.*

Drawer Exploded View

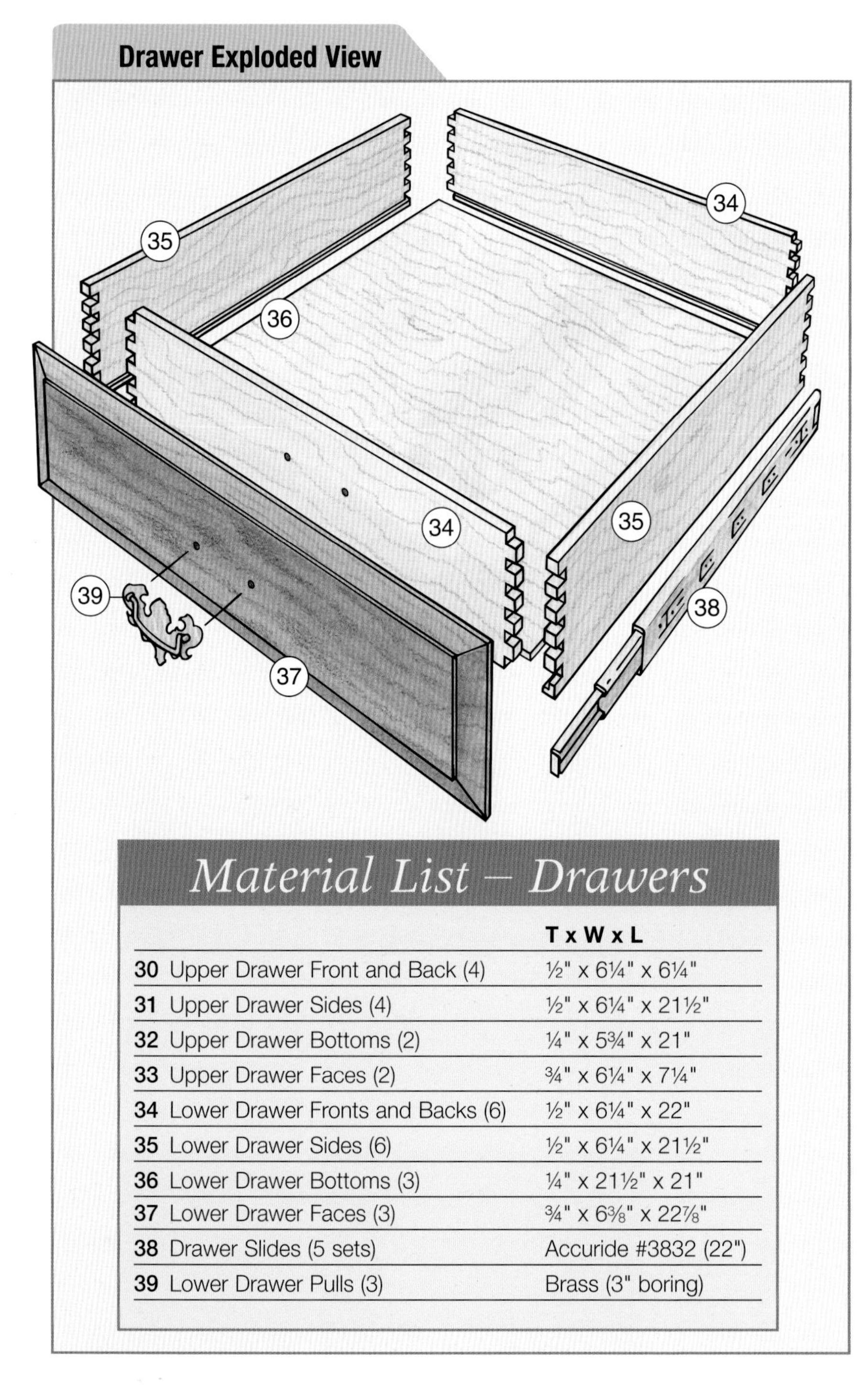

Material List – Drawers

	T x W x L
30 Upper Drawer Front and Back (4)	½" x 6¼" x 6¼"
31 Upper Drawer Sides (4)	½" x 6¼" x 21½"
32 Upper Drawer Bottoms (2)	¼" x 5¾" x 21"
33 Upper Drawer Faces (2)	¾" x 6¼" x 7¼"
34 Lower Drawer Fronts and Backs (6)	½" x 6¼" x 22"
35 Lower Drawer Sides (6)	½" x 6¼" x 21½"
36 Lower Drawer Bottoms (3)	¼" x 21½" x 21"
37 Lower Drawer Faces (3)	¾" x 6⅜" x 22⅞"
38 Drawer Slides (5 sets)	Accuride #3832 (22")
39 Lower Drawer Pulls (3)	Brass (3" boring)

you'll know when the banding is even with the panel. From there, switch to hand-sanding or use a sharp scraper to finish up.

Shelves and Drawers

By now the basic structure is complete and your entertainment center is taking shape. The next step is to make the removable parts of the project: the drawers, doors and shelves. Start by cutting the remaining sheet of plywood into the adjustable shelves (pieces 22 and 23). Cut the plywood to size and then rip more ¾" solid-wood banding to cover the front edge of each shelf. Glue on the banding and sand it flush with the plywood using the method described on page 127.

To make these drawers go the distance, I designed them with box joints. It's an easily repeatable joint that only requires a table saw and dado blade. The basic steps for making the jig and cutting the joint are outlined in the tint box on page 126. Once the fence is made, you can produce an unlimited number of boxes.

Begin working on the drawers by cutting all the parts to size from your sheet of ½" Baltic birch plywood (pieces 30, 31, 34, and 35), then cut the box joints. Next, use a ¼" dado blade to cut ¼"-deep grooves in the drawer walls for housing the drawer bottoms (pieces 32 and 36). Make the cuts ¼" from the bottom edge of each piece. After this is done, cut the bottoms to size and assemble the boxes, always making sure to check for squareness.

Raising Panels

Raised panels are a dominant feature on this entertainment center. They create a stately, classic appearance, and to help further this impression, we chose rift-sawn red oak for the panels. Rift-sawn wood has dramatic graining and is very stable, making it ideal for frame and panel construction. There are several methods for making raised panels, but most require special machinery or cutters. We took a simple, low-tech approach and raised the panels with a table saw (see tint box, next page 129). Before moving on, however, glue and clamp the rift-sawn stock into two long panels, then cut these panels apart to yield the individual door panels (pieces 41 and 42). Also, from another piece of rift-sawn lumber, cut enough stock for the lower drawer faces (pieces 37). Now follow the outlined steps in the tint box to raise the panels.

Completing the Drawers

Once the lower drawer faces are raised, cut the upper drawer faces (pieces 33) to size, then screw all the faces to the drawer boxes. Next, move on to fitting

Raised Panels

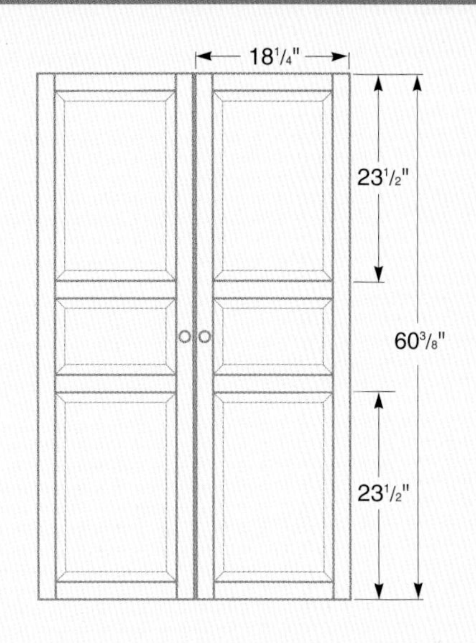

Begin raising the door panels by cutting four shoulders on the face of each piece with your table saw as shown in Step 1. Raise the blade 1/8" and clamp the fence 1 1/2" away. Make the cross grain cuts first. Once these cuts are finished, move the fence 1/2" closer to the blade and make the same cuts in the drawer faces.

To get the cleanest angle cut possible, take two passes. The first pass removes most of the waste, and the second pass just grazes the surface removing the last 1/32" or so of the wood. This procedure usually leaves a smooth surface that requires very little sanding.

Angle your blade 12° and raise it so the teeth reach the shoulder kerfs in the door panels. Clamp the fence 5/16" from the blade and cut across the end-grain edges of the panels, then cut the long-grain edges a shown in Step 2. Now move the fence 1/32" closer to the blade and trim the panels to their final shape. Follow the same procedure with the drawer fronts, but adjust the blade height and fence position to get the same results. When you're done raising the panels, sand the pieces to remove any burns or saw blade marks.

Step 1: *Set the blade height at 1/8" and clamp the fence 1 1/2" away to make the shoulder cuts in the door panels.*

Step 2: *With the blade tilted 12° and the fence 5/16" away, raise the end-grain edges of the panel first, then the long grain edges.*

and installing the drawers in the cabinet. Accuride drawer slides (pieces 38) are easy to install, but because this is a face frame cabinet, drawer filler strips (pieces 24) must be added for all the drawers. Cut the strips to size, then screw them to the carcass walls behind the face frame stiles.

Screw the slide members to the filler strips and the box sides following the instructions included with the packages. Remember to install the slides so the front of the drawer faces sit flush with the surrounding face frame. Wrap up the drawer-making process by drilling holes through the drawer faces and fronts for the pulls (pieces 39 and 40)—you'll need longer screws for the pulls that will reach through the extra stock thickness.

Euro Cabinet Door Slides

The upper guides have an adjustable lug that slides in and out of the track, allowing for easy removal of the door.

Considering how elegant the sliding doors look on our entertainment center, it's a wonder this hardware isn't used more often. Whatever the reason, Hafele, a German-based company (800-423-3531; www.hafele.com), has developed cabinet hardware for sliding doors that's easy to install, easy on the pocketbook, and makes opening the doors virtually effortless. Once installed, the plastic track and nylon rollers are hardly noticeable, and the door operation is completely silent. The track easily press-fits into dadoes at the top and bottom of the cabinet opening, and ribbing on the sides of the plastic extrusion holds the track tightly in place. All the guides have adjustments to help you plumb the door to the cabinet. The guides are rated to carry a hefty 44 pound load.

Door Exploded View

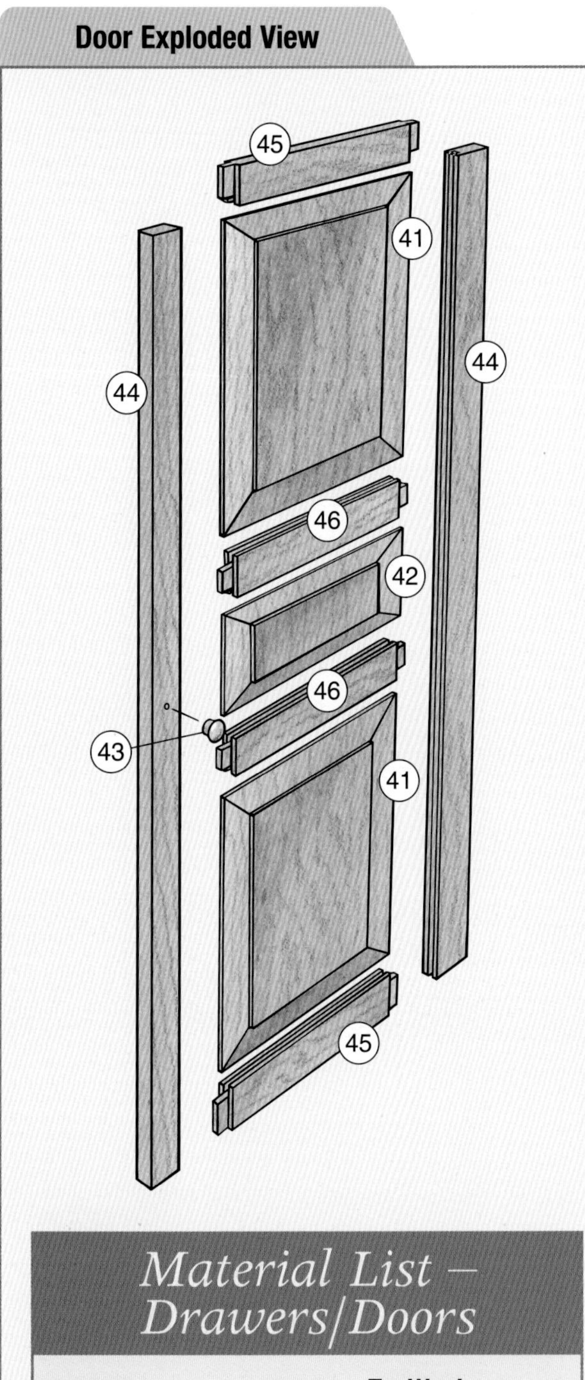

Material List – Drawers/Doors

	T x W x L
40 Upper Drawer Pulls (2)	Brass (2½" boring)
41 Large Door Panels (4)	¾" x 15" x 22¼"
42 Small Door Panels (2)	¾" x 15" x 9⅞"
43 Door Knobs (2)	1¼" Dia. (Brass)
44 Door Stiles (4)	¾" x 2" x 60⅜"
45 Top and Bottom Rails (4)	¾" x 2" x 15⅛"
46 Door Middle Rails (4)	¾" x 2" x 15⅛"

Making the Doors

You've raised the door panels already, so now it's time to tackle the door frames. Rip ¾"-thick stock for the stiles and rails (pieces 44, 45, and 46) and crosscut the pieces to length.

Now plow grooves in the edges of the stiles and rails to serve as mortises for the joints and for holding the panels in the doors. Set up your table saw with a ¼" dado blade and raise it ½", then clamp the fence 3⁄16" from the blade. Cut all the grooves, and remember that the middle rails require a groove in both edges.

Switch to a ½" dado blade and prepare to cut the rail tenons. Clamp a clearance block to your fence and move the fence to align the block with the edge of the blade (see Figure 3). Make sure the stock completely clears the block before contacting the blade. Raise the blade ¼" and cut a tenon on a scrap piece of ¾" stock. Check the fit of the tenon in a groove, and make any necessary adjustments to improve the fit. Once you're satisfied, proceed to cut all the tenons.

You're getting close to gluing up the doors, but first you have to cut rabbets on the back of the door panels so they'll fit in the frame grooves. Use your dado blade to cut ¾"-wide by ⅛"-deep rabbets along all the panel edges. Check the fit of one edge and, when it's right, proceed with the rabbeting. When all of the panels are ready, test-fit the door assemblies. Make sure all the joints are tight and the panels fit in the grooves without being too tight or too loose. While the doors are together, mark a line across each joint as an alignment reference. When you get to the real assembly you'll be able to easily re-align the pieces.

If everything goes well during the trial run, collect your glue and clamps for the assembly. Spread glue in the grooves only at the joint locations, and put a drop or two at the center of each panel edge—gluing the panel in this way will keep it centered in the frame while still allowing freedom of movement outward from the center.

Sand the door frames flush after you take off the clamps, then completely sand the doors to 180 grit and test their fit in the cabinet. With the door resting on the middle rail there should be a gap of about ⅛" from the top of the door to the top rail. If the gap is slightly more, the adjustments on the door hardware should compensate for the difference. After fitting the doors properly, lay them upside down on your bench and drill the 35mm holes for installing the door hardware, however, don't install the hardware until after the finish is applied to the doors.

Milling the Carcass Mouldings

The shell of the entertainment center is completely built now, but adding a few decorative mouldings will dress it up tremendously. The baseboard (piece 26) and middle moulding

Figure 3: *Use a ½"-wide dado raised ¼" to cut the tenon cheeks. For safety, be sure to clamp a clearance block to the fence.*

(piece 27) are simply pieces of solid stock with routed edges (see the full-size drawings on the next page). Once these pieces are routed, miter the mouldings to fit around the front and sides of the cabinet. Install the mouldings with glue and small brads, then after staining and sealing the wood, fill the nail holes with color-matched putty or wax.

The crown moulding (piece 28) consists of four individually routed pieces glued together to form a stacked lamination. We first routed the edges of four boards that were each 12' long. The bits we used to rout the boards are shown at right. Next, we ripped each of the boards to different widths and glued them together to form a crown molding. Try to keep the glue squeeze-out to a minimum, especially on the front of the moulding, and use a damp rag to clean up any squeeze-out right away. Or, wait for the glue to cure for a few minutes to a rubbery consistency and then scrape it off instead of wiping. When the glue dries, miter-cut the crown moulding to fit around the entertainment center and used 6d nails and glue to install it. Like the other mouldings, fill the nail holes after the finish is applied.

Adding Final Details and Finish

By now you should be as proud as punch looking at the work you've done. The last 50 or so hours in the shop have been busy and rewarding, and you're going to have a lot to show for it. Cut the back panels (pieces 17 and 18) to fit each of the three entertainment center sections, then check the fit of the back pieces and set them aside for sanding and finishing.

As far as the finish is concerned, we stained the oak cabinet a medium brown color by mixing Minwax's special walnut stain with equal amounts of their natural stain. After the stain dried for two days, we sprayed on two coats of clear lacquer. If you don't own spray equipment, you could use aerosol lacquer or just brush on a polyurethane or varnish finish.

Finally, add the door tracks, shelf standards and reinstall the drawer slides on the carcass. Press the door rollers and guides into the holes on the back of the doors. Screw on the drawer pulls and door knobs (pieces 43) and move the cabinet into place. Adjust the entertainment center's levelers with an Allen wrench, then pop the drawers and doors into their tracks. Use a flathead screwdriver to adjust the drawer rollers until they move effortlessly.

Sizing Things Up

As you fill your entertainment center with stereo and TV equipment and set out some of your favorite books and photos, you'll probably be amazed at the distance you've come. The design of the cabinet, with its two sliding doors, really fills the bill for creating both useful and decorative display space. With the doors pushed to the side, the center compartment takes on the look of a professional studio, and with the doors pushed to the center, your collectibles suddenly become the focus of the room. In either case, the door positions won't look awkward or interfere with the dual purposes of this hard-working cabinet.

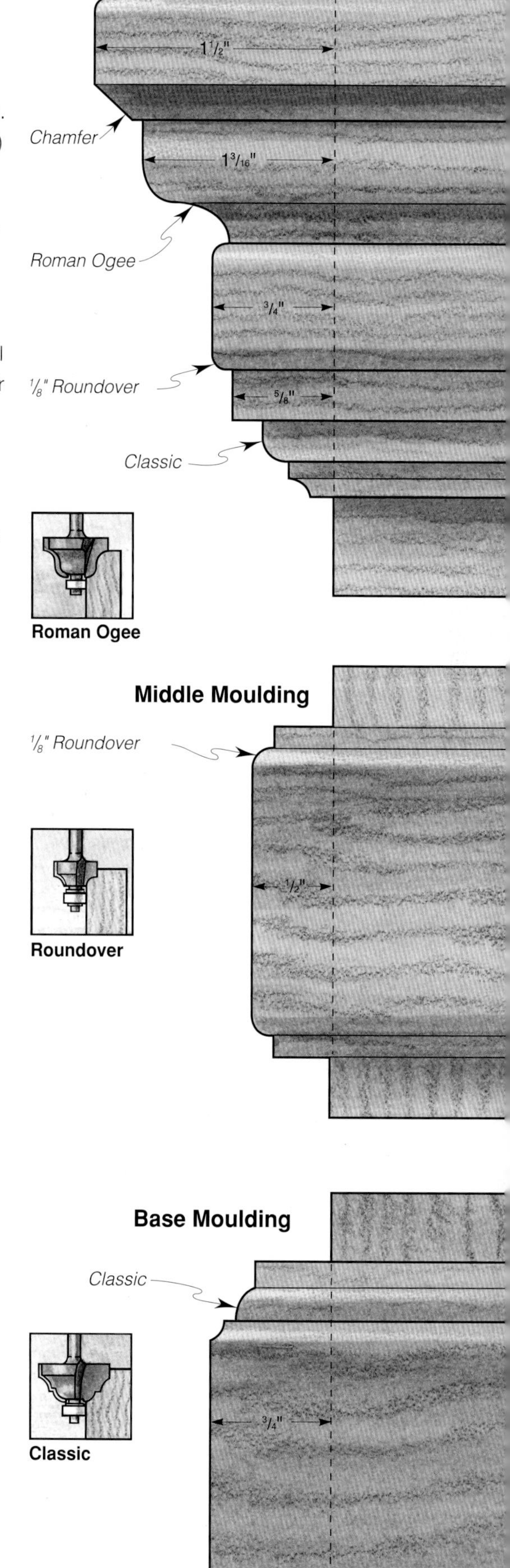

Entertainment Center

Cherry dentil moldings crown this third generation of our most requested plan, and building it yourself can save you thousands of dollars.

by Rick White

It's hard to avoid the technology revolution. No matter how determined you may be to leave the TV off, by eight o'clock on most evenings you may well be sitting in your favorite chair, remote in hand. Like it or not, television and videos have become fixtures in twenty-first century America's living rooms and dens. And if you have music lovers or teenagers in your home, it's not just a TV, VCR, and DVD player that occupy center stage. You also have to deal with stereo components. All of this technology can really clutter things up, unless you have a home for it.

This is the third entertainment center I have built. Many readers wrote in telling me of their experiences building the first two projects. I decided it was time to take the idea to the next level. Many readers offered great suggestions for a new generation of this project, and I've included the best of them in this design. For example, almost everyone wanted more drawers, and larger ones, too. The next most popular suggestion was making the center sectional, so it could be moved from the shop to the living room, then assembled.

We retained at least one really solid idea from the previous entertainment center designs: Flipper doors on the TV compartment that disappear when it's time for the big game.

The Center Cabinet

It will help organize your work if you think of this project as three separate units—a center cabinet and two wings (see the Exploded View Drawings on pages 133 and 134). The wings are mirror images of each other, so there are really only two unique elements to consider.

Each center cabinet side is made up of a plywood panel (piece 1), a hardwood front edging (piece 2), and a plywood back edging (piece 3). By extending the panels with the back edging strip, you can cut both side panels from a single sheet of ply. Cut all of the entertainment center's pieces to size: these dimensions are given in the Material Lists on pages 135,138, and 141. With that done, use clamps to edge glue the back trim to each panel. Dowels or biscuits will help to keep the two parts aligned during glue-up.

The cabinet top and bottom (pieces 4) and the four fixed shelves (pieces 5) are all the same width. All six pieces will later be set into dadoes cut into the cabinet sides. For now, locate the six ⅜" deep dadoes in each side by referring to the Technical Drawings on pages 136 and 137. Cut these dadoes with your portable router and a clamped-on straightedge (see Figure 1), using a ½" diameter straight bit. Work from front to back so any cross-grain tearout occurs at the back, then use

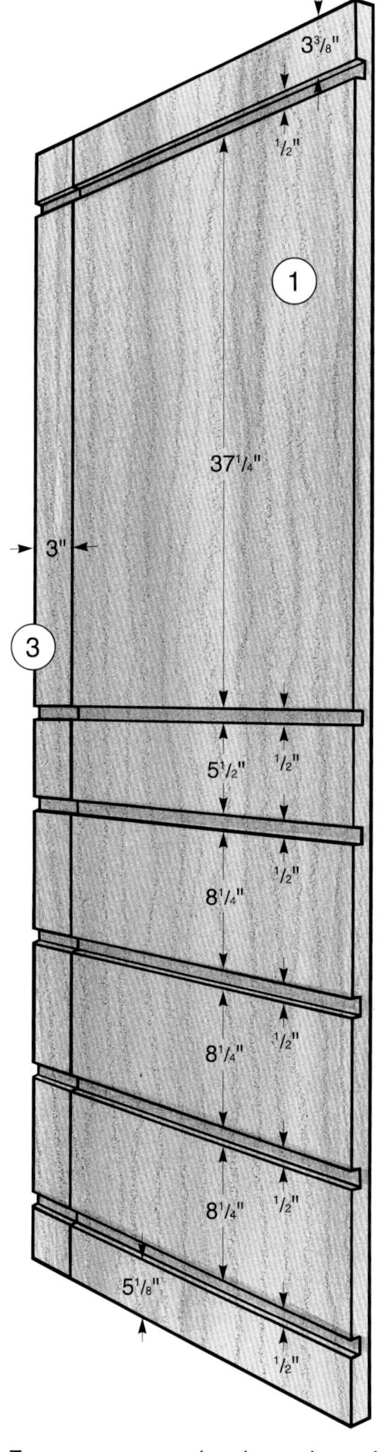

To conserve expensive cherry plywood, *I cut two 23¾" wide panels from a single sheet of stock, then added a hardwood molding to both back and front edges to build each side panel out to its full dimensions.*

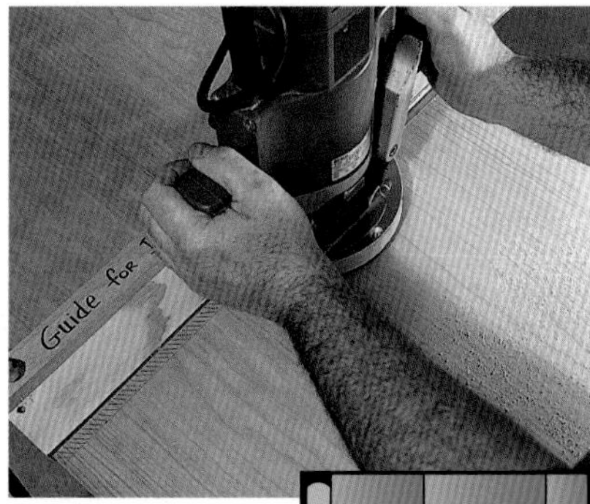

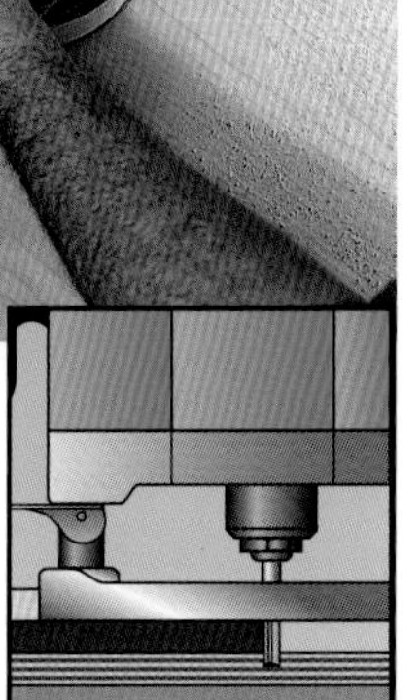

Figure 1: *To cut the shelf dadoes in the cabinet sides, run a router against a straightedge jig clamped to the workpiece.*

the same technique to cut a 3/8" wide by 1/4" deep rabbet down the back edge of each side: This will accommodate the 1/4" thick plywood back (piece 6), and cutting it removes the tearout from the previous operation.

Finish up the sides by attaching the 1/4" thick front trim to each panel (use clamps and glue to avoid having to fill nail holes later on), then move on to the shelves.

Mill the Shelves and Dividers

Start your milling by forming a 3/8"-long tongue on each side of each shelf, and on the top and bottom. These 1/2"-wide tongues make for a clean joint, and the easiest way to form them is on your table saw, as shown in Figure 2: Simply cut a 1/8" rabbet into both the top and bottom faces of each piece (see the Technical Drawings).

The top and top shelf need no more milling than these tongues, but the three shelves and bottom are connected to dividers (pieces 6). The dividers separate pairs of drawers, and both the locations and dimensions of the dadoes that hold them can be found on the Technical Drawings. Cut them with your portable router and a straightedge, then turn your attention to the trim that goes on the front edge of each of the fixed shelves and dividers. This trim (pieces 7) is just 3/4" wide hardwood stock on the lower shelves and it can be applied with glue and clamps. The trim on the top shelf (piece 8) is actually a dentil molding, so named because it looks like teeth. Form it by cutting a series of 5/16" dadoes spaced 3/4" apart on your dentil molding stock at the table saw. Index the spacing of the dadoes by making a reference mark on your miter gauge so the dadoes will be uniformly spaced.

Assembling the Center Cabinet

There are no great secrets to this assembly process—just make sure everything is square before your glue starts drying. If you're not used to building cabinets, it may help to know the best way to square up a rectangle is to measure it diagonally from top right to bottom left, and then from top left to bottom right. When both diagonals are exactly the same, your assembly is square.

Use screws (pieces 9) to pull the sides tight to the shelves. The trick here is to drill pilot holes through the sides, large enough for the screw shanks to slide easily though. Then drill smaller holes in the shelf so the threads can grip. This will allow the screws to pull the two pieces of wood tightly together. After drilling both sets of holes, counterbore for the screw heads and wooden plugs (pieces 10).

Glue and screw the carcass together (Rick likes to attach all the fixed shelves to one side with a few screws first, then glue and screw the second side in place. Then he removes the first side, glues it up, and screws it back in place). Add bracing (pieces 11, 12, and 13) behind the top drawer and toekick (refer to the Technical Drawings for locations), then tack the back (piece 14) in place with a 1" tack every 6".

Frame and Panel Doors

The input we got from readers suggested keeping doors on entertainment centers to a minimum. For some people, that was a matter of aesthetics, while others felt that building doors can be a complicated process. That, however, is certainly not the case with these doors: They're simply a pair of 1/4" thick plywood panels (pieces 15), framed in 3/4" solid hardwood stock.

You've already cut the stiles (pieces 16) and the rails (pieces 17) to size, so stay at your table saw to create the grooves in these pieces for the plywood panels. Do this with

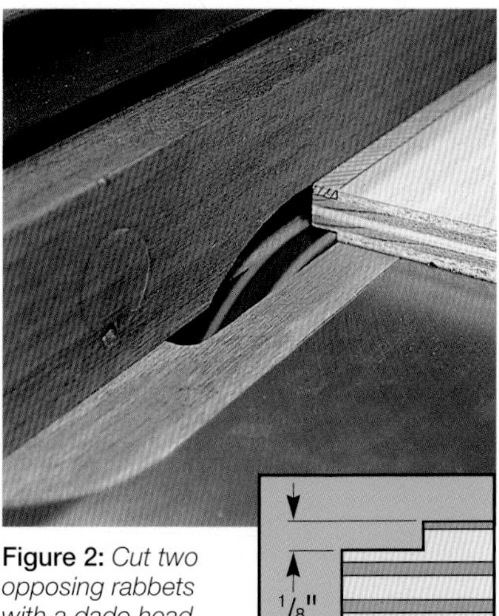

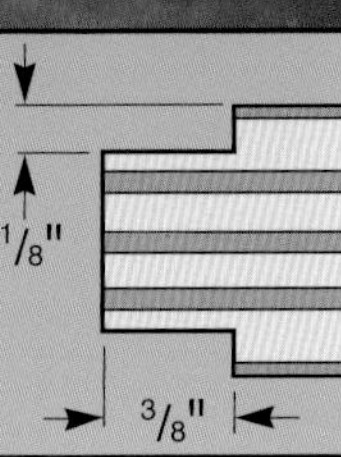

Figure 2: *Cut two opposing rabbets with a dado head to make the tongues on the edges of the shelves.*

Exploded View

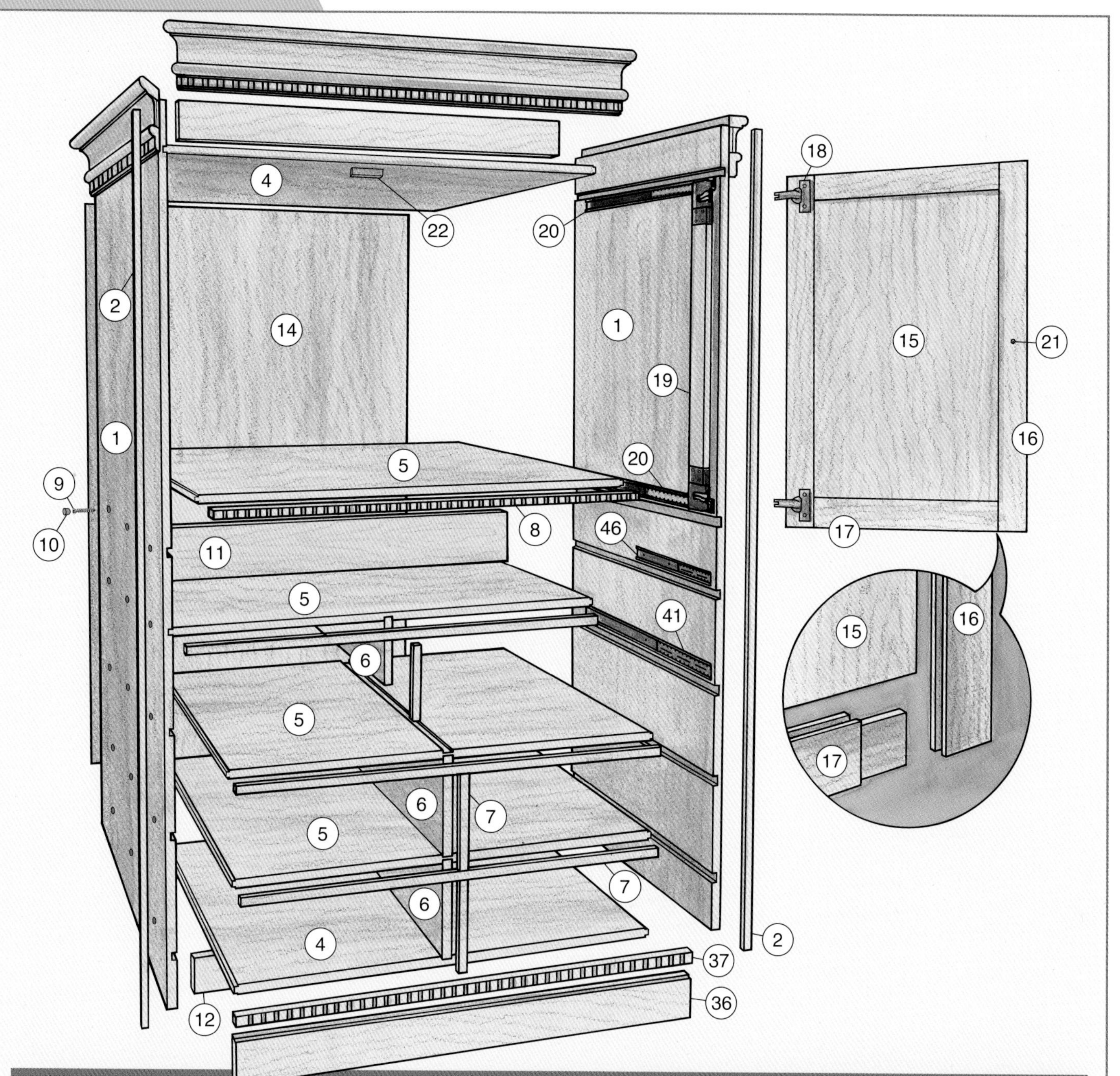

Material List – Center Cabinet

	T x W x L
1 Sides (2)	¾" x 23¾" x 79"
2 Side, Front Edging (2)	¼" x ¾" x 79"
3 Side, Back Edging (2)	¾" x 3" x 79"
4 Top & Bottom (2)	¾" x 37¼" x 26¾"
5 Fixed Shelves (4)	¾" x 37¼" x 26½"
6 Dividers (3)	¾" x 8½" x 26½"
7 Shelf and Divider Edging	¼" x ¾" x 144"
8 Top Shelf Dentil (1)	¾" x ¾" x 36½"
9 Screws	#8 x 2" SquareX
10 Plugs	Flat Top
11 Top Shelf Brace (1)	¾" x 5¼" x 36½"

	T x W x L
12 Toekick Long Brace (1)	¾" x 5" x 36½"
13 Toekick Short Brace (1)	¾" x 5" x 10"
14 Back (1)	¼" x 37¼" x 72"
15 Door Panels (2)	¼" x 14¼" x 33½"
16 Door Stiles (4)	¾" x 2" x 37"
17 Door Rails (4)	¾" x 2" x 17¾"
18 Door Hinges (2 pair)	Concealed, 35mm.
19 Follower Strips (2)	See kit instructions for size.
20 Flipper Door Slides (2 pair)	24"
21 Teardrop Handles (2)	2" Solid Brass
22 Door Stop (1)	½" x ¾" x 2⅝"

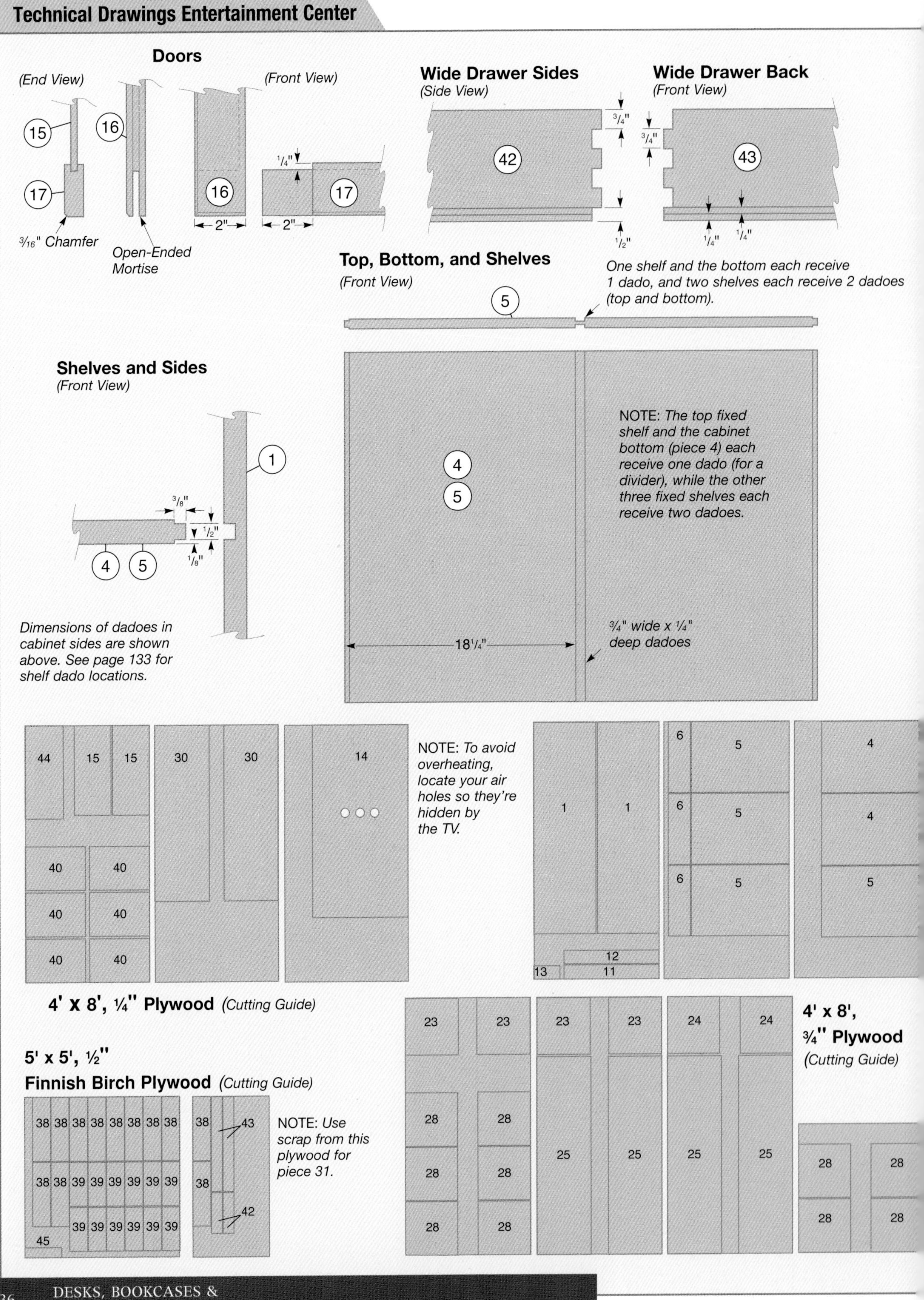
Doors
(End View)
(Front View)
15
16
17
16
17
3/16" Chamfer
Open-Ended Mortise
1/4"
2"
2"
Wide Drawer Sides
(Side View)
42
3/4"
1/2"
Wide Drawer Back
(Front View)
43
3/4"
1/4"
1/4"
Top, Bottom, and Shelves
(Front View)
5
One shelf and the bottom each receive 1 dado, and two shelves each receive 2 dadoes (top and bottom).
Shelves and Sides
(Front View)
1
3/8"
1/2"
1/8"
4
5
Dimensions of dadoes in cabinet sides are shown above. See page 133 for shelf dado locations.
4
5
NOTE: The top fixed shelf and the cabinet bottom (piece 4) each receive one dado (for a divider), while the other three fixed shelves each receive two dadoes.
18 1/4"
3/4" wide x 1/4" deep dadoes
44
15
15
40
40
40
40
40
40
30
30
14
NOTE: To avoid overheating, locate your air holes so they're hidden by the TV.
4' x 8', 1/4" Plywood (Cutting Guide)
1
1
12
11
13
6
5
6
5
6
5
4
4
5
5' x 5', 1/2"
Finnish Birch Plywood (Cutting Guide)
38 38 38 38 38 38 38 38
38 38 39 39 39 39 39 39
39 39 39 39 39 39
45
38
38
43
42
NOTE: Use scrap from this plywood for piece 31.
23
23
28
28
28
28
28
28
23
23
25
25
24
24
25
25
4' x 8', 3/4" Plywood
(Cutting Guide)
28
28
28
28

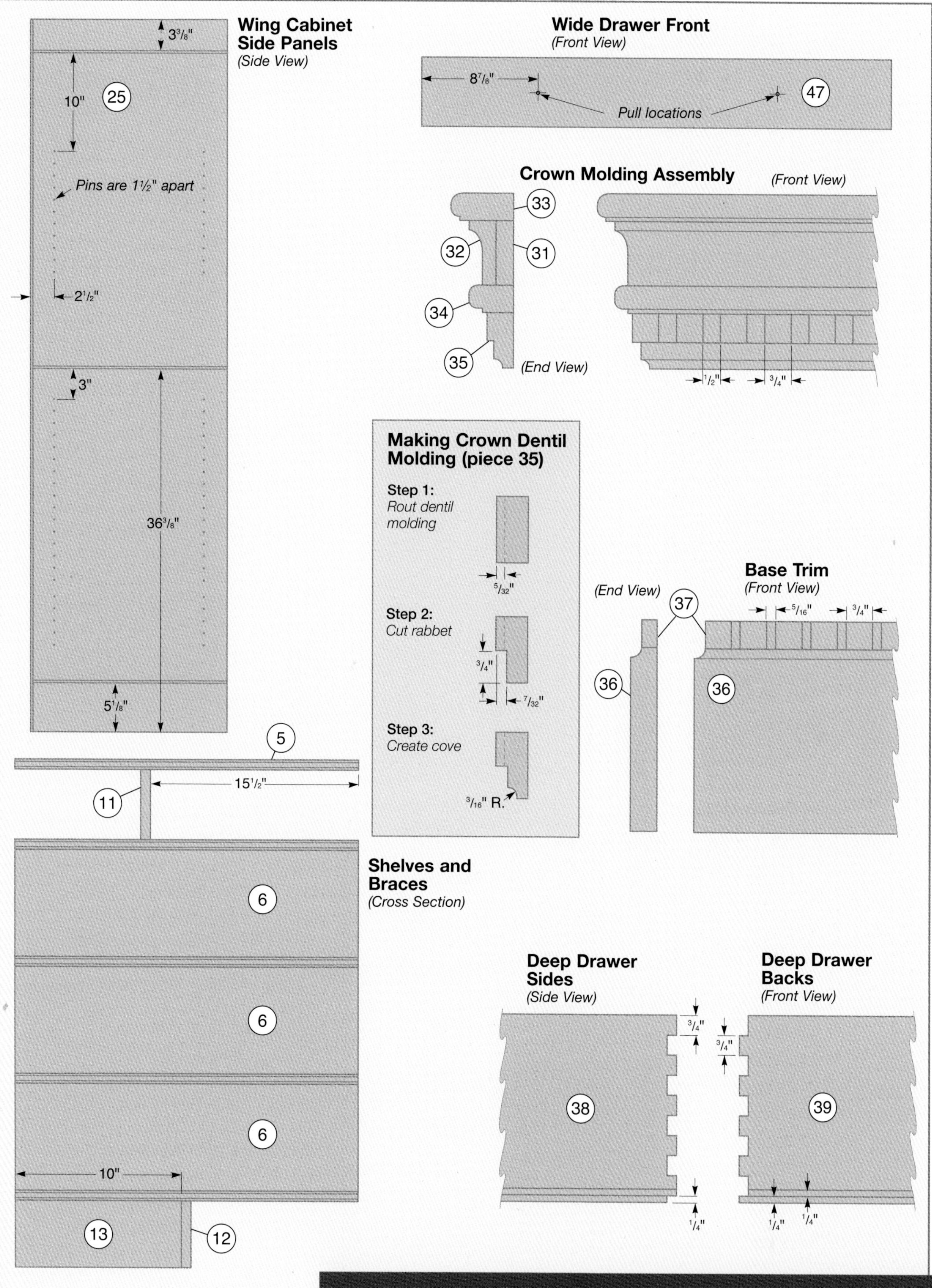
Wing Cabinet Side Panels
(Side View)
3 3/8"
10"
25
Pins are 1 1/2" apart
2 1/2"
3"
36 3/8"
5 1/8"
Wide Drawer Front
(Front View)
8 7/8"
Pull locations
47
Crown Molding Assembly
(Front View)
33
32
31
34
35
(End View)
1/2"
3/4"
Making Crown Dentil Molding (piece 35)
Step 1:
Rout dentil molding
5/32"
Step 2:
Cut rabbet
3/4"
7/32"
Step 3:
Create cove
3/16" R.
Base Trim
(Front View)
(End View)
37
5/16"
3/4"
36
36
5
15 1/2"
11
Shelves and Braces
(Cross Section)
6
6
6
10"
13
12
Deep Drawer Sides
(Side View)
Deep Drawer Backs
(Front View)
3/4"
3/4"
38
39
1/4"
1/4"
1/4"

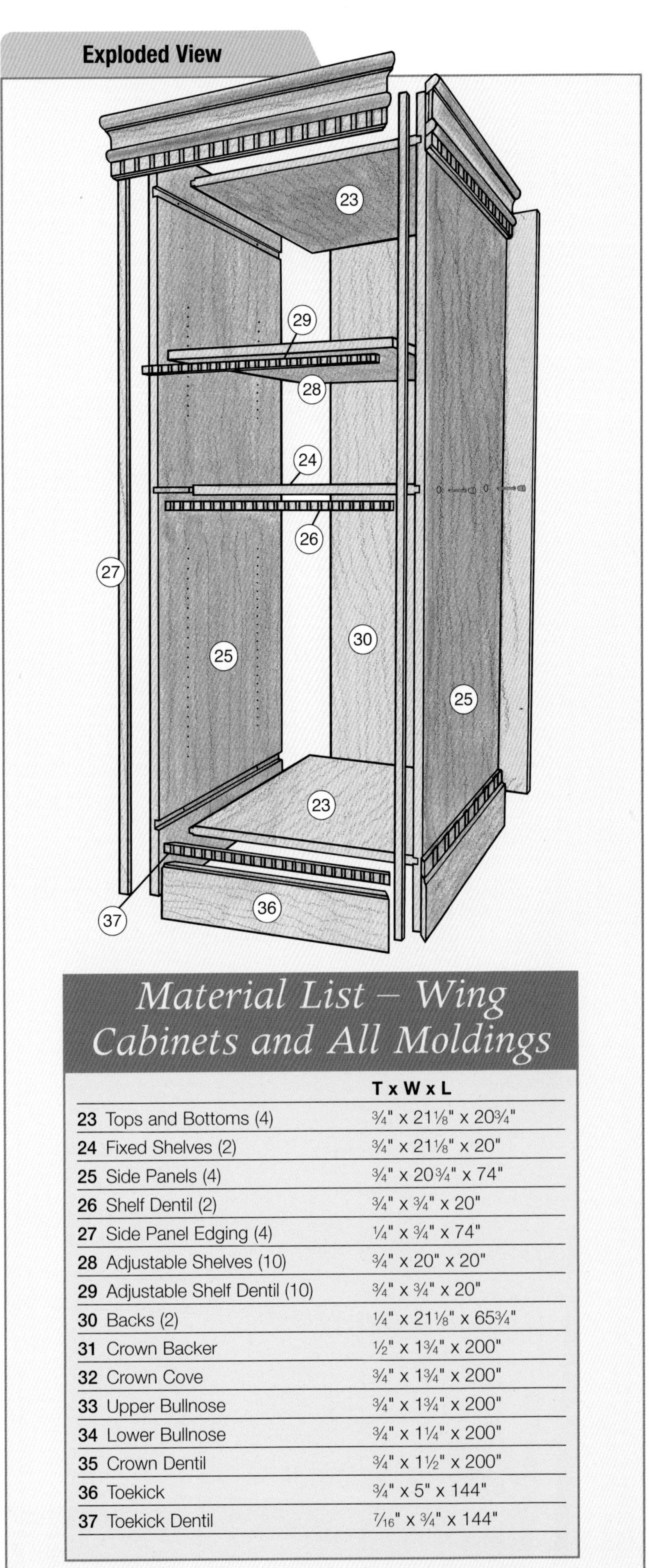

Material List – Wing Cabinets and All Moldings

	T x W x L
23 Tops and Bottoms (4)	¾" x 21⅛" x 20¾"
24 Fixed Shelves (2)	¾" x 21⅛" x 20"
25 Side Panels (4)	¾" x 20¾" x 74"
26 Shelf Dentil (2)	¾" x ¾" x 20"
27 Side Panel Edging (4)	¼" x ¾" x 74"
28 Adjustable Shelves (10)	¾" x 20" x 20"
29 Adjustable Shelf Dentil (10)	¾" x ¾" x 20"
30 Backs (2)	¼" x 21⅛" x 65¾"
31 Crown Backer	½" x 1¾" x 200"
32 Crown Cove	¾" x 1¾" x 200"
33 Upper Bullnose	¾" x 1¾" x 200"
34 Lower Bullnose	¾" x 1¼" x 200"
35 Crown Dentil	¾" x 1½" x 200"
36 Toekick	¾" x 5" x 144"
37 Toekick Dentil	7⁄16" x ¾" x 144"

a ¼" dado set, centering your cut on the workpiece (see the Technical Drawings). You should keep in mind that some mills supply plywood that is nominally ¼" thick, but it may only be 7⁄32" or so in actual thickness. Adjust your dado set accordingly.

Use the same dado setup to create the joinery that holds the frames together. Referring to the Technical Drawings for layout dimensions, adjust your blade height and use the table saw's miter gauge to create tongues on the ends of the rails that are exactly the same thickness as your plywood.

The open-ended mortises that are cut into the ends of the stiles (refer to the Exploded View detail of the doors on page 135 for an illustration of these mortises) can also be cut with your ¼" dado head, although these cuts should be made with the aid of a tenoning jig or similar support that holds the workpiece vertical to the table. Make several passes to remove all the waste, checking the fit as you work.

When the rails and stiles are all milled, dry-fit your door assemblies. If everything looks right, glue and clamp them together (checking that they're square by measuring diagonals), but don't glue the panels in place—they have to move freely.

Wait until after the glue has dried to mill a 3⁄16" chamfer all around the outside face of each door (see the Technical Drawings), which you can do either on your router table or with a guided bit in a portable router.

The Flipper Door Hardware

Each door is mounted with a pair of European style hinges (pieces 18) to a strip of wood called a follower (piece

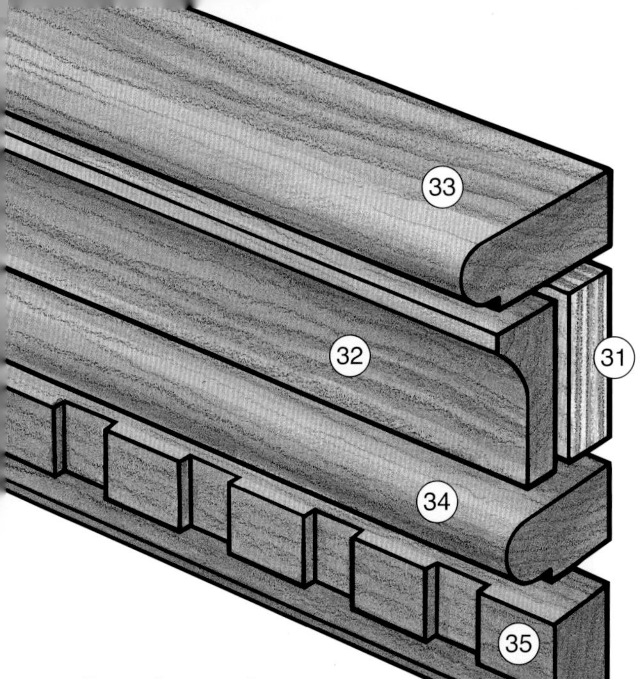

Dressing up the top of the three cabinets
is easier than it looks. The compound crown molding is made up of five elements—four of which are milled with common router bits.

19). This strip of wood is then screwed top and bottom to slides (pieces 20) that are not unlike standard drawer slides. The door glides in and out on these slides (see Figure 3), kept on track by a pair of plastic retainers that come with the kit.

Full instructions for installation are included with the hardware. You'll need two sets of slides, two pairs of hinges, and a 35mm Forstner bit to install the hinges. I suggest using a drill press to accurately control the depth of cut when drilling the hinge cup recesses in the doors.

Clearance was an issue with the two flipper doors. I needed a handle that had a low enough profile to allow the doors to be slid all the way back into the cabinet when open. The brass teardrop handles (pieces 21) not only fulfill that function, but also add a touch of elegance in keeping with the crown and dentil moldings. A small wooden stop (piece 22) keeps the doors in line when they are closed.

The Wing Cabinet Carcasses

Each wing cabinet is a mirror image of the other, rather than an identical copy. Remembering this will be critical when you're applying moldings later on, but it's also important now: It allows you to choose the least attractive of the four available faces to put up against the center cabinet, where it will be hidden.

As in the center cabinet, dadoes hold each wing's top and bottom (pieces 23) and fixed shelf (piece 24) in place. The locations of these dadoes in the side panels (pieces 25) can be found on the Technical Drawings, and they, too, are cut with a portable router and guide.

Figure 3: *Although installing the flipper door hardware looks complicated, it's really not. Full instructions are included with the hinges. To order, see page 141.*

Dentil molding (piece 26) is applied to the front edge of each fixed shelf with glue and clamps—make sure the dado "teeth" at either end of the moldings are the same size. The same method is also used to apply ¼" thick trim (piece 27) to the front edge of each side panel. When the glue is dry, sand the edging flush and install the top, bottom and shelf in each unit using screws and glue.

I made adjustable shelves (pieces 28) for the wing cabinets, after first applying dentil molding (pieces 29) to each shelf front. The wing cabinet backs (pieces 30) are simply tacked in place every 6" with 1" tacks.

The Crown Assemblies

Let's face it—a cabinet is just a square box until you add moldings and doors. To dress up the top edge of these three units, I added a compound molding (see Drawing, this page) made up of five elements. This compound is applied to the front and both sides of the center cabinet, and to the front and one side of each of the wings.

The first element in this compound is a strip of plywood (piece 31), which is glued and screwed in place, flush with the top edge of the cabinet side. A cove molding (piece 32) is glued directly to the exposed face of this plywood. To make this cove, rip hardwood stock to the correct dimensions and install a ¾" core box bit in your router table. With the bit protruding about ⅛" above the tabletop, set the fence so that there's a ¼" gap between the bit and the fence. Then run the workpiece through several times, raising the bit ⅛" between passes until it makes a ⅜" deep cut in the hardwood (see Figure 4).

Completing the molding is a simple matter of ripping off the excess stock below the cove using your table saw (see Figure 4, inset), then giving the workpiece a thorough sanding. With that done, glue and clamp your cove in place and turn your attention to the next molding element, the bullnose.

The same bullnose profile is used in two places: Above the cove molding it forms a cap (piece 33), and below the cove it becomes the transition (piece 34) between the top and bottom of the crown assembly. Both upper and lower bullnose moldings can be milled from a single length of ¾" thick by 1¾" wide stock. Use a ⅜" radius roundover bit in your router table or portable router to radius the top edge of the stock, then raise the bit ⅛" to create the bottom, beaded profile, as shown in Figure 5. Note that the lower bullnose is not as wide as the upper, so cut them to length and rip the lower one to width.

Earlier, you used dentil molding for the shelf edges, and the same type molding is used here in the crown assembly (piece 35). It's tucked in under the lower bullnose. There are three steps to making it.

First, trim the workpiece to size and cut your dentil profile on the cleanest face. Change your dado set width and cut a rabbet on the bottom half of this same face (see the Technical Drawings). The third step is to create the small cove with a ¼" radius bit in your router table.

Cut the moldings to length, miter their ends if needed and dry-fit them. When everything fits, glue and clamp them in place.

Figure 4: *To create the cove molding, make the first cut on your router table with a cove bit, then remove the rest of the waste on your table saw (see inset).*

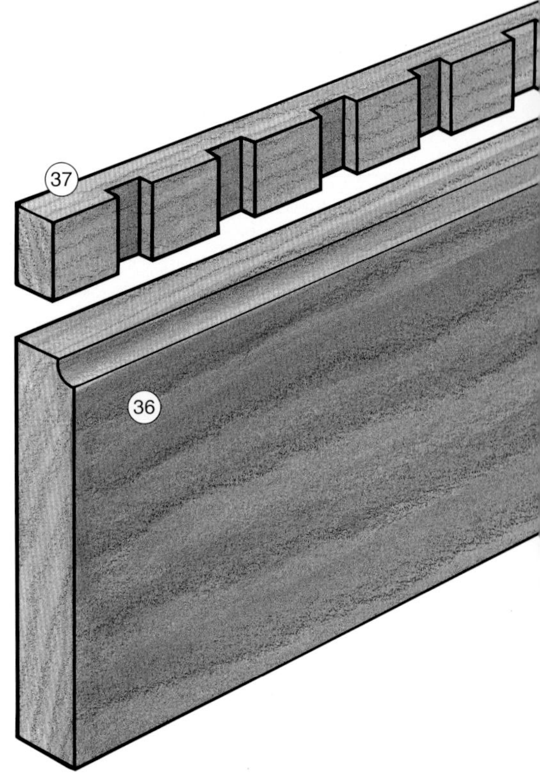

The Base Trim

There are only two parts to the compound molding that dresses up the bottom of the entertainment center: A baseboard (piece 36) and a cap of dentil molding (piece 37). The baseboard is simply squared-up stock with a small cove cut into it along the top edge. This ¼" radius cove, like the ones in the crown molding, can be formed on your router table (see Figure 6) with a core box bit. Then cut it to length, miter as needed, and attach it to each carcass with glue and clamps. Do the same with the dentil cap.

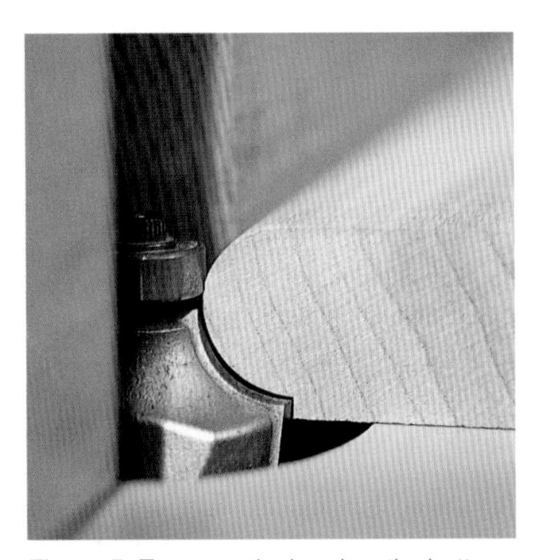

Figure 5: *To create the bead on the bottom edge of the bullnose molding, raise the roundover bit ⅛" when making the second cut.*

Building the Drawers

I used finger joints to hold the sides of the deep drawers (pieces 38) to the fronts and backs (pieces 39). The dimensions for these finger joints can be found in the Technical Drawings, and the cuts are easily made on your table saw, as shown in Figure 7. Run a ¼" wide dado in all four pieces of each drawer to hold the bottom panel (piece 40), then glue and clamp the deep drawers together, letting the drawer bottoms float freely. Install the slides (pieces 41) according to the manufacturer's instructions (see Figure 8).

Figure 6: *The base molding is a board with a cove cut in its top edge with a round nose or cove bit and a cap of dentil molding.*

I used the same finger joinery to hold the wide drawer's sides (pieces 42) to its front and back (pieces 43), then installed the bottom (piece 44) and used 4d nails and glue to secure the divider (piece 45) in place. Screw in the slides (pieces 46) before positioning the drawer faces (pieces 47 and 48) and attaching them with screws from the inside.

The seven drawer pulls (pieces 49) are centered on the deep drawer faces. The wider top drawer receives two pulls (see Technical Drawings).

Before finishing the entertainment center, drill holes for the shelf pins (pieces 50) at the locations shown in the Technical Drawings. Then remove the hardware, sand the entire project and apply the topcoat of your choice. Finally, it's a good idea to drill air holes (see Technical Drawings) in the back of the TV compartment—they're hidden by the TV to prevent it from overheating.

Figure 7: *Cut the finger joints with a dado head, using an index pin on your miter gauge's auxiliary fence (see inset) to space the cuts evenly.*

Figure 8: *Try this specially designed jig (available from Rockler Woodworking and Hardware) to install the drawer slides correctly.*

Exploded View

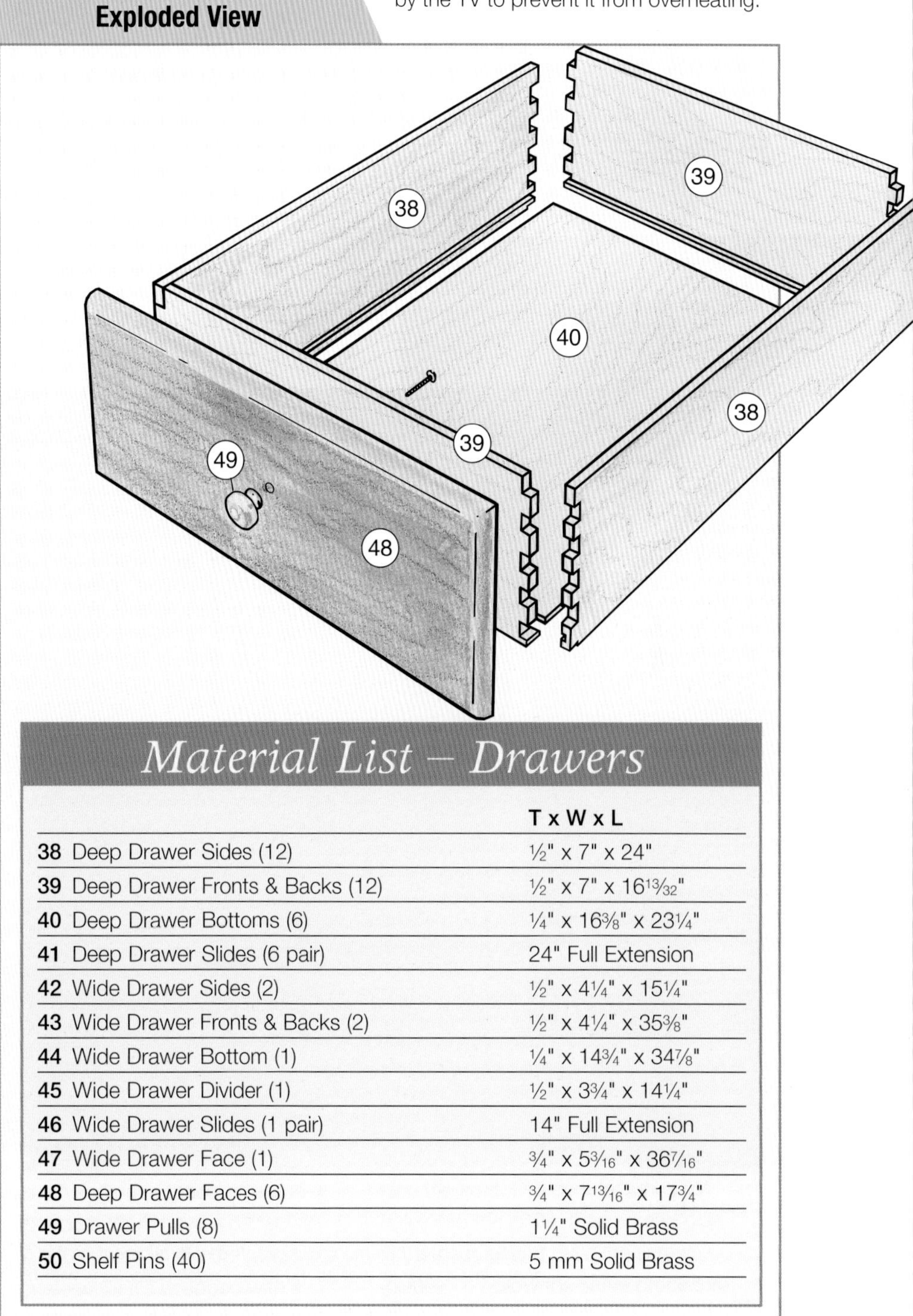

Material List – Drawers

		T x W x L
38	Deep Drawer Sides (12)	$\frac{1}{2}$" x 7" x 24"
39	Deep Drawer Fronts & Backs (12)	$\frac{1}{2}$" x 7" x $16\frac{13}{32}$"
40	Deep Drawer Bottoms (6)	$\frac{1}{4}$" x $16\frac{3}{8}$" x $23\frac{1}{4}$"
41	Deep Drawer Slides (6 pair)	24" Full Extension
42	Wide Drawer Sides (2)	$\frac{1}{2}$" x $4\frac{1}{4}$" x $15\frac{1}{4}$"
43	Wide Drawer Fronts & Backs (2)	$\frac{1}{2}$" x $4\frac{1}{4}$" x $35\frac{3}{8}$"
44	Wide Drawer Bottom (1)	$\frac{1}{4}$" x $14\frac{3}{4}$" x $34\frac{7}{8}$"
45	Wide Drawer Divider (1)	$\frac{1}{2}$" x $3\frac{3}{4}$" x $14\frac{1}{4}$"
46	Wide Drawer Slides (1 pair)	14" Full Extension
47	Wide Drawer Face (1)	$\frac{3}{4}$" x $5\frac{3}{16}$" x $36\frac{7}{16}$"
48	Deep Drawer Faces (6)	$\frac{3}{4}$" x $7\frac{13}{16}$" x $17\frac{3}{4}$"
49	Drawer Pulls (8)	$1\frac{1}{4}$" Solid Brass
50	Shelf Pins (40)	5 mm Solid Brass

Center Door Exploded View

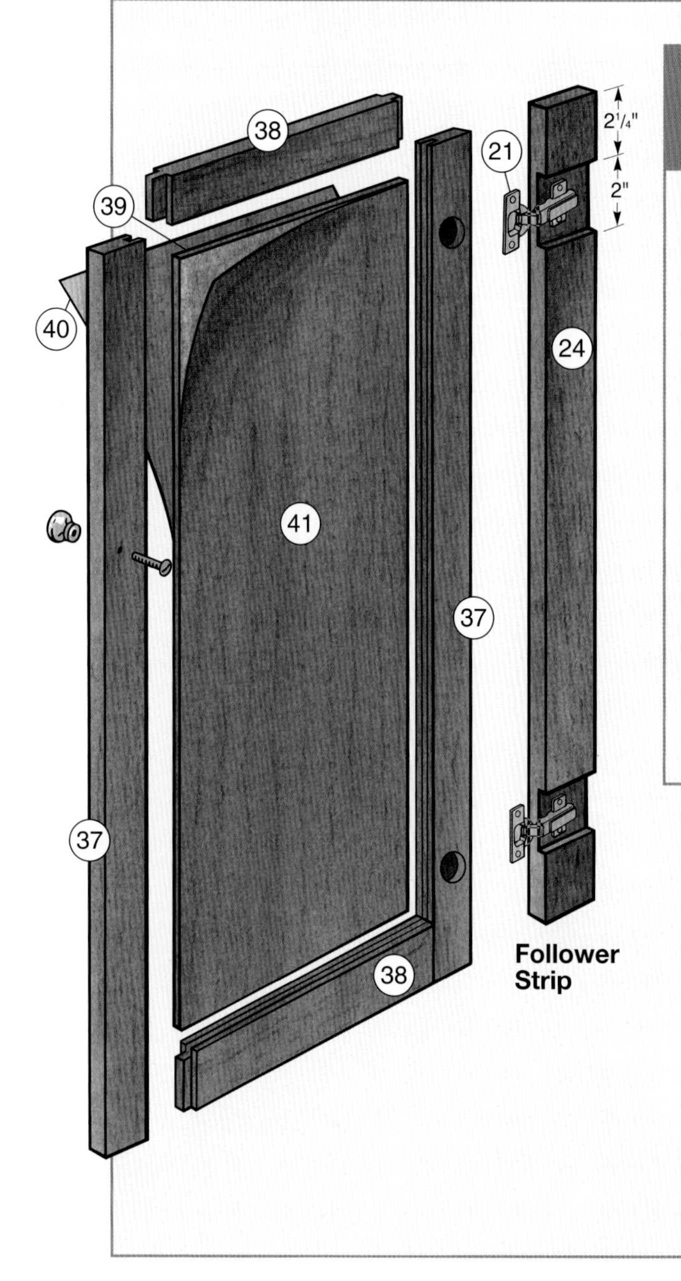

Tips for Installing The Center Doors

Follower strips (left) provide the mounting platform for the hinges and slides, and they support the doors throughout their travel. Cut the dadoes in the strips exactly ⅜" deep, as this will affect the fit of the doors and their swing around the pivot rollers (right). For all other installation requirements, refer to the instructions that come with the hardware.

Screwing stops (above right) to the dividers will end the door's travel before the door knobs hit the front face of the cabinet. Drilling the pilot holes off center gives the stops a wide range of adjustability.

Pivot Roller

Material List – Center Doors

	T x W x L
37 Center Door Stiles (4)	¾" x 2¼" x 36⅜"
38 Center Door Rails (4)	¾" x 2¼" x 13"
39 Substrates (2)	¼" x 13" x 33"
40 Face Veneer (2)	1⁄32" x 14" x 34"
41 Back Veneer (2)	1⁄32" x 14" x 34"

tops to the rails just as you did with the television stand. Glue the fronts to the tray tops and secure the tray slides (pieces 34) to the brackets and rails.

The holders (pieces 35) for storing video tapes, cassettes, DVDs and CODs have their own adhesive tape. All you have to do is peel off the protective cover and press them into place—but not until after you've completed the finishing. Wrap up by cutting the back (piece 36) to size and mounting it on the cabinet carcass with 4 ½" screws driven into countersunk pilot holes.

Finishing and Final Installation

To stain and finish the entertainment center, take off all the hardware, remove the back and set the project in a dust-free room—you may have to settle for cleaning up your shop like we did. I colored the cabinet using brown mahogany stain and topcoated the stain with sanding sealer and varnish. Two coats of varnish is plenty for normal use. Put the stain on with a rag or brush and wipe it off after a few minutes. Be sure to watch for any glue spots, and remove them with a sharp chisel. Some stains are quite forgiving—you can stain

Mahogany Crotch Veneer

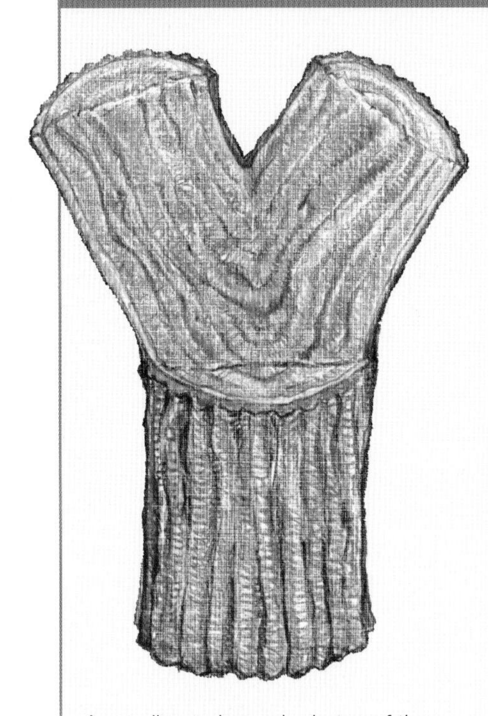

According to legend, pirates of the high seas buried their treasures on Caribbean islands. What they couldn't know, however, was that another treasure lay hidden right in front of their noses. Had they anticipated its value to the woodworking trades they surely would have added the small amount of beautifully figured wood hidden deep in the crotch of the mahogany trees to their ill-gotten booty.

Mahogany, although not the only tree that produces a desirable crotch grain pattern, offers some of the most spectacular results. Nearly all harvested crotch wood is sliced into exceptionally thin veneer in order to stretch the rare material to its absolute limits. While each specimen is unique, names like plume, flame, feather and rooster tail generally apply to this kind of grain pattern.

Crotch veneer is cut perpendicular to the V created by the spreading branches in the log, as shown in the drawing at left. Each slice has a wild grain pattern going in all directions, much like burl veneer does. Of course, this usually means that no matter how you glue it to a core material, eventually the veneer will crack and split.

Working with crotch veneer requires a little more effort than plain-sliced or quartersawn veneers. Due to its irregular grain patterns, crotch veneer is often wrinkly, making it necessary to flatten the veneer prior to gluing. Homemade treatments can be mixed, or you can go easy on yourself by just buying an off-the-shelf product. Generally speaking, you brush the treatment on the veneer, then clamp it between sheets of fiberglass mesh screen, newspaper and plywood. After a couple of days, you can remove the veneer and glue it to your core material—but don't wait too long or the veneer may distort once again.

Special handling is required when smoothing and finishing crotch veneer. Planing is almost impossible on such wild grain, so you'll need to rely on scraping and sanding instead. Since crotch veneer has random areas of exposed end grain that absorb stains and finishes unevenly, you may want to apply a wash coat of shellac to guarantee a uniformly colored surface.

Mahogany crotch veneer is relatively expensive. For example, a square foot of plain-sliced veneer costs about $1, whereas crotch mahogany sells for about five times that much. When you have the right application, however, its stunning beauty is well worth the extra hit to your pocketbook.

—by Gordon Hanson

the exposed spots right away and they will blend in well. Sand between each topcoat with 400-grit wet/dry paper.

Remount the doors and hardware after allowing the final coat of varnish to dry for a couple of days. When you decide how you want your stereo equipment arranged, drill access holes in the cabinet dividers and cut notches in the shelves for passing wires from one component to another. We've found that 1½"-diameter holes work well. Following drilling, reinstall the back panel and press your holders into place.

This new entertainment center satisfies a different set of requirements from many of the designs we've published before. It takes up less space on a family room floor, it's more classically inspired and the construction is less complicated. It's also much easier to move around the room without needing a small army of help to do it. We hope it's just the fit you've been looking for.

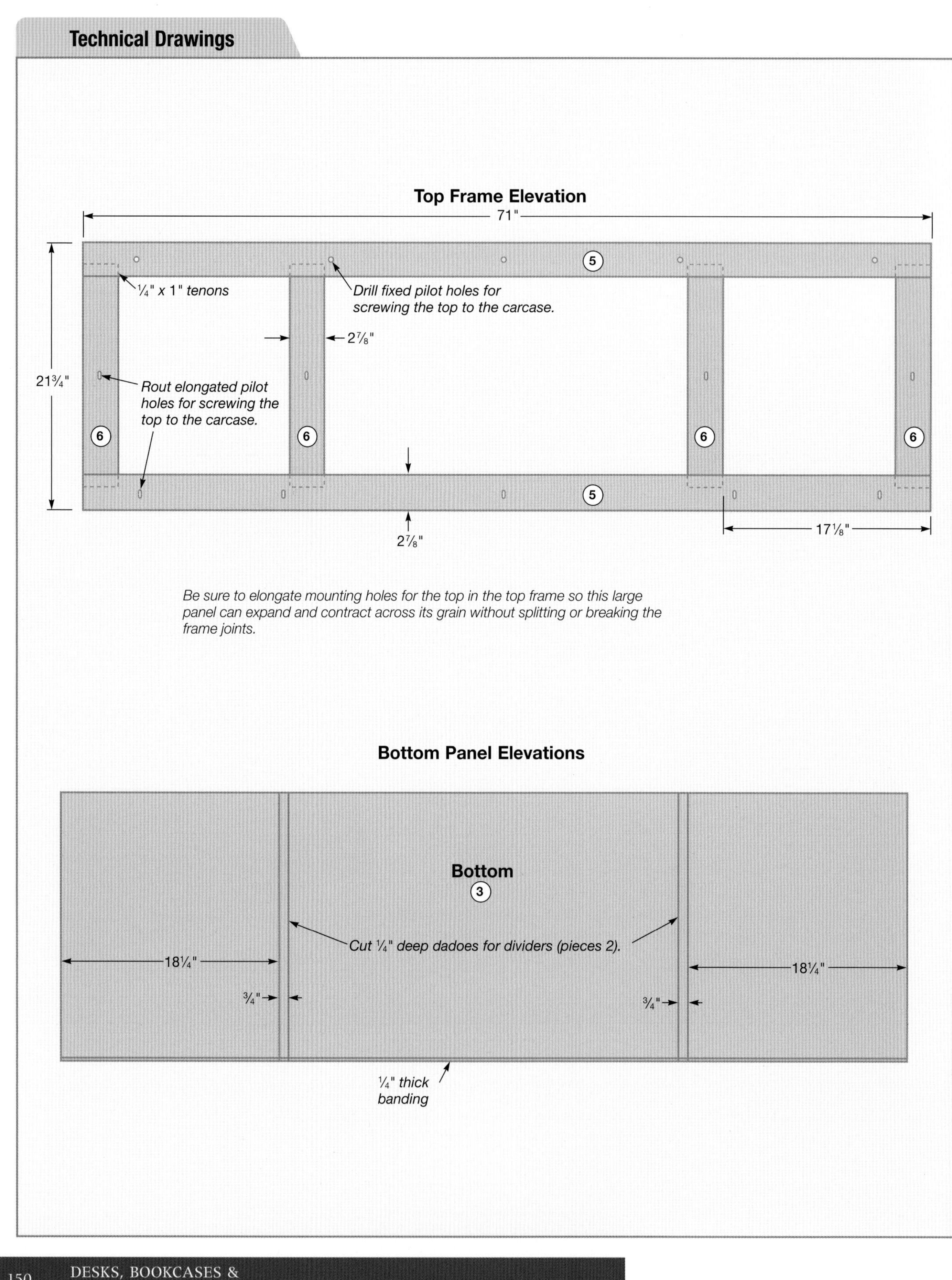

Be sure to elongate mounting holes for the top in the top frame so this large panel can expand and contract across its grain without splitting or breaking the frame joints.

Side and Divider Panel Elevations

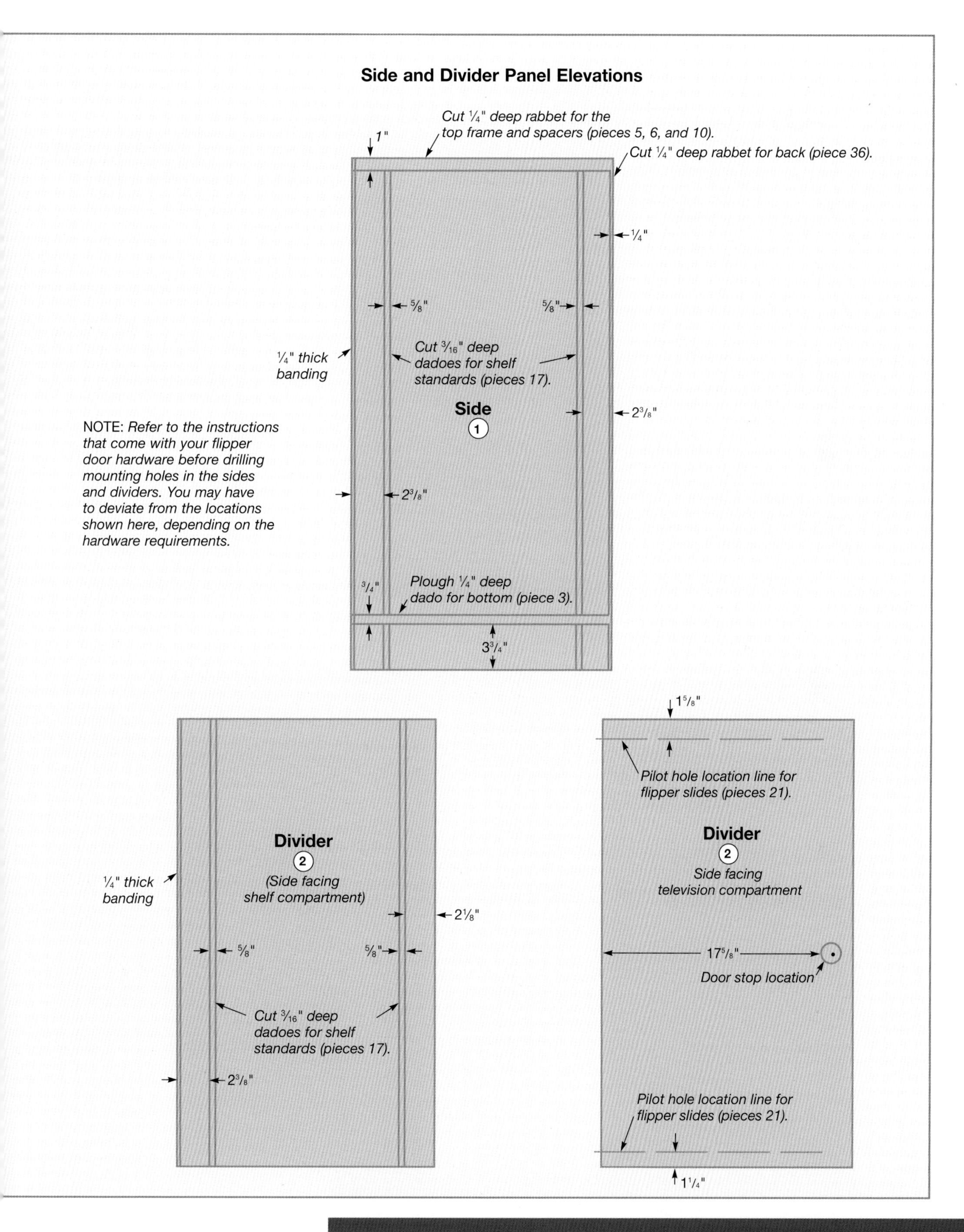

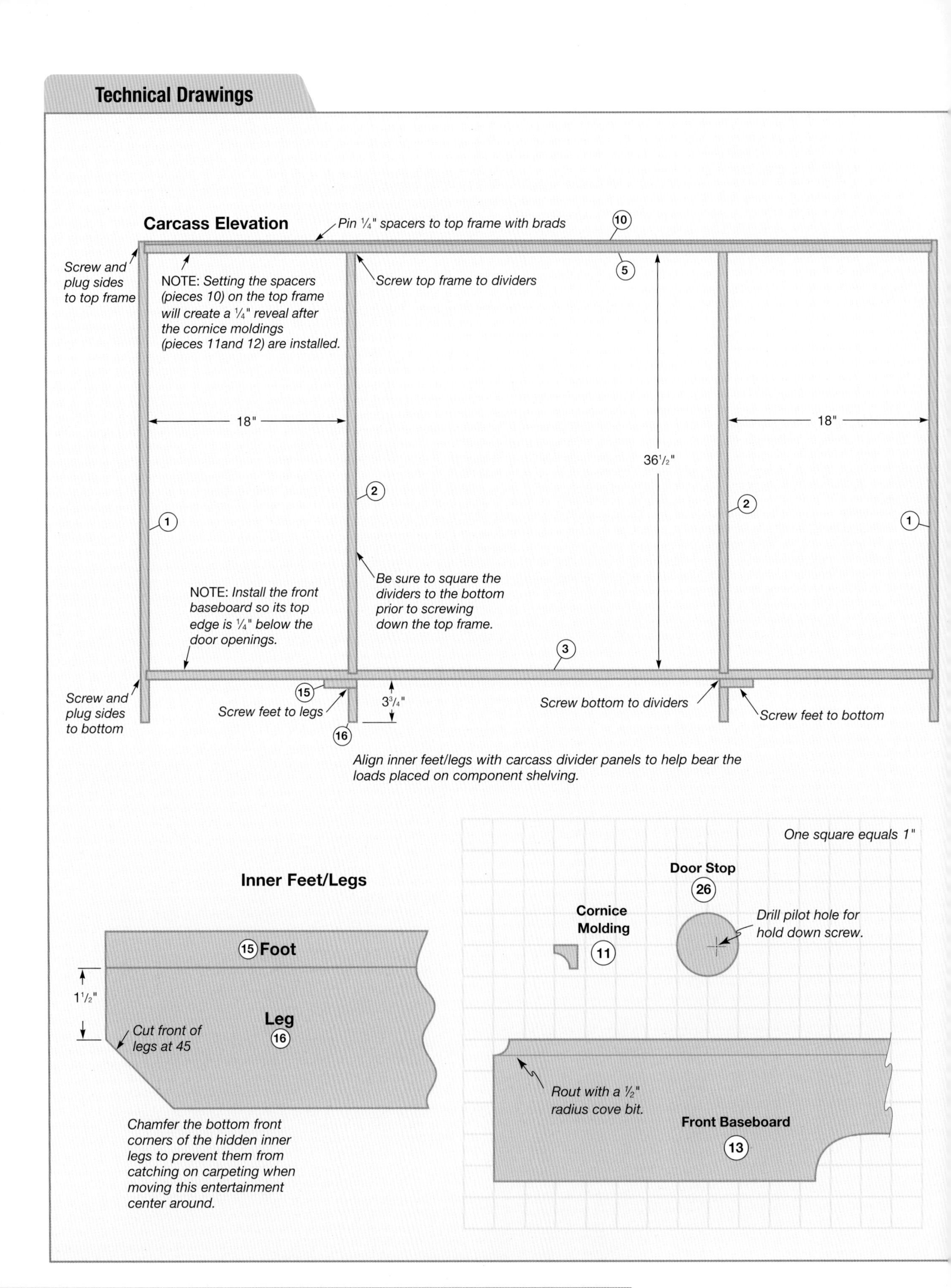
Carcass Elevation
Pin 1/4" spacers to top frame with brads
Screw and plug sides to top frame
NOTE: Setting the spacers (pieces 10) on the top frame will create a 1/4" reveal after the cornice moldings (pieces 11and 12) are installed.
Screw top frame to dividers
18"
36 1/2"
18"
Be sure to square the dividers to the bottom prior to screwing down the top frame.
NOTE: Install the front baseboard so its top edge is 1/4" below the door openings.
Screw and plug sides to bottom
Screw feet to legs
3 3/4"
Screw bottom to dividers
Screw feet to bottom
Align inner feet/legs with carcass divider panels to help bear the loads placed on component shelving.
Inner Feet/Legs
Foot
Leg
1 1/2"
Cut front of legs at 45
Chamfer the bottom front corners of the hidden inner legs to prevent them from catching on carpeting when moving this entertainment center around.
One square equals 1"
Door Stop
Cornice Molding
Drill pilot hole for hold down screw.
Rout with a 1/2" radius cove bit.
Front Baseboard

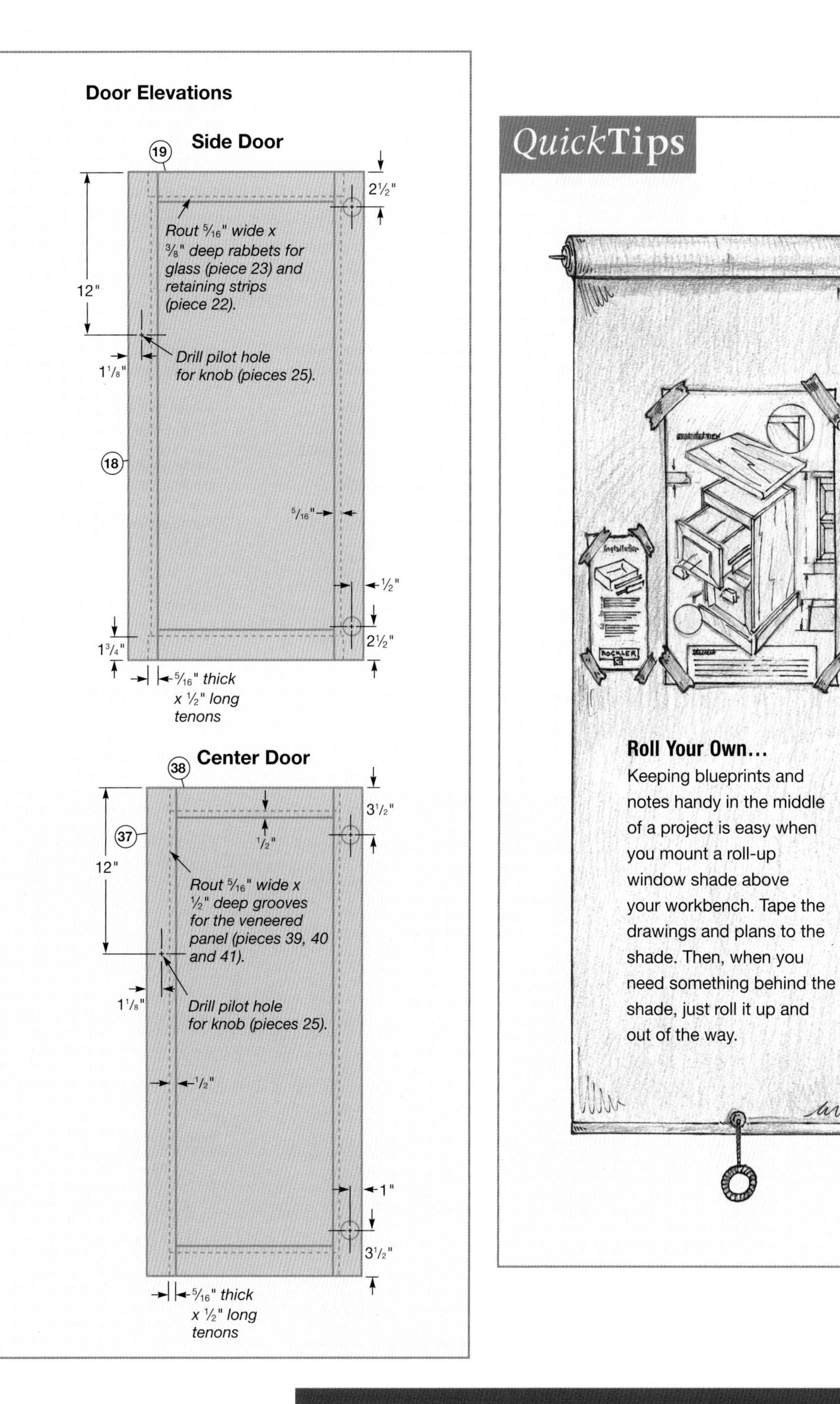

QuickTips

Roll Your Own...

Keeping blueprints and notes handy in the middle of a project is easy when you mount a roll-up window shade above your workbench. Tape the drawings and plans to the shade. Then, when you need something behind the shade, just roll it up and out of the way.